Su

BORN TO SHOP

PARIS

*The Ultimate Guide for
Travelers Who Love to Shop*

9th Edition

Wiley Publishing, Inc.

For Pascale-Agnes Renaud Sahler, who has taught me Paris for 20 years.

Published by:

Wiley Publishing, Inc.

909 Third Ave.
New York, NY 10022

ISBN 0-7645-6653-9
ISSN 1066-2790

Editor: Marie Morris
Production Editor: Donna Wright
Photo Editor: Richard Fox
Cartographer: Roberta Stockwell
Production by Wiley Indianapolis Composition Services

For information on our other products and services or to obtain technical support, please contact our Customer Care Department within the U.S. at 800-762-2974, outside the U.S. at 317-572-3993 or fax 317-572-4002.

Wiley also publishes its books in a variety of electronic formats. Some content that appears in print may not be available in electronic formats.

Manufactured in the United States of America

5 4 3 2

CONTENTS

MAP LIST

ABOUT THE AUTHOR

Suzy Gershman is a journalist, author, and self-confessed shopping goddess who has worked in the fashion and fiber industry for more than 25 years. The Born to Shop series, which is now 18 years old, is translated into eight languages, making Gershman an international expert on retail and trade. Her essays on retailing have been used by the Harvard School of Business; her reportage on travel and retail has appeared in *Travel & Leisure, Travel Holiday, Travel Weekly,* and most of the major women's magazines. When not in an airport, Gershman can be found in Paris, Provence, or Texas.

TO START WITH

This is the first edition of *Born to Shop Paris* as a hometown book. That's right, *mes amis,* I am now living part-time in Paris. This new edition has an insider's perspective that I've never been able to offer before.

The beauty of this edition is not only that it's devoted solely to Paris, but that it's on a different publication cycle than *Born to Shop France*. Because I revise the two guides in alternate years, I have an opportunity to revisit my sources, always ensuring that you get *le dernier cri,* or the last word.

Paris has changed a lot since I've been living here. In fact, Paris has changed the most since we switched to the euro. The changeover was easy, but the fact that prices have gone up will make you want to reevaluate your shopping goals.

Because of these changes, and my belief that you too will change your shopping patterns when traveling, I have changed the organization of this book enormously. I have also altered some of the focus, especially when it comes to hotels, restaurants, and bargain shopping.

Chapter One

....

PARIS *VITE*

PARIS IS BEST

Ah, Paris—how I love to live here (even part time), and how I love to shop, now that we have euros and I can actually tell how much I am spending . . . or saving. Ah, Paris—how I loathe making this list.

Putting the best of Paris into one list is an impossible task; it seems that every store I walk into is the best store in Paris. Just being here, pressing your nose to the windows of the stores, is a best-in-show experience. Now that I spend several months a year here, I run around with a notebook in my handbag and the constant feeling that I must write down my latest find to share with my readers. The notebook is bigger than this edition.

With that in mind, the selections in this chapter have been chosen for people in an incredible hurry who have no time for leisurely strolling and shopping. If you have more time, you owe yourself the luxury of checking out the finds described elsewhere in this book. But if you must hit and run, I hope these choices will be rewarding.

Paris

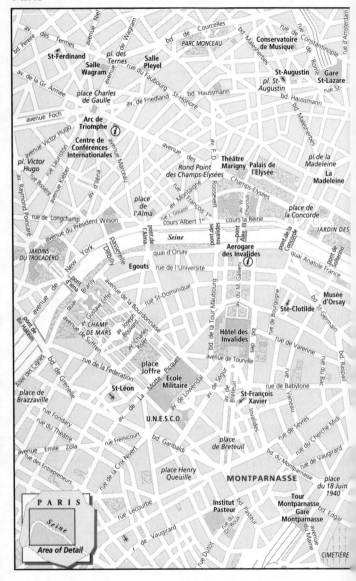

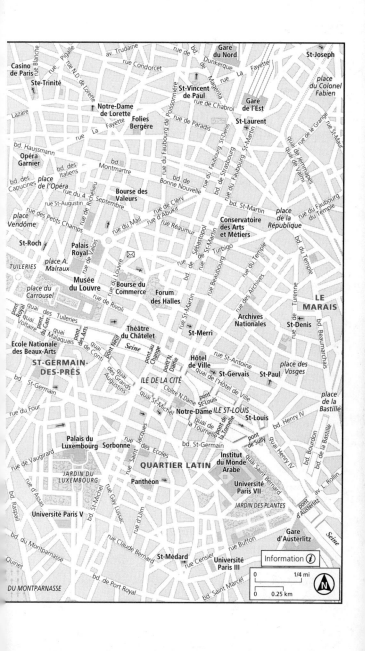

The Best Specialty Perfume Shop

SALONS SHISEIDO
*Jardins du Palais Royal, 142 Galerie de Valois, 1er
(Métro: Palais-Royal).*

This tiny shop with high ceilings and royal purple decor is the showcase of makeup genius Serge Lutens. He used to create makeup for Christian Dior and has been with Shiseido for decades. His perfumes are also divine. Even if you buy nothing, just look around and breathe deeply. The Jardins du Palais Royal is another terrific shopping experience, so check it out while you're here.

The Best Duty-Free Perfume Shop

CATHERINE
7 rue Castiglione, 1er (Métro: Tuileries or Concorde).

This small, intimate shop is family run and can get crowded because it's very popular (good news travels). Catherine offers "instant détaxe" (you get your savings up front) and one of the best discount policies in Paris. It has an excellent selection of scents and specializes in hard-to-find perfumes. It carries makeup and beauty goods by Chanel, Dior, Lancome, and Sisley— which is the steal of the century at French prices. Also note the excellent souvenirs and the best Hermès copies for the price in town.

Confused about the whole duty-free issue? There's lots more information in these pages.

The Best Mass-Market Perfume Shop

SEPHORA
70 av. Champs-Elysées, 8e (Métro: F-D-Roosevelt).

Sephora is a large French chain with stores in Paris, throughout France, in many European capital cities, and even in the United States. This branch, the French flagship, is open Sunday.

Everything in the large shop is color coordinated. Fragrances have their own section, with scads of testers and lots of scent strips. There's far more than perfume; in fact, you're better off not buying perfume here, since you'll get a better price from a discounter or duty-free shop. What Sephora is good for is bath and beauty products (an enormous selection, including its own line of shampoos and body lotions, makeup, and hair accessories). This is a great place for girls, preteens, and women of all ages. The inexpensive sample-size (15ml/0.5 oz.) products make fabulous gifts.

You'll also find books, a *parapharmacie,* a mix-your-own perfume counter, and a computer to teach you everything you need (or want) to know.

The Best Kitsch

It's not hard to find kitsch in Paris—just stroll the tourist traps along the rue de Rivoli.

The Best French Gift Statements

I have several:

- Glass and crystal items from the big French makers, such as **Baccarat** or **Lalique.** They make fashion statements and accessories, such as Lalique belts or stick pins. "Exotica" is the Lalique line of leather belts with smoky glass buckles. About $200 (184€), but you can apply for a détaxe refund. Lalique's stick pins, named "Nerita," are also quite chic and cost a bit less. See chapter 9, "Paris Home Style."
- Anything from **Didier Lamarthe.** Its handbags have limited distribution in the U.S. (through Nordstrom only). Most bags cost $100 to $150 (92€–138€). See chapter 7, "Basic Paris Resources from A to Z."
- If you know don't mind splurging (over $100/92€ or so), head to **By Terry,** the tiny makeup atelier of Terry de Gunzberg. Terry mixes color for YSL, has another makeup and beauty line with her sister (Nuxe), and does both custom

and off-the-peg makeup in her little shop. The custom makeup is *tres cher*, but the little silver palette with the travel selection is *tres chic:* It holds two blushes, three eye shadows, and a powder, and costs about $125 (115€). See chapter 8, "Paris Beauty."

- Semiprecious-rock aromatherapy in bath-oil form ($65/59.80€) from **Lora Lune.** You put the stones into your tub, pour in the magic oil, and soak; by osmosis, you get energy from the stones. Neat, huh? See chapter 8.

The Best Gifts for $10 or Less

- Anything from **Sephora,** preferably the house brand of bath goodies. See chapter 8.
- Hot-chocolate mix ($5/4.60€) from **Angelina,** the most famous tea shop in Paris. 226 rue de Rivoli, 1er (Métro: Tuileries).
- A box of Mère Poulard **cookies** ($1.50/1.40€). These indescribably good cookies are imported from Mont St-Michel. Available in any grocery store.
- A bag of **coffee** ($3/2.75€). I buy Carte Noire, and there are other brands; Grand Mère has a cute package. Available in any grocery store.
- A jar of **mustard** ($2/1.85€). I buy Maille brand. Check out the cassis and red fruits flavors. Most fun when bought at Maille's own store. Place de la Madeleine, 1er (Métro: Madeleine).
- Box or bag of **tea.** Grocery stores carry Elephant brand; at Mariage Frères, 4€ ($4.30) will buy you a small bag of deliciously fragrant leaves. Mariage Frères has several stores, plus a boutique in Galeries Lafayette.
- Anything from **L'Occitane,** the Provençal soap maker, including soaps for 3€ ($3.25). If you're willing to carry it, try the lavender scented water to fill up your steam iron. Available in all major department stores or in L'Occitane shops. See chapter 8.
- A bar of French milled **soap,** from a made-in-France brand *(bien sur)*, teamed with *gant de toilette,* a French-style

washcloth. The two pieces together don't have to cost more than 10€ ($10.80). I like Roger & Gallet soaps, especially the more unusual scents, such as the cherry-and-tomato combination. Available in any department-store linen section.

The Best Status Gifts for Under $25

- **Hermès** soap, sold in the Saddle Shop. See chapter 7.
- **Lanvin chocolates.** Available in any grocery store.
- **Champagne.** There are plenty of good champagnes. In addition to the ones you've heard of, there are several good ones that aren't as well known in the U.S.—I swear by nv (non-vintage) Alain Thienot, found at Nicolas or Monoprix. Also note that France sells more sizes of Champagne by more makers than you can imagine, so you can bring home several minibottles and not exceed your liquor allowance.
- Anything from **Diptyque,** the candle, soap, and scent maker. This luxury brand is not that well known in America (its first U.S. shop opened recently in Boston) but is a cult item to celebs and serious shoppers. See chapter 9. Also available at Au Printemps.

The Best Shopper's Break

SALON DU THÉ BERNARDAUD
11 rue Royale, 8e (Métro: Concorde).

Pick your own dishes! The staff at this tea salon brings you a tray of gorgeous Bernardaud china, and you pick the style of china you would like your tea served on. How's that for a great gimmick?

The Best Gifts for Kids

- Manitoba Jeunesse publishes adorable French **books** (6€/$6.50)—*Ma Maison, Ma Ferme,* and *Mon Ecole*—that lie flat like any book, but can be built into a house!
- **Monoprix,** a chain of "popular stores," is packed with items, ranging from a selection of books (Disney translations

are nice) to Legos. I also buy kids' clothes here. Locations throughout Paris.

- **Sephora** carries little animal-shaped bath gel thingamabobs (50¢/.45€); each animal shape is a different scent, and there must be 20 of them. See chapter 8.
- **CanCan Barbie.** *Barbie La Dentiste* speaks French, *c'est vrai*, but I like CanCan Barbie better. Similarly, Elmo giggles in French—he's pricey (about $40/37€) but adorable. I found him at Galeries Lafayette.

Best New Boys' Toy Store

LEROY MERLIN
Centre Georges Pompidou, 3e (Métro: Châtelet).

Look out, BHV. The department store with the iconic hardware-filled basement faces a challenge from the French version of Home Depot. Paris's first Leroy Merlin is conveniently located in the Centre Georges Pompidou.

The Best Store for Teenage Girls

ETAM, CITE DE LA FEMME
73 rue de Rivoli, 1er (Métro: Pont Neuf).

An entire department store of style: fashion, beauty, even home touches and a cafe. It occupies a makeover of one of La Samaritaine's landmark buildings. Low prices.

RUNNERS-UP FOR TEENS & TWEENS

H&M
54 bd. Haussmann, 9e (Métro: Havre Caumartin).

The Swedish phenomenon has copies of the latest looks for men, women, and children. Affordable prices. This is the flagship; there are other, smaller branches around town.

LE SHOP
3 rue d'Argout, 2e (Métro: Etienne Marcel).

The music is too loud for me—need I say more?

ZARA
44 av. Champs-Elysées, 8e (Métro: F-D-Roosevelt); 128 rue de Rivoli, 1er (Métro: Hôtel de Ville); place de l'Opéra, 1er (Métro: Opéra).

There are several Zara (pronounced in the French manner, "Zah-rahhhh") shops around town, as well as representation in major department stores.

The Best Fantasy Designer Find

LEE YOUNG HEE
109 rue du Bac, 7e (Métro: Rue du Bac or Sèvres-Babylone).

The Korean name should be a giveaway. These French clothes are inspired by Korean traditional garments, and have an edge of whimsy that doesn't make them practical for my lifestyle. If, however, I were going to a ball or getting married, this is where I'd go. She also has a shop in Seoul.

RUNNER-UP

MR. GAS
44 av. Etienne Marcel, 1er (Métro: Etienne Marcel).

Gas has been around for years: It's a teeny-tiny jewelry shop that sells colorful, creative whimsies. Now, "Mr. Gas" has added a clothing store next door. Funky, exotic, and hip. Large sizes need not apply.

Gotta-Have-It Trendy Gift

Blame it on Pablo Picasso or Coco Chanel, but the traditional striped fisherman's T-shirt has become an iconic fashion statement. This time the colors are not so traditional (although you'll have no trouble finding navy-and-white or red-and-white stripes). **Monoprix** usually has a fair selection. Specialty stores and brands to check out include **Le Phare de la Baleine,** passage l'Havre, 9e (Métro: St-Lazare), part of a small chain of stores that specializes in marine looks from Brittany; **Amour Lux,** a brand name sold all over France (I buy mine at Galeries Lafayette) that makes the shirts in wild colors; and **St. James,** 13 rue du Rennes, 6e (Métro: St-Germain-des-Prés), a brand that has freestanding stores and perhaps the best colors, but the highest prices.

Best Kate Spade Inspirational Find

HERVÉ CHAPELIER
390 rue St-Honoré, 8e (Métro: Concorde); 1 rue du Vieux-Colombier, 6e (Métro: St-Germain-des-Prés); 3 rue Gustave Courbet, 16e (Métro: Victor Hugo); 53 bd. de Courcelles, 8e (Métro: Courcelles).

I think Kate's great, but take a look at Hervé Chapelier and his brightly colored nylon tote bags. The major department stores stock a lousy selection, so head to his freestanding stores. The best location is the flagship, not far from the rue Royale in the heart of the best shopping in town.

Best One-Trick Pony

ANNE FONTAINE
64 rue des Sts-Pères, 6e (Métro: Sèvres-Babylone); 50 rue Etienne Marcel, 2e (Métro: Etienne Marcel); 12 rue Francs-Bourgeois, 3e (Métro: St-Paul); and many more.

Ms. Anne has shops all over town and boutiques in the major department stores. She sells only two things: white blouses and black blouses. She also has shops in select U.S. cities.

Best Department Store Rehab

GALERIES LAFAYETTE
40 bd. Haussmann, 9e (Métro: Havre Caumartin or Chaussée d'Antin).

What becomes a legend most? This store's return from the dead is nothing short of amazing. Not only is the main store a totally different place, but the Men's Store has been renovated, the gourmet grocery store has been expanded, and Galeries has just taken over space formerly owned by Marks & Spencer for even more ways to wow us.

Best New Retail Block

Get a look at the corner of boulevard Malesherbes and rue Royale—not the part that indents, but the real street part at the beginning of Malesherbes, in the 8e. Here you'll find three totally new buildings filled with wonderful things to see, sniff, and touch. The stores are Sia (home style), Resonances (gifts and novelties), and Shiseido, the Japanese beauty maven. A whole new energy comes to a corner of Paris that makes you think that U.S. marketing concepts can work on other shores. Métro: Madeleine or Concorde.

Most Hyped Store in Paris

COLETTE
213 rue St-Honoré, 1er (Métro: Tuileries).

This store seems to be extraordinary to the French, who can't stop talking about it even though it's been open now for 5 years. If you're an American, excuse me, but there is no *there* there. The merchandise is almost all American and therefore nothing to write home about. However, the downstairs cafe is adorable, well priced, and a fun place for a nosh.

The Next Colette for Those Who Care

DIX SEPT
17 rue de Sèvres, 6e (Métro: Sèvres-Babylone).

Part art gallery, part Colette wannabe, part trendorama—this is the store everyone is looking at in order to have a new store to look at. The space was once the swimming pool of the Hôtel Lutétia.

Hottest New Line You've Never Heard Of

Yumé, which means "dream" in Japanese, is Kenzo Takada's newly launched line. Takada is back from retirement with all sorts of new ventures, and a new store to be unveiled in the Madeleine area at a site to be determined. In 2003, Kenzo will also have a huge place in the newly renovated La Samartaine department store.

Novelty Item to End All

I've been writing about *sirops* and flavored waters for the last year, but this takes the, uh, cake. Perrier has launched three new flavored waters—in different colors. Yes, you have to lug home a bottle, and at 3€ ($3.25) per bottle it's not really a bargain . . . but for the person who has everything, what a gift!

Chapter Two

....

PARIS DETAILS

WELCOME TO PARIS

What a difference a day makes . . . or a year . . . or a euro. We've still got the Eiffel Tower and the Arc de Triomphe, but there are lots of small changes. If this is your first visit to Paris, you won't notice anything too different from the way you dreamed it, except for the money. No one dreams in euros, right?

Hmm, I take that back. Because of the money, there aren't as many bargains as there were just a year or two ago. So if your dreams included low, low prices, you may want to rethink that right now.

If you are returning to Paris, you'll notice that a lot has changed, much of it instigated by that cute little euro. Yes, the euro will make traveling within the European Union easier, but it sure has brought up prices in France. Prices have risen 15% to 45%, and I don't just mean on luxury goods. A cup of coffee has always been 5F. Now it costs anywhere from 1€ to 1.50€ ($1.10–$1.60); that's an increase of 15% to 25%.

Parity is the name of the euro game—the whole point is for the euro and the U.S. dollar to stand at parity—and you may find yourself equating dollars and euros and wincing. A magazine I bought for years for 25F no longer sits next to my bed because it costs 4€ ($4.30). My brain said, "Four dollars for *that* rag?"

Dollars and euros are not at parity as we go to press, but the realities of translating prices have already hit home and hit the wallet. And speaking of wallets, the new chic accessory is a coin pouch, because there are so many more coins in euros than there were in francs. But don't panic—I have many tricks up my *manche*. I live here part-time now, so I have the inside scoop. There's a whole chapter on money (see chapter 3, "Money Matters"), but for now, sit back and relax—I'm about to show you my hometown.

Paris is, of course, one of the world's premier shopping cities. Even people who hate shopping enjoy it in Paris. What's not to like? The couture-influenced ready-to-wear? The street markets? The most extravagant kids' shops in the world? Jewelers nestled together in shimmering elegance? Fruits and vegetables piled in bins like more jewels? Perfumes and cosmetics at a fraction of their U.S. cost? Antiques and collectibles that are literally the envy of kings? It's not hard to go wild with glee at your good luck and good sense for having chosen such a place to visit. If the prices are higher, well, you'll just have to be a little smarter.

PARIS NEWS

If you don't get to Paris once a year, here's a quick checklist of what's new and what's hot; there's more information on these venues in the pages that follow.

- The **Left Bank** is better than ever. "There goes the neighborhood," I thought when I discovered that **Louis Vuitton** had moved onto the place St-Germain-des-Prés across from the church of the same name; then came **Etro, Giorgio Armani,** and **Dior.** Ruined? *Au contraire.* While a teensy bit of the funky flavor is easing away, the new stores offer a deluxe feel that's just divine. I've never been a fan of Vuitton merchandise, but now I beg you, don't miss this store. You don't have to buy anything (although there's is much to tempt you)—simply stare. More designers have come on board; Armani has taken several spaces and now brings us **Armani Casa,** 195 bd. St-Germain (Métro: Rue du Bac), a whole new store that offers a whole lot of chic between the plates.

- Not everyone loves Tom Ford or the Gucci-ization of YSL. Shocking, but true. Yves Saint Laurent quit—his word is "retired"—rather than have to put up with it.

- Karl Lagerfeld shrugged in a non-Gallic fashion throughout the YSL tsk-tsking and now says, "Hey, what about me?" Kaiser Karl has lost 90 pounds and is writing a couture diet book.

- West may have been best for snobs and young men, but **eastern Paris** is where it's happening for the young, the hip, and the hot. In the 18e, 80% of the population is under 25. If you aren't planning to move but want to enjoy the hottest shopping, check out the Canal St-Martin, the rue du Faubourg St-Antoine (which starts right after Bastille), and even the **Village Bercy.**

- There's another turf war going on in "midtown" Paris. It involves the renovation and upmarket twist to **La Samaritaine,** the arrival of **Etam's** flagship teeny-bopper department store, and the previously old-fashioned **BHV,** which seems headed for the importation of brand names, to take on La Samaritaine. Watch this war—it should be fun!

- **Colette** has been a major creative force in Paris; its success has spawned many wannabes, and even Galeries Lafayette has a Colette-like gallery. On the Left Bank, next to the Hôtel Lutétia, check out **Dix Sept,** named for the street address— a multilevel art gallery in what was once the swimming pool of the Lutétia.

- Everyone is **going to the dogs.** Not only are there dog products galore, but now dog gourmet and dog perfume. I am working on a doggy spa for one of the department stores. Au Printemps, another department store, just opened a Dog Generation Boutique. Life's a bitch, huh?

- **Marks & Spencer** closed its French shops and sold them to Galeries Lafayette. Galeries Lafayette made some into

Monoprix stores—check out the new one on the rue de Rivoli, not far from BHV department store and the Hôtel de Ville (Métro: Hôtel de Ville)—and sold some to the Swedish ready-to-wear chain H&M. The key to the deal was the flagship M&S space across the street from Lafayette Homme on boulevard Haussmann, which will become Lafayette Maison but keep the British deli-cum–grocery store on the ground floor. Film at 23H.

- In the department-store star wars, the almost totally reinvented flagship Galeries Lafayette is unrecognizable if you haven't been there in the past year or so. It has a new wine library and two new restaurants, and everything has moved around—you won't even remember how old-fashioned it used to be. To compete, Au Printemps has totally redone its first floor, the luxury floor of the store.

- As history buffs may recall, Bon Marché reinvented itself many years ago when it was bought by LVMH and turned into a retail icon more tony than New York's Barneys. Now the La Samaritaine department store, near the Hôtel de Ville, has been bought by LVMH and hopes to compete by the end of 2004. Frankly, my dear, I don't give a dime—I like it the way it is.

- Speaking of trends, all the stores have cute new cafes. Café Brico, in the basement of the department store BHV, is a must-do. Monoprix is opening soup bars; its flagship Left Bank location has the only cafe in the 300-plus-store chain.

KNOW BEFORE YOU GO

The French Government Tourist Office in the U.S. is an excellent source for visitor information and trip-planning advice. Its 900 number, France On Call (☎ 900/990-0040), costs 50¢ per minute. Everyone who answers the phone speaks English, and the average call takes 5 minutes. The office will mail any booklets or brochures you request (some of which contain discount coupons), and provide firsthand information. It does not make bookings but will guide you to a local travel agent if you need one.

If you prefer, you can call one of the U.S. offices, in **New York** (☎ 212/315-0888), **Chicago** (☎ 312/337-6301), **Dallas** (☎ 214/720-4010), or **Los Angeles** (☎ 310/271-6665).

MORE INFORMATION, PLEASE

It's not hard to get information on Paris and on France. All you need to get around Paris is a copy of *Paris par Arrondissement,* a book of intricate maps. This is your source for street maps, bus lines, and the Métro. Mine fits in the palm of my hand and is so complete, I can look up an address in the front of the book, then check a chart to find the nearest Métro stop for that destination. For some reason these babies are not available in the U.S., so buy yours at any bookstore in Paris, and at some street kiosks that also sell newspapers. They come in large formats too.

If you want to learn more on immediate events, try local magazines. *Le Figaro* publishes a weekly insert, *Figaroscope,* about everything that's going on in the city, including special flea markets and shopping events. It appears in the paper every Wednesday. My fave is *Zurban,* a small-format weekly publication. It includes movie listings and information about upcoming cultural events. Like *Figaroscope,* it's in French, but movie times (which use the 24-hr. clock) are easy enough to check. *Zurban* also lists such special events as big flea markets. Buy it at any news kiosk.

Electronically Yours

The Internet is a fabulous source for researching your trip to France. Hotels, airlines, and travel agents all have their own Web sites. Most major brands also have Web sites, as do the French *grands magasins*—the big department stores. As we go to press, none of them offers e-commerce, but it's on its way.

Some previously hard-to-find information, such as train schedules (**www.sncf.fr**), is easily available online.

So many businesses have Web sites that it's impossible to
give you a list. The best-known English-language site, **Bonjour
Paris** (www.bonjourparis.com), offers the best content. Full dis-
closure: I sometimes write for Bonjour Paris.

Electronically Yours, Part 2

- Get your Internet service provider's French toll-free access
  number before you travel. Some hotel concierges can fur-
  nish it.
- If you are continually cut off and disconnected, don't curse
  AOL. It could be the phone lines and the difference between
  digital and analog connections (don't ask). Take your laptop to the hotel's business center and tap into their T-line
  (the equivalent of an American T1 line). It saves the day for
  me every time.
- There are plenty of **Internet cafes** and centers around town.
- New or newly renovated hotels have dataports in the rooms;
  these may facilitate connecting. For $5.25 at Radio Shack,
  I bought a French modem connector, which is a good investment. In older hotels, an engineer will come to your room
  with one of these and install it for you. Regardless of the
  type of connection, you may not be able to get online. I once
  made the Hôtel de Crillon take all my connection fees
  (totaling about $6/5.50€) off my bill because I could not
  connect. Turns out, it was a digital line and AOL needs an
  analog line, but I didn't know about these things.

GETTING THERE BY PLANE

From the U.S.

While getting to Paris may seem easy enough—after all, most
of the major carriers fly there—I've got a few secrets that
might make getting there more fun and less expensive.

The cheapest airfares are always in winter. Furthermore, winter airfares often coincide with promotional gimmicks. They might include buy one ticket, get one half-price; buy one ticket, bring along a companion for a discounted price; or kids fly free. Also during winter, airlines may reduce the number of frequent-flyer miles you need to reach a particular destination. This seldom applies to Paris, but Brussels often goes "on sale."

Winter always brings airfare price wars; when **Air France** announced a $289 weekend fare to Paris last winter, I think half of New York tilted into the Atlantic in a mad rush for tickets. And, of course, all the other airlines flying to France matched the fare. Tough travel times have made even more low fares available.

Meanwhile, winter weekend European travel is a popular niche. Just about every country has deals that allow for Thursday or Friday departures and Monday or Tuesday returns. The problem with these tickets is that you can't add the week in between; you are limited to *le weekend longue*. Conceptually speaking, people who live on the Eastern seaboard are flocking to Europe on weekends like birds to Florida.

And don't forget online sales and online purchases—two different subjects. Most airlines allow you to register for e-mail announcements of bargains on your favorite routes. I just had a tickle from Delta telling me I could fly from New York to Nice for $428 round-trip—not much more than it would cost me to get there from Paris.

Between the airlines' online fares, discounters' online fares, and airfare wars usually announced in the newspapers, you should be able to find a number of good deals.

A few tricks I have learned during airfare wars: If you buy a ticket, and a price war then makes the same ticket available at a lower price, don't just sit there and stew. The airlines will rewrite your ticket, subject to a service charge. The charge is usually $75 to $150, but you may save money overall.

Another strategy: Buy a cheapie ticket, then pay the fee to change to different dates, which may not have been included during the price war.

Check out consolidators, who unload unsold tickets on scheduled flights at discount prices (which vary with the season, like regular prices). You won't earn frequent-flyer miles. These tickets are great for last-minute travelers who do not qualify for 21-day advance purchase prices. You need only about 4 business days' notice.

Don't forget the big-time tour operators. Rates are lower if you book through French tour operators or wholesalers like **Nouvelles Frontieres** (**www.nouvelles-frontieres.fr**), a major chain of French travel agents, which calls itself **New Frontiers** in the U.S.

Flying from the U.K.

If you think you'll just make a quick little hop from London to Paris on a whim, you may be shocked to realize that the regular airfare is outrageously high, depending on the day and time you fly. For a regular round-trip ticket, figure on paying £200 ($300–$350) per person. If you buy your ticket 14 days in advance and stay over a Saturday night, the fare will drop.

If you need one-way transportation between London and Paris but are keen on flying, an advance round-trip ticket that includes a Saturday-night stay will be less expensive than a one-way ticket. Just throw away the unused portion. *C'est la vie.*

Flying to Brussels

Don't look at me like that! Brussels is just an hour and 20 minutes from Paris, thanks to speedy new train lines; you can easily fly into Brussels and out of Paris (or vice versa), or even go to Paris for the weekend from Belgium. Sometimes, when there are airfare deals and promotions, all seats in and out of Paris are sold. Try Brussels for one leg and see if you can beat the system by being a little bit clever.

Flying from Nice

Many people like to combine the south of France with Paris, especially because the Delta nonstop flight from New York makes it so easy. Getting to Paris can be complicated if you don't work it all out before you decide what to do and how to book the trip. If you are flying Delta on the triangular route, so to speak, you will need a train, a car, or a plane ticket to get you to Paris. Or you can book with Air France. Since Air France has no direct flights from the U.S. to Nice, it offers an alternative that should be priced competitively when it includes Nice—you just want to lay over between legs. Note that because Delta and Air France have merged many of their flights and services, you may be able to book a mixed ticket at a good price. The point of the game is to avoid overpaying for the Paris-Nice link.

GETTING THERE BY TRAIN

There are many, many train fares for travel to and from Paris. Several **BritRail USA** packages allow you to choose which method you'd like to use for getting from the U.K. to the Continent; the Continental Capitals Circuit connects London with Paris, Brussels, and Amsterdam.

Rail Europe (☎ 888/382-7245 in the U.S.) sells passes geared to travel to specific countries (such as the France pass) that enable you to save money on train travel. The price of some products includes an automatic discount (about 30%!) off your Chunnel train (Eurostar) ticket. Note that the Eurostar ticket is not part of any pass currently available; it must be bought as an add-on. Rail Europe also offers multiple-country train passes, as well as other train-drive promotions and products. It's a one-stop agency that can arrange everything, and you'll have the train pass in hand when you land in Europe. Note that if you travel on TGV (fast) trains in France with a train pass, you will need an additional reservation (3€/$3.25).

Rail Europe not only has tons of train passes but also books transatlantic flights, hotels, car rentals—the works. One of the greatest things about its system is that there are different prices based on age (youth passes, seniors, and so forth), as well as on the number of people traveling together. Not just "the more the merrier"—the more the cheaper.

ARRIVING IN PARIS

If you are arriving from the U.S., you will fly into Charles de Gaulle International Airport, or CDG (☎ **01/48-62-22-80** for English-language info about transport; www.ratp.fr). It consists of Terminal 1 and Terminal 2. Terminal 1 has various satellites; Terminal 2 has pods designated A to D. I have been lost in those pods, and it was not pretty.

Note: Flights to and from the U.S. no longer use Orly Airport.

A taxi to the 1er from CDG costs about 50€ ($54). This price includes tip and the traditional surcharge for luggage. Most French taxis are small; if you have a lot of luggage, hold out for a Mercedes taxi. If you have a lot of family plus a lot of luggage, expect to need two taxis. Or you can send one person and all the luggage in a taxi, and let the other members of the family take public transportation.

Air France offers bus service to and from Etoile (take a taxi to your hotel from there) and both airports. You can take Roissy Rail, which lets you off in town at the Gare du Nord or Châtelet.

Several other bus lines serve routes that can get you into the best part of Paris for connecting to your hotel.

If you want private car service, see p. 27.

CALLING AROUND

When calling a phone number inside Paris, dial the entire number, including the "01." When dialing from outside of France, drop the "0." International calls to Paris all begin with "33-1."

GETTING AROUND PARIS

Paris is laid out in a system of zones called *arrondissements,* which circle around from inside to outside. When France adopted postal codes, Parisians incorporated the *arrondissement* number into their codes as the last two digits. Codes for addresses in the city of Paris begin with "75," and the last two digits match the arrondissement. A code of 75016 means the address is in the 16th arrondissement (16e). The first arrondissement is written *1er;* for others, the number followed by a small *e* (2e, 3e, and so forth) signifies the arrondissement.

Knowing the proper arrondissement is essential to getting around rapidly in Paris. It is also a shorthand system for many people to sum up everything a place can or may become— simply by where it is located, or by how far it is from something that is acceptably chic.

Think about arrondissements when planning your shopping expeditions. Check the map frequently, however: You may think that, say, 1er and 16e are far apart, but you can walk between them, and have a great time doing so. (Take the rue du Faubourg St-Honoré toward the Champs-Elysées and you even get a tour of the 8e).

With its wonderful transportation system, Paris is a pretty easy city to navigate. Tourists are usually urged to ride the Métro, but buses can be a treat—you can see where you're going and get a free tour along the way. *Paris par Arrondissement* usually includes bus routes as well as a Métro map. Métro maps are available free at hotels and are printed in almost every guidebook. Keep one in your wallet at all times.

By Métro

There are many Métro ticket plans. If you can speak a little French and visit Paris often enough to take the time to do this, buy a *carte orange.* It is exactly what it sounds like: a small orange card, with a passport-type photo of you. (Bring a photo, or use the photo booth in the station.)

The *carte orange* is not for everyone, because it covers an entire week. It is good for unlimited travel on bus or Métro *for a 1-week period, Monday to Monday.* It is not for sale after Wednesday.

Once you have your permanent orange card, with your photo, you only have to buy a weekly coupon—I've had the same orange card for about 15 years. The *carte orange* is about half the price of the weekly tourist ticket, **"Sesame."** Bargain shopping begins at the Métro station, *mes amis.* However, the *carte orange* does not pay for itself if you don't use it a lot. Now that I live part-time in Paris, I rarely use mine.

Note: You probably cannot get your first *carte orange* unless you speak enough French to negotiate the purchase and can answer a few questions. Touristy tourists will be guided toward other, more expensive arrangements, such as the Sesame. I ask the hotel concierge to write down everything I need, and then I slide the paper under the window at the ticket booth at the Concorde Métro station. Only a handful of stations process the *carte orange* for first-timers, and Concorde is one of them. Remember, you will need a passport photo. Also remember where you put the card when you return home; I keep mine with my passport.

If you want individual tickets, buy them by *carnet.* The 10-ticket *carnet* is for sale at any station, and is good for the bus or the Métro. An individual Métro ticket costs about $1.20 (1.10€) a ride; with the *carnet,* the price drops by about 10% (to .96€).

The *Paris Visite* transportation pass provides travel for 3 to 5 days (depending on what you buy); it costs up to $30 (27.60€) but includes rides to the airport, outlying suburbs, and even Versailles. It's an awfully good deal if you plan to use it. The pass comes in a black case in which you insert something that looks like the coupon used in a *carte orange.* Another *Paris Visite* pass is good for unlimited 1-day travel. It costs about $5 (4.60€), but remember, the *carte orange* costs about $10 (9.20€) and it's good for a whole week. You can't go to

Paris by Arrondissement

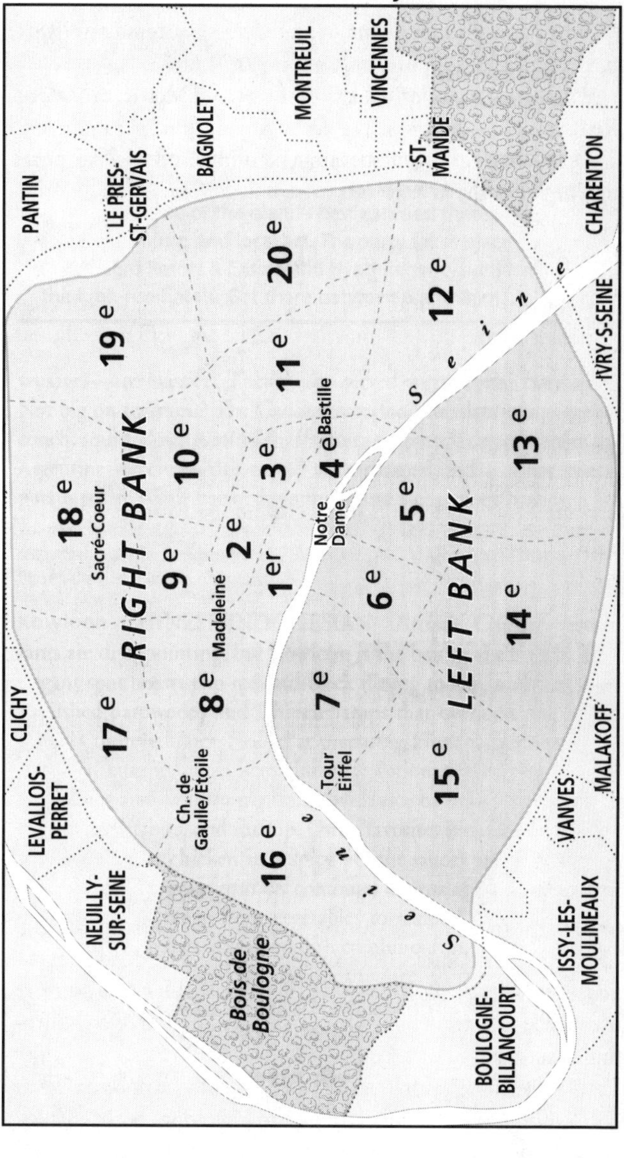

Versailles on the *carte orange,* but a regular round-trip RER ticket to Versailles costs only about $5 (4.60€).

Passes are for sale at RATP stations (big Métro stations or RER stations—I look at the acronym and think "rapid transit"), SNCF (French national train) stations, and ADP (airports de Paris) booths at both airports.

By RER

If you use the RER trains within the city of Paris, you can use a regular Métro ticket; some *Paris Visite* coupons are valid on RER out of town, as far as Versailles even.

By Bus

Paris buses take the same coupons as the Métro, and cash. They are much slower than the underground, but you get to see the sights.

By Taxi

The taxi meter drops at 2€ ($2.15) and goes up, up, and away—extras for luggage, for extra people, for dogs. Taxi drivers may also take you on a scenic route in order to bring the fare up, blaming traffic. Sit back and enjoy it. Tip at least 1€ unless the cheat has been a violation to common sense.

By Car

If you plan to visit the countryside or Disneyland Paris, you may want to rent a car. As long as you avoid driving around the place de la Concorde, you'll be fine. As an added convenience, most major car-rental agencies will allow you to drop the car at a hotel, saving you the time and trouble of returning it yourself.

If you intend to drive around Paris (silly you), be sure you know about parking regulations and how to work the meters, which provide a ticket that proves you've paid. (Display it prominently in your windshield.) Just because you don't see a meter like we have in the U.S. doesn't mean that parking is free. Also, you may need a new-fangled parking *carte* from a news kiosk to get the ticket.

If you prefer a car and driver, contact **Paris Millenium** (☎ **01/30-71-93-03;** fax 01/30-71-97-91; www.chez.com/paris millenium); ask for Mathieu, who speaks perfect English. There are special *Born to Shop* rates for airport transfers and shopping tours.

E.T., PHONE MAISON

- The most expensive way to phone home is from your hotel room.
- Using a pay phone is not particularly difficult, especially if you use a French Telecom *telecarte.* You can buy one at any newsstand.
- Another way to save is to use a direct-dialing service through your long-distance carrier at home. For **AT&T,** call ☎ **0-800-99-00-11;** for **MCI,** call ☎ **0-800-99-00-19;** for **Sprint,** use ☎ **0-800-99-00-87.** These systems are more expensive than I like, but many people pay for the convenience and like the well-advertised connect numbers.
- Many stores have introduced telephone cards along the American model, with an access code and a discounted rate for local or international calls. I bought mine at Printemps; FNAC and many other stores sell them. You can use this card from a hotel, and it's amazing. I spoke to a friend in the U.S. for over a half-hour for less than $10 (9.20€). These cards require some reading in French; if your French isn't good, ask the hotel concierge to read the card to you, or have someone at the store explain it.
- Renting a mobile phone, especially a bi-band, is a popular way to keep in touch. You may rent in the U.S. or in France, often through your car-rental firm or hotel. If you rent the phone before you leave the U.S., you can give out your number in advance. Call **InTouchUSA** (☎ **800/872-7626**),

a service that will help you reach out and touch—and can also evaluate your own phone's capabilities.

- You can buy a bi-band portable phone in France; it will work everywhere in the world but the U.S. They are sold without monthly charges, which is obviously the type a tourist would want to buy. Prices begin at around $30 (28€). Instructions are available in dozens of languages; the guide that comes with the phone, however, may be only in French.
- If you have a three-way phone from the U.S., you can be reached in Europe on your home number—just remember to change the band when you arrive. Arranging an international plan with a U.S. long-distance carrier brings the costs of those calls down to a few cents a minute.

E-MAILING HOME

If you do not normally travel with your computer, you can still use e-mail. Most luxury hotels have Web television, as well as a business center where you can log on. Paris also has tons of cybercafes (p. 129).

POSTCARDS HOME

Postcards in Paris are as original and arty as the city itself. There are thousands of designs and styles to choose from, but watch out—many of them cost $1 to $2 (.90€–1.85€) each! The large, enormously cute Disney cards (sold in Paris, not Disneyland Paris) cost even more. The better the postcard design, the higher the price.

You can buy postcards for less if you shop carefully; you may even luck out and find 15 cards for 2€ ($2.15). Walk along the rue de Rivoli, where the tourist traps are thick, checking prices as you go. The price per card drops as you head uptown (away from Concorde, toward the Louvre), and the bulk deals get better. Tourist traps near Notre Dame also sell postcards and often offer bulk deals.

You can buy stamps at a PTT (post office), at a tobacco shop, or from your hotel concierge. Postage to the U.S. (even for a postcard) is .63€ (68¢); local postage, which includes other EU countries, is .47€ (51¢).

Traditionally, stamps in France do not have the price printed on them. They are color-coded: the orange stamp is for EU (including local) mail, and the blue stamp is for international and non-EU items.

SHOPPING HOURS

Shopping hours in Paris are extremely irregular and independent. Welcome to France. Thankfully, they are big-city hours, so you needn't worry about a lot of downtime, as in Italy or the French provinces. There are plenty of shopping opportunities even on Sunday and Monday, and some serious late-night shopping.

Generally speaking, *stores are open Monday, or part of Monday*. Stores that are closed on Monday morning—usually, small establishments—open anytime from noon on, sometimes 1, 2, or even 3pm. Department stores and branches of the major chains are open on Monday morning; about 50% of the stores on the Left Bank in the prime shopping areas are open.

During the rest of the week, most stores consider 10am to 7pm standard hours, but there are many exceptions to this rule, such as it is. Some stores open at 10am, except 1 day of the week, when they open at 9:30am. Some stores are open until 10pm on Thursday only. A few stores are open until 8 or 9pm every weekday, especially in high-traffic areas.

My favorite is Au Printemps, which opens not at 9:30am but at 9:35am! It's impossible to know or keep track of every store's hours. Other stores have a few weird twists to their hours, like Hermès—which closes for lunch on Monday and Saturday.

mer, many stores close for lunch on Saturday but stay open later in the evening. Some stores are open for lunch during the week but close for lunch on Saturday.

France has about 15 bank holidays a year; stores may close on these holidays. Beware the month of May! Not only does May have about 10 holidays in it, but it's hard to know when stores will be open. May 1 is a huge holiday, and everything is closed. May 8 is a less important holiday, and stores may or may not be open—check ads in *Le Figaro*. Your hotel concierge may not know. Also note that openings may be related to the part of town. On May 8, I was shut out in the 16th arrondissement, but found stores in most other neighborhoods open. Go figure.

The entire month of August may be unusual. Most of France closes down on August 15 for the Feast of the Assumption, but some stores close for the entire month, or just from August 14 to August 31. Bastille Day, July 14, is a holiday, and stores are closed—but some small retailers open, if only for a few hours, to take advantage of the crowds in the streets.

Bonne chance, as we say.

SUNDAY IN THE PARK WITH GEORGES

....

Although traditional Parisian retail closes on Sunday, there is still an enormous amount of shopping. Aside from the flea-market business, which has always been hot on Sunday, nowadays entire neighborhoods are jumping.

Check out:

- The **Louvre,** with the adjoining mall Carrousel du Louvre, the Antiquaires des Louvre, and all the touristy shops on rue de Rivoli
- The **Marais,** including the retail street rue Francs Bourgeois
- The **Champs-Elysées,** where most stores open on Sunday at noon (except Monoprix, which does not open on Sun)
- The **Ile St-Louis**

Many stores that open on Sunday are closed on Monday.

Antiquing on Sunday is a national hobby; don't forget to check the newspapers, or ask your concierge about special weekend shows or events. From February through May, the weekends are dense with special events, many of which highlight shows for antiques, *brocante* (used items, not necessarily antiques), or both.

When the weather is good, shops in the main flow of tourist traffic may open on Sunday to catch the extra business. Every now and then a duty-free shop will open; tourist traps near popular attractions are almost always open on Sunday afternoons. By 5pm on Sunday, though, it's hard to find any place that's open.

EXCEPTIONAL OPENINGS

The French government allows retailers five exceptional openings on Sundays during the year. These are most often taken around Christmas, but there's usually one in September or October for back-to-school shopping. Often, openings on holidays in May are also known as exceptional. Exceptional openings are usually advertised in French newspapers like *Le Figaro*.

SALE PERIODS

Officially, the French government sets the dates of the sales, and there are only two sales periods: one in winter (Jan) and one in summer (June–July). However, many retailers, strapped for cash, offer assorted promotions and discounts these days. A few, like Hermès, have special events held outside the store. These events are advertised and listed in papers; check the page called *Le Carnet du Jour* in *Le Figaro* for sale ads.

The big department stores turn their sale promotions into mega-deals, with banners all over the front of the stores and enticing titles. You don't need to speak French to get the picture—the ads and banners make it quite clear.

The thing that I find most frightening about French sales is that they last a set time and are then over. The sale merchandise does not stay marked down! I fell in love with a tablecloth at a department store. On sale it cost $150 (138€), which I thought was a little high for my budget, so I decided to think about it. When I went back, it cost $200 (184€).

PERSONAL NEEDS

Pharmacies are marked with a green neon cross; at least one in each neighborhood must be open on Sunday. When a pharmacy is closed, a sign in the window indicates the nearest open pharmacy.

Machines in all Métro stations and pharmacies sell condoms.

If you need a book in English, try **Brentano's,** 37 av. de la Opéra (Métro: Opéra), or **W.H. Smith,** 248 rue de Rivoli (Métro: Concorde). Both sell American and British books and periodicals. Most luxury hotels sell daily or Sunday London newspapers. A small cadre of Left Bank bookstores sell books in English and serve as hangouts for expats. Check out **Village Voice, Tea & Tattered Pages,** and **Shakespeare & Co.**

AIRPORT SHOPPING

Both Orly and CDG have more than their share of shopping opportunities—in fact, the shopping is so brisk that the airports have their own shopping bag. Stores at CDG are fancier than those at Orly (which handles no international traffic), but you will have no trouble dropping a few, or a few hundred, euros.

Prices at the airport duty-free shops may be slightly cheaper than at comparable retail stores in Paris, but not much. There are usually better bargains in Paris, especially if you qualify for détaxe. Do not be confused by the new duty-free laws; you are entitled to buy duty-free goods if you are leaving the EU. If you are traveling to another EU country, you may not get the discount.

Those in search of cosmetic and fragrance bargains should already have bought them in Paris at the duty-free shops, which offer 20% to 40% savings. You will save only 13% at the duty-free stores at the airport. The selection at the airport may be better than the selection on your airplane, but the airline's prices can be better. It pays to take the duty-free price list from your plane when you arrive and save it for comparison when you're shopping at the airport at the end of your trip. I also keep a Saks Fifth Avenue price list in my wallet for each of the fragrances that I like. Saks prints them constantly in mailers, bill stuffers, ads, and so on. You'd be surprised how often a duty-free price can be the same as the Saks Fifth Avenue price!

Legally speaking, you may not buy duty-free goods if you are leaving for another EU destination. To be precise, you can buy them, but you will pay the full retail price. If you are departing the EU, you may buy at the duty-free price (13% less than regular retail).

Chapter Three

....

MONEY MATTERS

UNIFICATION & YOU

The EU (European Union) has officially united its currency into the long-anticipated euro. Surely you've seen this coming, so don't freak—I'll get you through this easy as *tarte Tatin*.

If euros on price tags confuse you, calm down. The euro-to-franc ratio is close to the dollar-to-franc ratio when the exchange rate was 6 to 7 francs per dollar. To get a quick fix on a price, you can consider euros and dollars at parity (1€ = $1).

WHY EUROS?

I will oversimplify this: The population of the U.S. is approximately 280 million. The population of the current member countries of the Euro zone is approximately 300 million. The whole point of the unification of the EU and the "*monie unique*" (the euro) was to be able to compete with the U.S. on a more or less equal footing. The goal is for the euro to gain parity with the U.S. dollar—so spend now while you're saving.

About Those Euros

As we went to press, 12 member countries were participating in the euro scheme. The UK has been debating the issue for years and may join around 2005, but many votes need to be taken before then. Other countries want to join the euro zone; geographically they rest between Switzerland and Greece. Those Scandinavia countries that did not join the euro system seem to have no second thoughts at this time.

In France, you might want to pronounce the word *euro* in the local accent, or people may not know what you are talking about. Say: uhr-oh. If you speak enough French to add numbers to it, remember to slur the plurals—*euro* begins with a vowel, so *deux euros* is pronounced doose-uhros; *dix euros* is dees-uhros.

Travelers will find that euro bills are the same through the zone, but the coins are minted locally—they have different art on them and are of differing weights. (This caused problems in highway toll machines but shouldn't affect you in Paris.) Collectors note that coins with the portrait of Pope John Paul II are expected to be very valuable.

Coins of the Realm

Locals can't stop talking about the way euro coins outnumber franc coins. A booming industry produces plastic containers that sort and hold coins, coin purses, and wallets with individual coin slots. Some coins will strike you as annoying (for various reasons), but remember that many of them were invented so no one could feel cheated in the transition period. It's expected that some of the smaller coins will go out of circulation.

The 20-cent piece is the size of the old franc and similar in size to the 1€ coin, which may drive you nuts. There are more 2€ coins than 1€ coins in circulation, so you end up parting with 2€ when you didn't really want to (for instance, when tipping).

FAKES & FRAUDS

If you are worried about fake euros, you are not the only one, and, yes, they have been spotted. Some appeared *before* the launch of the euro. Talk about dumb. Here are some characteristics of the real thing:

- All bills are made with a cotton fiber blend, so you can feel the texture.
- The bills have an iridescent band that seems to dance in different colors in the right light.
- A hologram band within the strip has the amount printed on it.

Price Tags

By law, prices in the euro zone were listed in both euros and local currency for 3 years before the launch; in some stores—at least, as we go to press—prices are still in francs and euros, which helps people get grounded on what the price is. In the provinces, God only knows when they'll get the hang of the whole thing.

Naturally, once the euro price had to be set, enterprising businesses began to fool around with price tags. Restaurants were first—they converted prices to easy euro figures, listing amounts in francs as the odd man out. Within the next 2 years, all prices will have shifted to easy euro figures, and the franc prices will disappear.

With the launch, some products and businesses announced that they were rounding prices up or down (and when they round *down,* they make a big deal out of their nobility). Others translated prices from francs to euros, which gives you odd price tags. The only price regulated by law is the price of bread.

Tax is included in the euro zone, so the price on the tag is the price at the checkout counter.

Up, Damn Price

In the adjustment period, most prices have gone up. While across the board the increase is about 20%, some of the rises have been more dramatic—mass-market shampoo has gone up 23%, milk is up 47%, and batteries are up 62%. The cost of the daily newspaper *Le Figaro* is down a fraction; McDonald's has lowered prices on the Big Mac.

As a shopper, you will soon feel the pinch. There are still bargains, but the cost of living has gone up. It's my bet that tourists will reconsider their shopping habits, if only because people are more aware of how much they are spending now.

ALAS, MY DETAXE

One of the other goals of the EU is to bring value-added tax throughout member countries to the same 15%. This is not going to be easy, especially where the tax is as high as 22%. However, everyone is trying. In the spirit of cooperation, the French recently dropped TVA from 20.6% to 19.6%.

However, when you file for a tax refund, you rarely get back 19.6%. Instead, expect 12% or maybe 13%. For an explanation of détaxe, see "Détaxe Details," below.

SPENDING DOWN

If you still have French francs in your drawer, now is the time to get rid of them. Bills can be exchanged for euros at any Bank of France until 2012, coins until 2005. The French franc is no longer legal tender in France (or anywhere), so give yours to charity or stop by the bank.

Locals had a 6-week period for "spending down" their euros, when francs and euros were accepted. That period is gone. So love me tender and take your old tender to the Bank of France. No other bank will accept francs.

CURRENCY EXCHANGE

If you have no francs and are a euro virgin, you'll get the hang of this in no time. You can buy traveler's checks in euros, which will be good for later trips to other destinations.

You can also use your ATM card from the U.S. to withdraw euros from a French ATM, although your bank at home will probably charge you $5 each time you do. There are bank windows and ATMs at the airports, so you can have euros for your taxi into town.

For tipping, the $1 bill is still a good thing to have on hand, especially if you are stuck in that nowhere land created by the loss of the 10F piece.

HOW TO GET CASH OVERSEAS

ATMs

Sacré cash card! This is without doubt the easiest and possibly best way for exchanging money—*le bank machine.* Bank cash machines are everywhere in Europe. Just look for the Cirrus and NYCE logo—some bank machines are only for local bank cards. Also note that when you see several bank machines in a row, they may not be the same. Sometimes only some of the machines give money back; the others are for customers' transactions. Read the signs above each machine.

As much as I love ATMs, I find myself betwixt and between on the fee-versus-safety issue. If you try to save the $5 fee, you may end up with a lot of cash in your wallet and feel nervous.

Amex

Card members may draw on their American Express cards for cash advances or may cash personal checks. *Never travel without your checkbook.*

It's relatively simple: You write a personal check at a special desk and show your card, it is approved, and then you go to another desk and get the money in the currency you request. Allow about a half-hour for the whole process, unless there are long lines. The same desk usually handles cash advances.

With some types of cards, you can write a check in dollars at a hotel and get back euros.

Visa

Some Visa cards allow you to take cash loans from your bank while you are in a foreign destination.

Traveler's Checks

I still think they are great, and I *love* having "free money" for my next trip if I didn't use all the checks I bought. I get mine through AAA so I don't have to pay a fee.

DEBIT CARDS

U.S. and French debit cards work on different formats. You will probably use your U.S. debit card more like a credit card for your end of the transaction in France, although the payment will be automatically deducted from your debit account. You will probably have to sign a paper, however. I got a notice from my U.S. bank saying that my debit card could be used internationally only six times. I was in hot water.

(To use a French debit card, you punch a code into a machine—you sign nothing. Your U.S. debit card will not work this way in France.)

TIPS ON TIPPING

Tipping in Paris can be confusing, because all restaurant and hotel bills include a service charge. While you do not have to add a tip to a restaurant check, it's often done—simply round up the bill or plunk down an extra euro or two or five. It's all the waiter will see of your real tip; think 5% of the total.

Also note that tipping has suffered with the loss of the 10F coin, which used to be the perfect tip. If you are cheap, tip in dollars. If you are going French style, substitute 2€ for 10F and just suck it up.

That Was No Tip

So my girlfriend Dorrie and I go to the flea market at Vanves, and stop at one of the cafes on the main drag when market is about over. Tourists speaking many different languages fill the cafe. We have lunch and speak French. The bill is 25.65€. We put 30.65€ on the tray and wait for change. We wait and wait. Finally we ask where's the change, dude . . . and the waiter says, "Change? I thought that was the tip for my colleague and myself."

No one—no one—in France leaves a 5€ tip on a 25€ meal, nor do Americans add exact change to get back exact change if they don't want exact change.

Tourists beware.

You may, however, do some rounding up—say 3€ for two pieces of luggage to the bellboy. The hotel doorman can get 1€ for getting a taxi, or you can leave an envelope at the end of your stay at the hotel, with a total of 5€ or 10€ for the doormen.

SEND MONEY

You can have money sent from home, a process that usually takes about 2 days. Money can be wired through **Western Union** (☎ 800/325-6000 in the U.S.). Someone brings cash or a certified check to the office, and WU does the rest—this may take up to a week. You can also get cash with an international money order, which is cleared by telex through the bank where you cash it. Money can be wired from bank to bank, but this works only when your American bank has branches in Europe or a relationship with a French bank. Banks usually charge a large fee for doing you this favor.

In addition, American Express can arrange for a Money Gram (☎ 800/543-4080 in the U.S.), a check for up to $500 that family or friends at home can send. You cash it at the American Express office in Paris.

DÉTAXE DETAILS

••

Détaxe is the refund you get on TVA, the 19.6% value-added tax on all goods sold in France (except goods needed for home repairs, which carry a 5.5% tax). TVA is similar to sales tax in the U.S. The French pay it automatically. Tourists can get a refund on it.

There are more and more ways of getting that refund.

The basic détaxe system—the process of getting a refund on this tax—works pretty much like this:

You are shopping in a store with prices marked on the merchandise. This is the true price that any tourist or any national must pay. If you are a French national, you pay the price without thinking twice. If you are a tourist who plans to leave the country within 6 months, you may qualify for a détaxe refund. Currently the minimum by French law for a détaxe refund is 183€ ($197.65) for a person spending this amount (or more) in one store on a single day. Each store has the right to establish the amount (over 183€) you must spend to qualify for the refund.

You may no longer save up receipts over a period of time— to get the refund, you spend the money in the same store on the same day. For this reason, planning one big haul at one of the department stores is often your best bet.

If you go for the détaxe refund, budget your time to allow for the paperwork. It takes about 15 minutes to fill out each store's forms, and may take 20 to 60 minutes for you to receive the forms back, because the store must process them. But you never know—I've zipped through the line in less than 5 minutes. Allow more time than you need, just in case.

My secret? Return to the department store the moment it opens, and head directly to the détaxe desk.

You will need your passport number (but not necessarily the passport itself) to fill out the paperwork. The space that asks for your address is asking for the name of your hotel. You do not need to provide its address. After the papers are filled out, they will be given back to you with an envelope, usually addressed to the store. Sometimes the envelope has a stamp on it; sometimes it is blank (if the latter, you must affix a stamp to it before you leave the country). At other times, it has a special government frank that serves as a stamp. If you don't understand what's on your envelope, ask.

At the airport, go to the Customs official who services the détaxe papers. Do this before you clear regular Customs or part with your luggage. There are two ways to do this: 1) Check your luggage but keep your purchases separate and carry them on board with you; 2) Wheel your packed luggage to the Customs Office and be prepared to unpack the items.

The Customs officer has the right to ask you to show him or her the merchandise you bought and are taking out of the country. Whether the officer sees your purchases or not, he or she will stamp the papers, keeping a set (which will be processed) and giving you another set. Place this set in the envelope, and mail the envelope to the shop where you made your purchases. (Sometimes the Customs officer keeps the specially franked envelopes. Don't worry, they'll be mailed.)

Note: Since unification in 1993, you claim your détaxe when you leave your final EU destination to return to the U.S. If you are going on to Belgium from France, you claim everything as you exit Belgium and process your paperwork there. You'll get the French laws and the French discounts, but the paperwork itself is done at Belgian customs. Ditto for Britain, Italy, and elsewhere in the EU.

When the papers get back to the shop and the government has notified the shop that their set of papers has been registered, the store will grant you the discount through a refund. This can be done on your credit card (the shop will have made a dual pressing), or through a personal check, which will come in the mail (see below).

So that's how the system works.

Now, here are the fine points: *The way in which you get your discount is somewhat negotiable!* At the time of purchase, discuss your options for the refund with the retailer. Depending on how much you have bought, how big a store it is, or how cute you are, you may get a more favorable situation. At Galeries Lafayette, you have five different choices of how to take the refund (including as a credit on your next purchase).

Here are the two most popular ways to get your refund, in order of preference to the tourist:

- The retailer sells you the merchandise at the cheapest price possible, including the tax refund, and takes a loss on the income until the government reimburses him or her. For example: The bottle of fragrance you want costs $50 (46€). The détaxe is about $7.50 (6.90€). The best possible deal is for the retailer to charge you $42.50 (39.10€), give you the détaxe papers, and explain that he will not get the rest of his money unless you process the papers properly. Being as honorable as you are, of course you process the papers. This is "instant détaxe," and is the practice in most name-brand stores and parfumeries.
- You pay for the purchase, at the regular retail price, with a major credit card. The clerk makes a second imprint of your card for a refund slip, marked for the amount of the détaxe. You sign both slips. When the papers come back to the retailer, the shop puts through the credit slip. The credit may appear on the same monthly statement as the original bill, or on a subsequent bill. Just remember to check that the credit goes through.

With the old-fashioned and most basic method, you pay the regular retail price with cash, traveler's check, or credit card. You take the forms and go through the refund process described above, get on your plane, and go home. Several (usually about 3) months later, you get a check for the refund amount in the mail. This check is in the currency of the country in which you made the purchase and will have to be converted to dollars, a process for which your bank may charge you a percentage or a fee. Or you can go to a currency broker and get the money in the currency of origin to save for your next trip to that country. Either way, it's a pain in the neck.

Final note: The tax refund at department stores is 12%— the store takes the rest for fees. The refund at designer shops and boutiques is 13%; same thinking. Only a few rare stores actually give you a 19% or 20% discount. They say the spread is used to cover their expenses, but actually they make a heap of money off this and therefore encourage you to get the refund.

Money, Money Everywhere

So, if the department stores and boutiques are "making" about 7% off each refund, you can begin to figure that this refund business is hot stuff. Add to that the fact that it's confusing to beginners, time-consuming, and possibly annoying. Enter the professional refund services, which will happily help you through the process. Phew, you are thinking. For a fee, of course. Well, that seems fair enough, you say—nothing is free. Usually, it's a hidden fee or even a double fee in the guise of fee plus exchange rate.

This works several different ways and is totally legal, so I am not going to name names. Also, in some countries, the détaxe process is so complicated that even paying a double fee is a blessing. This is not the case in France.

The smartest way to get your détaxe refund is as a credit applied to your charge or bank card. Even if you paid for the purchase with cash, you can still have the refund applied to a credit card. Even if you are issued a "refund checque," you can endorse it on the back to be refunded to your credit card.

Détaxe on Trains & Ferries

If you leave Paris by train (such as the overnight train to Istanbul), you may be in a panic about your détaxe refund. Not to worry. As mentioned above, you now apply for the refund as you leave the EU. If your train is taking you to another EU country, you do not even have to think about filing for your détaxe refund in France.

If your train (or ferry) is taking you to a non-EU country, you will need to do the paperwork on board. No problem. Shortly after you board the international train, the conductor for your car will poke his head into your cabin, introduce himself (he speaks many languages), ask for your passport, and give you the Customs papers for the crossing of international borders. If you are on the sleeper, hc handles the paperwork in the middle of the night while you sleep.

U.S. Customs & Duties

To make your reentry into the U.S. as smooth as possible, follow these tips:

- Know the rules and stick to them.
- Don't try to smuggle anything.
- Be polite and cooperative (up until the point when they ask you to strip, anyway . . .).

Remember:

- You are allowed to bring in $400 worth of merchandise per person, duty free. (Books, which are duty-free, are not included.) Before you leave the U.S., verify this amount with a Customs office. Each member of the family, including infants, is entitled to the deduction.
- Currently, you pay a flat 10% duty on the next $1,000 worth of merchandise.
- Duties thereafter are based on the type of product and vary tremendously.
- The "head of the family" can make a joint declaration for all family members. Whoever is the head of the family should take responsibility for answering Customs officers' questions. Answer honestly, firmly, and politely. Have

receipts ready, and make sure they match the information on the landing card. Don't be forced into a story that won't wash under questioning. If you tell a little lie, you'll be labeled a fibber, and they'll tear your luggage apart.

- Have the Customs registration slips for your personal goods in your wallet or easily available. If you wear a Cartier watch, be able to produce the registration slip. If you cannot prove that you took a foreign-made item out of the U.S. with you, you may be forced to pay duty on it. If you own such items but have no registration or sales slips, take photos or Polaroids of the goods and have them notarized in the U.S. before you depart. The notary seal and date will prove you had the goods in the U.S. before you left the country.

- The unsolicited gifts you mailed from abroad do not count in the $400-per-person rate. If the value of the gift is more than $50, you pay duty when the package comes into the country. Remember, it's only one unsolicited gift per person. Don't mail to yourself.

- Do not attempt to bring in any illegal food items—dairy products, meats, fruits, or vegetables. Generally speaking, if it's alive, it's verboten. Coffee is okay. Any creamy French cheese is illegal, but a hard or cured cheese is legal as long as it has aged 60 days.

- Elephant ivory is illegal to import. Antique ivory pieces may be brought into the country if you have papers stating their provenance.

- Antiques must be 100 years old to be duty-free. Provenance papers will help, as will permission to export the antiquity, since it could be an item of national cultural significance. Any bona fide work of art is duty-free, whether it was painted 50 years ago or yesterday; the artist need not be famous.

- Dress for success. People who look like "hippies" get stopped at Customs more than average folks. Women who look like a million dollars, sporting fur coats, first-class baggage tags, and Gucci handbags, but declare that they have bought nothing, are equally suspicious.

Chapter Four

....

SLEEPING & EATING IN PARIS

MEMO TO BROTHER JOHN

....

If you are a regular *Born to Shop* reader, please note that the basics of this chapter have changed a bit: I am trying more than ever to stress value and to explain luxury only when it makes sense. Or gives you a baseline for comparison.

I am not one of those shoppers, however, who doesn't spend money on food and lodging. Sure, I'm always up for another pair of shoes, but what makes a memory whole isn't the joke about the fleabag hotel, but the secret smile of triumph that you juggled it all, made sense of it, and won the game.

ARE YOU SLEEPING?

....

Some of the world's best hotels are in Paris; thankfully, they are cheaper than those in London. But the really fancy ones have gotten a lot fancier in recent years—and more expensive. Even midpriced hotels can be expensive; furthermore, you can stay in a fabulous hotel or you can stay in a terrible hotel for the same amount of money. That's why I do so much hotel research and keep looking for the best buys.

The kind of trip you have is very much related to the hotel you book. Please take the time to research value and make sure you don't get burned. Also remember the importance of the $50 difference (p. 55)—sometimes you have to spend a little more to save a lot more. Even if you love your hotel, spend a little time during your visit to do some research for future trips. It's good to have backup plans.

When pricing hotels, especially during promotions, make sure to read the fine print and understand what you're getting. Some hotels require a minimum stay of 2 consecutive nights for you to qualify for a bargain price. Some "deals" are good only on weekends. Bear in mind as well that the price listed may be per person or per room. Also, several promotions may be offered simultaneously, leaving you confused as to which one is the best.

Remember that July and August are high season for airfare, but low season in terms of hotel rooms in Paris. Some of the best deals of the year can be made during this time, so ask around.

Here are a few more of my hotel booking secrets:

- **Think winter.** The rack rate, or official room rate, at a luxury hotel in Paris is generally between $300 and $500 (276€ and 460€) a night (or more) for a double. Don't flinch. A palace hotel normally charges at least $500 (460€).
- It's rare that anyone has to pay the **rack rate.** Paris is most attractive and most fully booked in May, June, September, and October. Those are not good months to get a break on a fancy hotel room. Think December. Think January. Even February. Or think tragedies that bring deals. When business is slow, hotels will deal.
- **Work with hotel associations and chains.** Most hotels are members of associations or chains that have blanket promotions. Leading Hotels of the World offers a fabulous corporate rate. Most hotels have rates frozen in U.S. dollars for at least a portion of the year, especially when they are in a promotional period but often in summer. These invariably have to be booked in the United States, but usually offer incredible value. Some hotels offer special rates for certain months; others offer these rates year-round!

- **Never assume that all hotels in a chain are equal.** Even if you are talking about big American chains, such as Hilton or Sheraton, you will find hotels in every category of style and price within the same chain. Concorde Hotels, one of the most famous chains in France, has plenty of moderately priced hotels as well as the Crillon, one of the fanciest and most expensive hotels in Paris. By the same token, it's not unusual for a booking agent from any chain to try to trade you from one hotel in the chain to another, especially in a similar price bracket. Don't do it without knowing the properties.
- **Think package tours.** Airlines and tour operators often offer you the same trip you could plan for yourself with the kind of hotels you really want to stay at, but for less money. Check it all out. Beware, however: On a package tour, you may not get as good a room as you would on your own, and your chances of being upgraded are lower.
- **Think opening day . . . or reopening day.** New and newly renovated hotels introduce themselves and woo back regular clients with amazing deals and perks. Pershing Hall, a boutique hotel in the 16e, offered excellent get-acquainted rates; the Ramada at Champs-Elysées ran a $199 (183€) opening special, then went to over $400 (368€) a night for the same room.
- **Think competition.** While the George V closed to transform itself into the Four Seasons, two neighboring hotels—the deluxe Prince de Galles and the Queen Elizabeth—enjoyed increased business. With the Four Seasons now open, try these hotels, which may try to lure you with price cuts.
- Don't forget **online deals.**
- Remember, especially if there are more than two in your group, that **renting an apartment** may give you more of the feel of living in Paris, and save money.
- **Compare apples to apples.** Get the best price you can from one or two luxury or palace hotels, and use that as your baseline so that you can figure out what you are really getting with other hotel offers.

ONLINE RESEARCH

Now that I live in Paris, I can't tell you how many people ask me either to recommend a hotel or to run over to some bizarre neighborhood and check out addresses they have clipped from magazines. This makes me nuts. I have learned to tell everyone to visit www.bonjourparis.com. Its hotel section allows you to see hotels in every price range and every neighborhood—and to look at pictures of the rooms. In fact, this is perhaps the best English-language website about Paris (and all of France); you can look up everything, and make reservations directly.

Most hotels or hotel chains also have websites that allow you to look at the property and make reservations.

HOTEL CHAINS & ASSOCIATIONS

If you prefer to book all your reservations in one phone call or don't want any surprises, almost every major hotel chain in the world has a property in Paris. I've found that the big American chains offer the type of room you would expect, while the offerings of the smaller European chains can be very uneven. I have listed only major chains or associations with properties in the most convenient neighborhoods for shopping.

A recent trend in the Paris hotel scene is for a big chain to come to town and open a smallish lodging with many qualities of a boutique hotel. The good news: These hotels usually have great locations, are easy to book, and can certainly be trusted. The bad news: Some of them cost almost as much as the palace hotels.

If you think that's something, ask your travel agent about **Bulgari Hotels & Resorts,** a new luxury chain being created by the Italian jewelry house Bulgari and the Marriott hotel group. Its Paris hotel won't open until 2005, but remember, you read it here.

On the other hand, I just got a call from a businessman in the U.S. who said his company is cutting back on expenses and

he must give up the **Hotel Meurice** (average room $600/552€)—
where would I send him? I suggested the **Hotel Inter-Continental,**
which is across the street from the Meurice and at that time
was offering a special of $179 (165€) a night per room. I also
mentioned the **Hotel Meliá Vendome,** around the corner from
the Meurice. The drop-dead-gorgeous member of the Spanish
hotel chain charges $325 (299€) per night. For more on these
hotels, see below.

U.S.-Based Hotel Chains

Hilton   There's a large Hilton right near the Eiffel Tower. This
isn't the best shopping location in the world, but it does have
many promotions and price breaks, including 3 nights for the
price of 2 on a Spring Weekend Breaks deal. Don't miss the
restaurant, Pacific Eiffel. There's also a Hilton at each Paris
airport. ☎ **800/HILTONS.**

Hyatt   The Hyatt Regency Madeleine, right near the
Madeleine, is almost a secret find. Café M is a good place to
take a shopping break and check out the hotel for another stay.
☎ **800/233-1234** in the U.S.

Inter-Continental   The chain's two Paris hotels are undergoing major renovations; one may be closed when you try to
book. When the renovations end, you can benefit from new
towels and welcome rates. Neither hotel feels like a member
of a chain. Both occupy historic buildings in fabulous locations,
and both offer among the best promotional rates in the business. You can even earn frequent-flyer points.

Both Inter-Continental hotels are great, but bear in mind
that Le Grand Hôtel Inter-Continental caters to tour groups,
has approximately 1,000 rooms, and can resemble Grand
Central Terminal at 9am. A very stylish Grand Central Terminal, but you get the idea. The rooms are tiny. The location,
especially for shoppers, is beyond sensational. The restaurants
are excellent. The nearby transportation choices are among the
best in Paris. ☎ **800/327-0200** in the U.S. for reservations.

Marriott   This chain has opened a nice little shopping hotel right above Sephora on the Champs-Elysées—you can't beat the location. The hotel is extraordinarily deep, so don't let the front door deceive you. The hotel strives to appear discreet, but go up to the lobby, explore the hotel, and you will be smitten. Sunday brunch outside on the terrace is a must. *Note:* This hotel invariably sells out and may not be very flexible on rates. ☎ **800/228-9290** in the U.S. for reservations.

Radisson   This chain recently opened a luxury boutique, the Radisson Champs-Elysées, hotel right off the Champs-Elysées at the top of Etoile, adjacent to the great shopping in the 8e and 16e. ☎ **800/333-3333** in the U.S.

Sheraton   In Paris, Starwood offers the **Prince of Wales** (Hôtel Prince de Galles), part of Sheraton's St. Regis Collection of grande dame hotels. The property is next door to the famed Georges V, with which it sometimes has a price war. Furthermore, it offers frequent promotions and airline mileage packages. The property is gorgeous in the intimate but gold ormolu tradition. ☎ **800/325-3535.**

International Hotel Chains & Associations

Accor   The largest hotel chain in the world, Accor is a holding company that owns many chains, among them the former Westin-Demeure chain and the Sofitel group. In the former Westin group are several small but luxe hotels, including the Castille, on rue Cambon, and the Astor, near St-Augustin. Both have multistarred chefs. I've always been nervous about Sofitel hotels, because there are thousands of them and they vary considerably. But they are moving more and more toward luxury as Accor juggles its many properties and public image. The newest property is a fancy boutique hotel, Sofitel Le Faubourg, 15 rue Boissy d'Anglas, off rue du Faubourg St-Honoré, 8e (☎ **01/44-94-14-14**), an unbeatable location for shoppers. There are a few small three- and four-star Sofitels in prime shopping areas, and they look good to me. Also ask about Sofitel Pullman, not far from Etoile. ☎ **800/SOFITEL.**

Best Western France This is one of the best secrets in Paris—the hotels, mostly three-star, are small, family owned, and often in residential areas. I've come to know them well—there are about five near my apartment in the 17e. Prices usually begin around $140 (129€). The chain has about two dozen hotel choices in Paris alone. ☎ **800/334-7234.**

Concorde Concorde is unusual because it's two chains in one: drop-dead luxury hotels that are among the fanciest in the world (Hôtel de Crillon, the Martinez, La Mamounia), and perfectly fine but not as luxurious four-star hotels. Some of these are in old buildings, in various states of repair and disrepair, and others are in brand-new, modern high rises.

The group publishes its own guide with color pictures of each property that helps in choosing but isn't fail-safe. You can't go wrong with the **Hôtel du Louvre,** one of my faves. The **Hôtel Concorde St. Lazare** is the best secret in Paris. The **Hôtel Ambassador,** with its split personality—half business hotel and half shopper's delight—is another one to consider. For business travelers, it's close to the Bourse, and shoppers are just 1 block from Galeries Lafayette. Concorde also manages the only large hotel on the Left Bank, the **Hôtel Lutétia,** which has a fabulous location for shoppers, a good restaurant (or two), and Ruhlman-style decor with a new health club and spa. ☎ **800/888-4747.**

Dorchester Group One of luxury-dom's smallest chains owns two important hotels in Paris, the Meurice and the Plaza Athénée. If you are visiting London and Paris, the group offers packages. ☎ **800/223-1230** (Leading Hotels of the World).

Forte Hotels Forte, which is the home of Trustehouse Forte hotels in Britain, also owns the Meridien hotel chain. Meridien specializes in teaming with Air France to offer fabulous winter weekend promotional rates. Its two hotels in Paris are in off-center locations, but the price may be right. Definitely worth looking into. ☎ **800/225-5843.**

Libertel & L'Horset This French chain has three- and four-star hotels, most of which are small and okay, some of which are small and rather fancy (or even very fancy). Their rates are excellent; many of the hotels have super locations. On the Right Bank, the **L'Horset Opera** is not swank but has a good location and reasonable rates. ☎ **800/448-8355** (Utell).

Meliá This Spanish chain isn't very well known to Americans. Its excellent reputation in Europe has been upgraded with the recent opening of several deluxe hotels. Its newest Paris property, Meliá Vendome, is between the Crillon and the Meurice, a block from Chanel and all the St-Honoré shopping. The hotel is breathtaking and well situated, but no bargain, with room rates around $300 (276€) per night (although that is a bargain to some). ☎ **800/336-3342.**

Millenium Hotels This international chain owns luxury hotels all over the world, as well as the Copthorne hotel line. Its best shopping property in Paris is near the big department stores on boulevard Haussmann. The hotel has fabulous electronic capabilities because it was gutted and built with phone, fax, and modem lines galore. A stay earns you air miles with Cathay Pacific. ☎ **01/49-49-16-00;** fax 01-49-49-17-00.

Relais & Châteaux Nothing stands for luxury more than this organization, representing small properties all over the world. Its Paris holdings include the Hôtel de Crillon. The phone situation is tricky—the toll-free number works only in some states. If it doesn't in yours, call the New York number. ☎ **800/ 860-4930** or 212/856-0115.

Warwick Warwick is a very small international chain with a great deal of variety among its hotels. Hôtel Westminster in Paris is a winner. ☎ **800/223-3652.**

BOOKING DEALS

Sometimes the big hotel associations have their own promotions or deals. I call **Leading Hotels of the World** (☎ **800/223-6800**) at the drop of my cell phone for corporate rates and specialty promotions. Less fancy is the **Utell** organization (☎ **800/448-8355**), which books thousands of hotels internationally and often has specials, especially weekend deals. They recently had an offering with **Hôtel Normandy** that made my heart stop—$215 (198€) per night (with breakfast) on weekends including May and June. I thought I was the only person who knew about the Normandy—a great find 1 block from the Hôtel du Louvre—which is getting press for its Saturday Chocolate Buffet.

THE $50 DIFFERENCE

Many people book the hotel with the lowest rate, figuring it represents the best value. But frequently, a more expensive hotel—or a slightly higher package rate—turns out to be cheaper, if you add in the extras. Does the more expensive hotel have a better location that saves money on transportation? Does the rate include breakfast, while the less expensive hotel's rate doesn't? The more people traveling with you (or sharing one room), the more vital this information is. Breakfast for a family of four can easily be $50 (46€). Hell, in a really good hotel, continental breakfast for two can be $50 (or more). Think also about what kind of breakfast the rate includes. Is it a continental breakfast or a buffet? You'll notice a big difference by the time lunch rolls around.

Make sure that the price includes tax and service, and figure that into your comparison. Sometimes U.S. dollar promotions do not include tax and service. Finally, remember that Paris has a per-night room tax; rate sheets rarely include it, and therefore you should not consider it when you're calculating your $50 difference.

THE GENERAL MANAGER'S SECRET

The general manager (GM in English, DG in French) of every hotel in the world has only one bottom line: to sell hotel rooms. He must attain a 40% occupancy rate just to break even.

In order to fill rooms, a GM will do whatever it takes. (A few palace hotels prefer to be empty rather than cut deals, but this is rare.)

I am not saying that every GM will cut a deal with you or that you should always call or fax the GM directly. I am saying that it pays to go out of your way to meet the GM, especially if you have decided to establish a regular relationship with a hotel. The GM has the ability to give you a better rate, to upgrade you to a better room, to send you a bottle of champagne or wine or a bowl of fruit, or to do something else that adds an extra touch of value to your choice. The GM has the ability to make you feel like a valuable customer, which will always enhance your stay.

Here's the best part: While the GM does not have time to have breakfast with you and the kids, he very much wants some type of relationship with you so that you will feel a connection to the hotel and will return. If he moves to another hotel (they all move to another hotel), he'll want your name and address so he can notify you.

If you have no time to meet the GM, write a follow-up letter after your visit and wait for his reply and business card. Networking pays, especially in a competitive market like Paris. Once you have his name and business card, the next time you want a reservation, contact the GM directly by fax. If you book with him and not a reservation service, the hotel saves a commission. You may turn that into a discount or an upgrade.

Should you choose a hotel without knowing the name of the GM, simply call the toll-free U.S. reservations number and ask for the name (and correct spelling) of the GM of your chosen hotel, and the fax number. Hotels change GMs quite often, so verify the name if you already have one. If your contact has moved on but you want to return to the hotel, write to the new GM, explain that you knew the former GM, and outline what he did for you.

TECHNOLOGICAL REPORT

If plugging in your laptop and getting online is important to you, you may want to consider the age of the hotel, or its most recent renovation. Older hotels do not have dataports, although they will send an engineer to your room with an adapter to modify your phone jack. All new hotels have dataports, phone connections for an assortment of computers, and even Web television.

Note that your phone cord may need an adapter. After I had great difficulty connecting, one hotel told me calmly, "Ah, yes, madame, that is because you are using a 45-35 line and in France you must use a 45-11. I will send it right to your room."

HOTELS BY SHOPPING DISTRICT

Concorde Coeur

HÔTEL DE CRILLON
10 place de la Concorde, 8e (Métro: Concorde).

One of the most famous palace hotels in Paris, the Crillon has just refurbished most of its rooms and suites and has added a fancy health club and a Guerlain spa. For more on the spa, see chapter 8, "Paris Beauty."

Instead of raving about how gorgeous this converted palace is, or how much fun it is to sit at the base of the Champs-Elysées and be a block from the rue du Faubourg St-Honoré, let me tell you a story that shows why the Crillon is considered one of the best hotels in the world.

I once arrived for a stay at the hotel and received a package from my girlfriend Jill, who then lived in St-Paul-de-Vence in the south of France. I wanted to thank her, but realized I had brought the wrong telephone book and did not have her number. Furthermore, I knew that she uses a professional name, which is not her legal name, so she was unlikely to be listed. Christian, the head concierge, first checked Minitel by the address (which I did know by heart), but found St-Paul too small to be cross-referenced by address. He checked under her professional name, but as I suspected, Jill had no phone listing in Minitel under that name. Next, Christian called the concierge of the Relais & Châteaux hotel in St-Paul and sent him to Jill's home. He asked Jill for her phone number, then called the Crillon and gave it to Christian. *Voilà!* You tell me where you can find another concierge like that.

The Crillon offers a number of packages and promotions with dollar rates, which can make the hotel almost affordable. In addition, there are weekend and honeymoon specials; one includes dinner and breaks down to be a good value. Dogs stay free and receive a tag that says, "If I am lost, return me to the Hotel Crillon." I wish I had a tag like that.

The restaurant is one of the most famous in Paris; the chef, Dominique Bouchet, has earned his stars, so it's safe to say that a stay that includes dinner is a memory in the making. The hotel has a shopping package complete with limo—as if you needed a car and driver to get the half block from the hotel to Hermès. ☎ **01/44-71-15-00;** fax 01/44-71-15-02. For reservations, ☎ 800/888-4747 in the U.S. Member, Leading Hotels of the World (☎ 800/223-6800); Relais & Châteaux (☎ 212/856-0115).

HÔTEL DU LOUVRE
Place André Malraux, 1er (Métro: Palais-Royal).

This smallish, old-fashioned hotel is a member of the Concorde group; it has just been spruced up. In one little plot of land, you have the owner of the Crillon as your landlord and the benefit of a fabulous discount program—you can get a room at the Louvre for around $200 (184€) per night.

The hotel overlooks the Garnier Opéra and is across the street from the Musée du Louvre. Its modern rooms are decorated in Laura Ashley–inspired French style. My favorite room has a gabled roof, blue-and-white *toile de Jouy* everywhere, and a gigantic bathroom with glass doors that overlook the Opéra.

Another room, sort of a suite dream, had a tiny room for my son, Aaron, on the left, and a master bedroom for my husband, Mike, and me. It was laid out more like a mini-apartment than a hotel suite and was beautifully decorated. Both of these fifth-floor rooms are great places if you're traveling with kids.

The only drawback to the Hôtel du Louvre is that tour groups have discovered it. But the location, the price, and the charm more than make up for the bother of sharing it with others. ☏ **01/44-58-38-38**; fax 01/44-58-38-01. For reservations, ☏ 800/888-4747.

HÔTEL MEURICE
228 rue de Rivoli, 1er (Métro: Concorde or Tuileries).

The sultan of Brunei bought this hotel and merged it into the Dorchester Group (with the Dorchester in London, and Paris's Plaza Athenée). After extensive renovation, the hotel has emerged fancier than before—and more expensive. There are more bells and whistles in a room than you can stand, including direct dataport, *bien sur.* The health club boasts the only Paris location of Le Source de Caudalie, the wine spa from Bordeaux that creates treatments from the anti-aging pepins of grapes from the château. Regulars, note that the hotel's front door has moved to the rue de Rivoli (next door to Angelina). ☏ **01/44-58-10-10**; fax 01/44-58-10-15. For reservations, Leading Hotels of the World, ☏ 800/223-6800 in the U.S.

LE CASTILLE
37 rue Cambon, 1er (Métro: Tuileries or Concorde).

The rooms are small, but they are fresh and gorgeous, with fancy bathrooms. The difference between a standard room and a deluxe room is negligible. The breakfast room is adorable. Rates vary enormously with the season, but you can sometimes make a weeklong deal; expect to pay about $300 (276€) per night. ☏ **01/44-58-44-58**; fax 01/44-58-44-00. For reservations, ☏ 800/949-7562.

Haussmann Haunts

CONCORDE ST-LAZARE
108 rue St-Lazare, 8e (Métro: St-Lazare).

Although this hotel books mostly tour groups and savvy Europeans on vacation with the kids, it is a great find with an even better location. Don't let train-station renovations upset you—the fact that the Gare St-Lazare is next door is a real plus. Location-wise, I am nuts for this hotel. It's near one of the major bus stops, near a train station, near three Métro lines, and within walking distance of everything you need. If you are in Paris for only a few days and want shopping right out your door, everything is a sneeze away.

The hotel has a nice cafe, a great breakfast buffet served upstairs, and a hidden billiards rooms (restored to Belle Epoque grandeur) that makes it the best buy in Paris at $200 to $250 (184€–230€) per night.

Note: I lived in this hotel before I got my apartment in Paris and have had an assortment of rooms. I once got a small and unattractive room possibly meant for Cinderella. Out of curiosity, I asked the front desk how much the room would cost for someone who didn't book it through a package (I was on a rate), and I was told that this room sold for almost $400 (368€) a night. I burst out laughing, although I would have been crying if I were paying that price (you can book the Crillon for not much more). When you pick a hotel based on price, make sure you are getting good value, and don't be shy if you don't like your room—ask to see others. ☎ **800/888-4747** in the U.S. or 01/40-08-44-44; fax 01/42-93-01-20.

Left Bank

HÔTEL LUTÉTIA
45 bd. Raspail, 6e (Métro: Sèvres-Babylone).

This is the only large hotel on the Left Bank, and a member of the Concorde chain. It was built in 1907 and now combines the Belle Epoque with the ocean-liner chic of the 1930s and a touch of modern art and contemporary sculpture. And the bathrooms are large.

The new general manager is keen on fair prices, upgrading the hotel, and providing plenty of shopping information to guests. The Lutétia has been totally redone in a style inspired by Jacques-Emile Ruhlman. There are a spa, a health club, and a business center. ☎ **800/888-4747** in the U.S. or 01/49-54-46-46; fax 01/49-54-46-00. www.lutetia-paris.com.

MONTALEMBERT
3 rue de Montalembert, 7e (Métro: Rue du Bac).

This is without a doubt the fanciest hotel on the Left Bank, but the rooms are tiny. If you want a charming, chic hotel in a great shopping location, search no further. Montalembert has only 50 rooms, each decorated to the nines. While rates are $300 to $400 (276€–368€) a night, several-night packages make the hotel more affordable. The same proprietor also owns the newer Hotel Bel-Ami. ☎ **800/447-7462** in the U.S. or 01/45-48-68-11; fax 01/45-49-68-99.

RELAIS CHRISTINE
3 rue Christine, 6e (Métro: Odéon).

Just down the street from the market at rue du Buci and rue de Seine, this hotel is charming beyond words. Outfitted in full medieval style, it's great for families because it has lofts and apartments. It's not inexpensive, but it's perfect. The hotel has no restaurant, but it's a block from everything, including the famous market. A sister hotel, Pavilion de la Reine, is at the place des Vosges. ☎ **01/40-51-60-80;** fax 01/40-51-60-81. www.relais-christine.com.

PARIS ON A ROLL

It's hard to get a really bad meal in Paris. The trick is to find a good meal that's not too expensive. You can count on me to have a nosh at every crêpe stand I pass; I've even been to McDonald's. I stand by that old tourist standby, **Café de Flore.** While it may cost $13 (12€) for coffee and croissants for two, it beats the $50 (46€) I'd have to pay for the same breakfast at my fancy hotel. And there's nothing better than the early morning air, a French newspaper, and a seat in one of the world's greatest theaters to start your day.

I have graduated from pizza to *panini,* the newest fast-food craze in Paris. I seem to eat one meal a day at a branch of **Toastissimo.** I still eat a lot of pizza; pizza places are easy to find in every neighborhood. I eat a lot of picnics bought from grocery stores I pass as I wander; you can shop the grocery stores of the rue du Buci or the rue Cler any day of the week, or wait for special market days.

I've also tested the offerings in the food court at **Le Carrousel du Louvre,** an American-style shopping mall attached to the Louvre. It's on the mezzanine level above the stores, and the food is great.

I cover additional simple, fast, and affordable lunch and dinner choices below. I also love to eat at Michelin-starred restaurants, particularly when my schedule's more leisurely and I can order from a fixed-price menu and save. So you'll find my favorite formal dining choices listed below as well.

SNACK & SHOP

If you are out alone or merely want a quick, easy lunch so that you can continue your explorations (and your shopping), you may want to stop by one of these addresses. I pick a "Snack & Shop" location based on a combination of factors: location in relation to good shopping, degree of visual stimulation, price, and quality of food. If you want to eat every meal in a Michelin one-star restaurant (see "Stars & Deals," below), or if you plan your day around where you'll have lunch, these suggestions may not be for you.

Right Bank

ANGELINA
228 rue de Rivoli, 1er (Métro: Concorde or Tuileries).

For shoppers in the first or around the Louvre: René Rumpel-
mayer opened this tearoom in 1903. Famous for its hot chocolate, the restaurant also is a great place for breakfast (starting
at 9:30am), lunch, or dinner. Salads and easy snacks are a breeze;
pastries and desserts are the house specialty.

Prices are low to moderate; there is a fixed-price full meal,
but I usually order a salad or light fare so that I can go for a
dessert. The first arrondissement is a great place to shop that's
convenient to the rue de Rivoli and the Louvre. Angelina also
has a branch on the third floor of Galeries Lafayette.

CAFÉ MARLY
Palais du Louvre, 1er (Métro: Musée-du-Louvre or Tuileries).

For those at the Louvre or nearby: Once before you die, you
have to eat or have coffee at the Café Marly, overlooking the
I.M. Pei pyramid in the courtyard of the Louvre. You may sit
outside, weather permitting, or in the small salons filled with
smoke and well-heeled locals, who come here even though it's
a major tourist haunt. Off-hours are less crowded; you can sit
with a coffee for hours, and pay only for the coffee. Light lunch
is easy to do, be it a hamburger or a salmon platter. Open daily
8am to 2am.

LADURÉE
16 rue Royale, 1er (Métro: Concorde).

For those shopping Faubourg St-Honoré or Madeleine: I'm a
regular for the quiche and salad at lunch. Eat upstairs or
downstairs, or order food to go. There's also a branch inside
Printemps. At the large branch on the Champs-Elysées, you
can eat on the sidewalk or have the full *carte* upstairs.

SALON DE THÉ BERNARDAUD
11 rue Royale, 8e (Métro: Concorde).

For shoppers in Designer Central: If you follow no other tip
from me, you owe it to both of us to visit this restaurant, preferably for tea. (You can also have breakfast, lunch, or dinner.)

What's so special about tea here is how it's served. A staff
member brings you a silver tray laden with teacups, you pick
the pattern you like best, and your tea—or snack or meal—arrives
on this pattern. Isn't that just the best gimmick ever? Bernardaud is one of the finest makers of French porcelain in history.

You can get here two ways: Step directly behind the Crillon, or walk through the small Galerie Royale mall. If you arrive
through the mall, you'll see just a few seats. You can take your
tea there or move to the inside dining area, with its celadon-
colored ragged walls. Don't forget to buy an ashtray for 10€
($10.80) when you leave. Open Monday through Saturday
8:30am to 7pm.

SHOP & DINE

CHEZ CATHERINE
65 rue Provence, 9e (Métro: Chaussée d'Antin).

If you are shopping Galeries Lafayette or on boulevard Haussmann: The portions of home cooking are large, so you might
want to come for dinner on a Thursday night when the department stores are open late. Closed during August, and for lunch
Saturday through Monday. ☎ **01/45-26-72-88.**

LA CHOPE DES VOSGES
22 place des Vosges, 3e (Métro: St-Paul).

If you're shopping the Marais: This is the place for you. This
visually charming restaurant in the heart of the Marais offers
lunch and dinner, as well as tea from 3 to 7pm. With its old-
fashioned front, stone interior, and wood beams, this is a cozy
multilevel space. Lunch is about $22 (20€).

THE "HERME" SECRET

Most visitors think Hermès and its little orange box. Now I ask you to think Pierre Herme, the most famous pastry chef in France, who recently opened his own shop. I am certain he will open a tearoom soon, but until then, take your treasures and sit on a bench in the nearby park.

72 rue Bonaparte, 6e (Métro: St-Germain-des-Prés).

Left Bank

DU BOUT DES DOIGTS
Hôtel Lutétia, 45 bd. Raspail, 6e (Métro: Sèvres-Babylone).

If you are shopping the heart of the Left Bank: This is the ultimate new girl in town, a specialty restaurant open only for weekday lunch and decorated to the teeth in Ruhlman chic. You eat French tapas with your fingers—although you do get a spoon for the chestnut soup, which is the best in Paris. ☎ 01/49-54-46-90.

HELENE DARROZE
4 rue d' Assas, 6e (Métro: Sèvres-Babylone).

If you are shopping the heart of the Left Bank: This famous chef (the daughter of another famous chef) has a controversial fancy dining room upstairs, but offers a great lunch off a set tapas menu downstairs. Once you opt for the stylish, well-served $25 (23€) menu, however, you can't make substitutions. Make sure you specify downstairs when you reserve. ☎ 01/42-22-00-11.

L'EPI DUPIN
11 rue Dupin, 6e (Métro: Sèvres Babylone or Bac).

If you are shopping Bon Marché or rue du Bac: The charming little bistro serves country cooking at lunch (except on Mon) and dinner. Reserve—it's hard to get in. Closed from the end of July through August. ☎ **01/42-22-64-56.**

LE FAST FOODING

You may not realize this, but *le sandwich* is hugely popular in Paris. Furthermore, the tax on fast food and take-out food is only 5.5%, whereas sit-down restaurants must charge almost 20%—although this could change. I'm wild for **Toastissimo** and its Italian-style *panini;* other popular chains include **Lina's,** with branches all over Paris (and all over France). Not all Lina's are created equal: Some are fancy, and the one in Galeries Lafayette has sit-down service and a real *carte.*

Perhaps the most interesting chain in France is **Paul,** because it offers so much—and because its branches are adorable and its food is well priced. Originally a bread baker from Lille, it now operates restaurants, cafes, and bakeries everywhere, including boulevard Haussmann next to the new Galeries Lafayette space (formerly Marks & Spencer) and across the street from Au Printemps.

A Belgian chain, **Le Pain Quotidien,** has become so international that it has a branch in Beverly Hills. Locations in Paris include 18 place du Marché St-Honoré, off rue St-Honoré near the Hotel Meurice. You can get a salad, sandwich, or hot meal.

DESIGNER & RETAIL DINING

Over the past few years, the fanciest designer boutiques in Paris have added cafes or small restaurants, often in the midst of the shopping experience. Lanvin started the trend, which has spread to regular retail: **Emporio Armani** has a large cafe (try the house risotto), as does the **St-Germain Monoprix,** next door to Armani. Monoprix is cheaper—you can eat lunch for about $10 (9.20€) a person (Métro: St-Germain-des-Prés).

Check out:

- **Barbara Bui Café,** 27 rue Etienne Marcel, 1er (Métro: Etienne Marcel). Fusion cooking with choices (including options for vegetarians) for about $15 (13.80€) per person. This designer is known for her cutting-edge chic, and the location is on a street of like-minded designers.
- **BCBG Max Café,** 14 bd. de la Madeleine, 8e (Métro: Madeleine). This cafe is upstairs, so you can walk through and check out the clothes. The *carte* is small but the food is nice. The crowd is so chic that you won't want to eat much, for fear of gaining weight.
- **Bleu Comme Bleu,** 2 rue Castiglione, 1er (Métro: Tuileries). This hair salon, spa, and boutique also serves lunch, tea, and afternoon snacks. The price per person is close to $30 (28€) for lunch.
- **Café Celio,** 2 rue Halevy, 9e (Métro: Opéra). Celio, a French firm similar to the Gap, has shops everywhere. The cafe is between Galeries Lafayette and Opéra, in an excellent location for shoppers. It offers light lunches and usually a quiche of the day, served with a salad.
- **Colette,** 213 rue St-Honoré, 8e (Métro: Tuileries). I am not a huge fan of this store, because I find it too American in its shopping choices, but the lunch space downstairs is fabulous. It features the best matchbook in Paris, zillions of flavors of water from around the world, and desserts by demigod Pierre Herme.
- **Etam,** 73 rue de Rivoli, 1er (Métro: Pont Neuf). This department store for teens has a cafe, 5em Sens, on the fifth floor, overlooking the rooftops of Paris. It serves a variety of dishes in the fusion–world food style; be sure to have the flavored iced tea.
- **Joseph,** 227 rue St-Honoré, 1er (Métro: Concorde). Hip and quick—salad, pasta, or the special of the day.
- **Lanvin's Café Bleu,** 15 rue du Faubourg St-Honoré (Métro: Concorde). The cafe is in the men's shop, on the lower level. I eat here often (it's a few steps from the Hôtel de Crillon), and just have a salad. The *carte* is limited but prices are good.

CARS 'R' US

Several car showrooms on the Champs-Elysées have opened cafes. I guess this is the same philosophy that leads a boutique to open a cafe. My favorite is Renault.

DEPARTMENT STORE DINING

The major department stores, which make an effort to bring in tourists of all nationalities, have restaurants geared to a quick meal or a well-earned coffee break. They also are trying to upgrade their image and keep you dining (and shopping) a little bit longer. Competition between them is hot, so when one store gets a big name, a new concept, or a renovation, the others strive to outdo it.

AU PRINTEMPS
64 bd. Haussmann, 9e (Métro: Chaussée d'Antin).

Café Flo, on the sixth floor, is part of a chain of restaurants and food shops with an excellent reputation; it has taken over the space directly beneath the cupola to offer easy meals. You can indicate your choice by pointing to a photo. Lunch starts at 10€ ($10.80); there is also a 13€ ($14.05) menu that includes wine. Ladurée is on another floor, and there's a coffee bar, Express Flo, on the teenage (third) floor.

BHV
54 rue de Rivoli, 4e (Métro: Hôtel de Ville).

This department store specializes in home style. Its world-famous do-it-yourself and hardware departments are in the basement, where you'll find the cute new **Café Brico.** Leave your husband here while you shop.

GALERIES LAFAYETTE
40 bd. Haussmann, 9e (Métro: Chaussée d'Antin).

Gourmet Lafayette, the store's gourmet grocery store next door, boasts two new restaurants: a soup bar and a "gastro" restaurant (meaning gastronomical, or good). The main store offers more choices, and in summer, you can also eat on the seventh-floor terrace. On the sixth floor is **Café Lafayette,** a sit-down restaurant, as well as a self-service cafeteria. There's a branch of the famous Angelina on the third floor; on the first floor you'll find the chic Lina's. If you'd rather go light, there's sushi on the fifth floor. Galeries surely will open new restaurants in the new store across the street.

LA SAMARITAINE
2 quai du Louvre, 1er (Métro: Musée-du-Louvre or Hôtel de Ville).

At **Toupary,** this very French department store's restaurant, the view is more important than the food. It also serves dinner, even when the store is closed—and the lights on the Seine are something to behold. Designed by the American designer Hilton McConnico, who is the rage of Paris design. Reservations (☎ **01/40-41-29-29**) are recommended.

Note that this store is undergoing major changes, and new restaurants and cafes will surely open.

FAMOUS FOOD HALLS

It's easy to take home a picnic from any of the famous food halls, and most of them also permit you to dine in. Also see the separate section on grocery stores, below.

FAUCHON
26 place de la Madeleine, 8e (Métro: Madeleine).

In the fancy Belle Epoque tea salon, you can sip tea, read, and write postcards in glory. Open Monday through Saturday 8am to 7pm. Check out upstairs as well.

HÉDIARD
21 place de la Madeleine, 8e (Métro: Madeleine).

This gastronomical house of wonders consists of a series of small dens and salons. It features tantalizing displays of everything from fresh and dried fruit and wine to spices. Upstairs is a chic restaurant. Reservations are advised. Closed Sunday. ☎ 01/43-12-88-99.

LENÔTRE
48 av. Victor Hugo, 16e (Métro: Victor-Hugo).

Although famous for its chocolate, Lenôtre has a salon for everything—chocolates, gourmet food, cocktail nibbles, coffee, and more. You can have a meal or a snack.

MUSEUM DINING

Check out **Le Grand Louvre,** in the Louvre. Open Wednesday to Monday noon to 3pm and 7 to 10pm. The must-see **Café Marly** is on the Louvre property (see above). Across from the Centre Pompidou, **Café Beaubourg,** 100 rue St-Martin, is an alternative to the museum's top-floor cafe, the Costes creation **George. Musée d'Orsay Restaurant,** 1 rue de Bellechasse (open Wed–Mon 9am–6:45pm), is gorgeous enough to write home about, as is the cafe in the **Musée Jacquemart Andre.** And don't miss **Les Monuments,** in the Palais de Chaillot, which houses three museums (but no madwoman).

GROCERY STORES

Neighborhoods frequented by tourists have grocery stores, so unless you're staying in one of the outlying arrondissements, you won't have to go out of your way to get to one. All the best shopping neighborhoods also have their share of grocery stores, where you can easily buy a picnic or do some of your souvenir shopping. The markets listed below are big, modern supermarkets chosen for their location; you will be near one or all of them as you explore Paris. And don't neglect any Monoprix you come across.

Left Bank

LA GRANDE EPICERIE
Le Bon Marché, 38 rue de Sèvres, 7e (Métro: Sèvres-Babylone).

This grocery store, part of Le Bon Marché, occupies a separate building. In the street-level grocery, you'll find everything imaginable, including brand names and regional foodstuffs from all over France and the EU. It has a good wine and champagne department, a bakery, and prepared foods. Don't mind the other American tourists. This is perhaps the best grocery store in Paris, and a source of endless delights and gift opportunities. I buy flavored *sirops* here.

MONOPRIX GOURMET
50 rue de Rennes, 6e (Métro: St-Germain-des-Prés).

This is an upscale branch of Monoprix, befitting the rising stature of the street address and the presence of Giorgio Armani next door. Don't be fooled by the small street-level space; downstairs is an entire world of food shopping. Open Monday through Saturday 9am to 9pm.

Right Bank

GALERIES GOURMET
Palais du Congress, 17e (Métro or RER: Porte de Maillot).

This midsized, modern grocery store is best for those who are at a convention in this area or want to shop on Sunday. It combines the talents of several big names in French food, and offers staples as well as gourmet choices.

LAFAYETTE GOURMET
52 bd. Haussmann, 9e (Métro: Chaussée d'Antin).

This store is inside Galeries Lafayette Men's Store, up one flight. You can do your gourmet grocery shopping and have lunch; serving areas form a circle surrounding a kiosk, and two new restaurants are in the store's Wine Library. This store is just as fancy but not nearly as expensive as Fauchon or Hédiard, the food temples along the nearby place du Madeleine. Don't miss it. Open Friday through Wednesday 9am to 8pm, Thursday 9am to 9pm. You can also enter from rue Provence in the rear.

MONOPRIX CHAMPS-ELYSÉES
109 rue de la Boetie, 8e (Métro: F-D-Roosevelt).

Handy but not as fancy as Lafayette Gourmet, Monoprix grocery stores can supply basic needs. This branch is open late, usually until midnight in summer and 10pm in winter. You'll also find grocery stores in most Monoprix locations, including place St-Augustin (Métro: St-Augustin).

STARS & DEALS

Several Michelin-starred chefs have created ways for you to enjoy their cuisine without having to pay an arm and a leg. Perhaps the best known for this is **Guy Savoy,** 18 rue Troyon 17e (Métro: Ternes), who finally got his long-anticipated third star recently and who offers a set menu at 176€ and 229€. If that doesn't strike you as a bargain, note that three-star chefs have been known to charge $500 (460€) per person. ☎ **01/ 43-80-40-61.**

VIOLIN D'INGRES
135 rue Dominique, 7e (Métro: Latour Maubourg).

Okay, this isn't in the heart of the Left Bank shopping, but it's not far. The three-star chef, Christian Constant, went out on his own and has a fabulous, *intime* one-star not far from the

Hilton. The prices are reasonable, and the food is touched by angels. The recently redecorated restaurant serves a seasonal *carte*. Can be a romantic night for two, but I've also done it for Girls Night Out. The chef's English wife, Catherine, is usually at the front desk; the chef is adorable but does not speak English. Learn French tonight. ☎ 01/45-55-15-05.

THE DISCIPLES

If you keep up with the latest chefs, you are probably into the young chefs I call "the Disciples." They trained with the most famous chefs in France and are now out on their own. Their restaurants cost less than those at a palace hotel and will put you on the cutting edge of table talk. This list is by no means complete: Guy Savoy, the king of this concept, has mentored almost a dozen chefs.

LES BOOKINISTES
53 quai des Grands-Augustins, 6e (Métro: St-Michel or Odéon; RER C: St-Michel).

The chef trained with Guy Savoy, and this restaurant is one of several in the Savoy Group. A fixed-price two-course lunch costs just over $25 (23€) per person (without wine); a three-course lunch is about $35 (32€). Reservations are imperative. It's closed for lunch on Saturday and Sunday, but serves dinner both nights; believe me, finding a great place to eat on Sunday night is hard. ☎ 01/43-25-45-94.

LES ELYSÉES DU VERNET
Hôtel Vernet, 25 rue Vernet, 8e (Métro: F-D-Roosevelt).

This restaurant is small, intimate, and formal, with a ceiling designed by Gustave Eiffel (yes, that Eiffel); it currently holds two Michelin stars. None other than Alain Ducasse trained the chef. A complete lunch is about $65 (60€) per person; dinner, about $70 (64€). It's right behind the Champs-Elysées; you can get there easily if you cut through Chez Clément, 123 av. des Champs-Elysées, another restaurant favorite of mine. Fax ahead at 01/44-31-85-69 for reservations with as much notice as possible.

L'HÔTEL ASTOR
11 rue d'Astorg, 8e (Métro: Madeleine).

The small, intimate dining room has two Michelin stars and is the baby of chef Joel Robuchon, who retired from Jamin and opened this hotel almost immediately. Though Robuchon does not do the regular cooking (he's the "director"), his influence is apparent. The famed mashed potatoes are all they are said to be. Chef Eric Lecerf offers several dégustation menus, or you can order off the menu. Leave room for the famous desserts—many of which were created by Robuchon. ☎ 01/53-05-05-20 for reservations.

ZE KITCHEN
4 rue Grands-Augustins, 6e (Métro: Pont Neuf or Odéon; RER C: St-Michel).

Ze Kitchen is right behind Les Bookinistes, to which it is spiritually related (the chef left one to open the other). The decor is moderne, the food light, and the scene with-it. Note that the address is rue, not quai—it's on a side street, not on the water. ☎ 01/44-32-00-32.

The Baby Ducasses

If you don't have a spare $300 (276€) or more per person for dinner at Restaurant Alain Ducasse, there are other ways to enjoy the creative genius of M. Ducasse. A bread and bakery restaurant is opening soon; watch this space.

59 POINCARE
59 rue Raymond Poincare, 16e (Métro: Victor Hugo).

This is the address of Alain Ducasse's former restaurant, ...e he planned a branch of his Monte Carlo bistro Bar & Boeuf. When hoof-and-mouth disease struck England, Ducasse made this more of a vegetable, lamb, and lobster space.

IL CORTILE
37 rue Cambon, 1er (Métro: Concorde).

Few people know about Il Cortile, which is worth investigating for its delicate palate and the wonderful, not at all touristy crowd. As you would guess, this is an Italian restaurant. You can dine outside in the wonderful hidden courtyard, weather permitting. ☎ 01/44-58-45-67.

SPOON FOOD & WINE
14 rue de Marignan, 8e (Métro: F-D-Roosevelt).

Spoon Food & Wine's "world cuisine" and mix-and-match menu began the world food craze in France. The restaurant has influenced many other local eateries. First-timers will have to concentrate on the menu to figure out the gimmick, and the waiters will frown if they think you've come up with a nasty combo. ☎ 01/40-76-34-44.

Chapter Five

....

RIGHT BANK SHOPPING NEIGHBORHOODS

THE BASTILLE IS UP

Paris is a city of neighborhoods. The word *arrondissement* is not synonymous with "neighborhood"—each arrondissement contains many neighborhoods, or *quartiers*. Some *quartiers* straddle portions of two arrondissements.

This chapter covers the best shopping neighborhoods on the Right Bank; chapter 6 features the best shopping neighborhoods on the Left Bank.

Now, a few words about orientation. I tend to categorize sections of arrondissements by their landmarks and stores. The Bronx may not be up and the Battery may not be down, but the way I look at it, the Bastille is uptown and the Arc de Triomphe is downtown. From the Right Bank, it's "crosstown" to the Left Bank.

As a tourist, you'll probably stick to a dozen or so neighborhoods that are must-see, must-return-to areas. Some you visit just for the shopping, but mostly you wander to take in everything they offer—sights, shopping, dining, and more. There are streets that fulfill all your fantasies of what Paris should be. While the city limits sprawl all the way to the highway loop Périphérique (and beyond), my parts of town are compact and easy to manage. See chapter 11 for shopping tours.

RIGHT BANK ARRONDISSEMENTS

The First (1er)

The 1er is a prime shopping area, with several high-rent neighborhoods. You'll find the city's fanciest designer boutiques on the **rue du Faubourg St-Honoré** (which crosses into the 8e), and some wonderful boutiques on the **rue St-Honoré** (an extension of the Faubourg St-Honoré that begins after the rue Royale). The 1er is also where you'll find tourist-trap heaven (the **rue de Rivoli**), some of the city's best museum shops, and the **Louvre** and its many shopping ops. The best secret of the 1er? The **Jardins du Palais Royal,** with fab shopping and strolling.

The Second (2e)

The 2e, known as Bourse, consists of the business district—basically the Wall Street of Paris—with some border areas for shoppers. You may not find yourself in the 2e unless you are doing business or have the heart of a *garmento* and want to visit the **Sentier** (garment center). There are tons of little wholesale-only shops in the Sentier, and if you have nerve you can ask if they'll sell to you—many will. Glamorous, however, it is not.

The **Galerie Vivienne** is in the 2e; one of the most famous *passages* in Paris, it sits at the edge of **place des Victoires.** There are also a few hidden upscale treasures in and around here. Victoires is on the border of the 1er and 2e, and its designer and avant-garde shops make it one of the highlights of Paris.

The Third (3e)

To most visitors, the 3e *is* the **place des Vosges**—not just the square itself, but the tiny, curvy streets, arcades, shops, and offbeat finds all around it, which make up the **Marais.** It's everything you've dreamed Paris would be. To be totally accurate, the **Picasso Museum** is in the 3e and the place des Vosges is in the 4e, but the spirit that connects them allows most visitors to lump them together.

The Right Bank

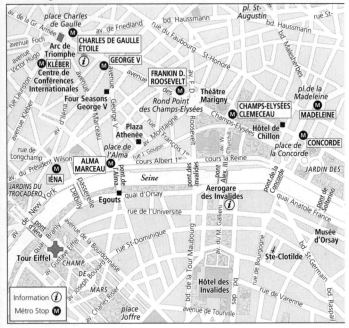

The 3e has several yummy museums in it and much historical perspective; it also has some edges of funkiness to it. There's a big covered market called the **Carreau du Temple,** where you can find old clothes (*fripes*) and some nice handcrafted items. It's open Tuesday through Sunday with a good number of discounters and rather shabby outlets that probably aren't worth investigating, especially if you are a rue du Faubourg St-Honoré kind of customer. Teens may be interested.

The Fourth (4e)

This neighborhood backs up on the Marais. The **Village St-Paul** (antiques galore) is in this *quartier,* and you are a stone's throw from Bastille and the new opera house. Once you cross the boulevard Bourdon at the canal, you are in the 12e, but never mind, you are now in an area of town considered very *branché* (with it).

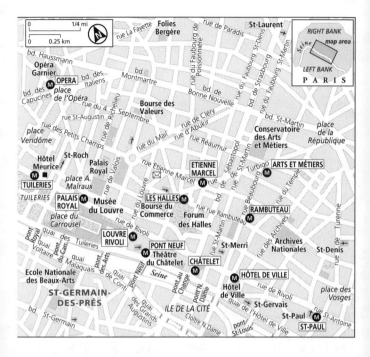

The 4e also encompasses the **Ile St-Louis,** whose local church is the **Cathédrale de Notre-Dame.** There is some pleasant tourist shopping near the church. You'll find touristy but fun shopping on the Ile St-Louis's main thoroughfare, rue St-Louis en Ile, which begins almost immediately after you cross the tiny bridge from the rear of the Notre-Dame onto the Ile St-Louis.

The Eighth (8e)

The 8e, nestled between the 1er and the 16e, connects the rue du Faubourg St-Honoré with the **Champs-Elysées,** stretching across some of the best shopping in the world. To me, the real soul of the 8e lies directly behind the Hôtel de Crillon, where you have not only the rue du Faubourg St-Honoré but also the boulevard de la Madeleine and the tiny rue Boissy d'Anglas, which abounds with great stores. The 8e is probably the single most shopping-dense district in Paris.

The Ninth (9e)

The 9e sits on the far side of the 2e and the back end of the 8e; it is famous to most of the world as the location of some big department stores, including the French icons **Au Printemps** and **Galeries Lafayette.** Originally, the 9e owed its fame to the St-Lazare train station, which brought shoppers to the big department stores on boulevard Haussmann.

The Tenth (10e)

Wholesale? Did you say you like wholesale? The 10e is one of the city's many wholesale neighborhoods. It's known for its fur, glass, china, and coiffure suppliers, but also for its hookers, hoods, and dealers, particularly around St-Denis. It has a strong ethnic mix as well. The **Bacarrat Museum** is on the rue Paradis.

But wait, this part of town is losing the hookers and getting the good lookers.

République is a formerly boring middle-class neighborhood that is now getting to be part of the new-chic (the New Republic?). There are some discounters, but mostly this is a neighborhood in the works, where those who specialize in the cutting edge would go out of their way to shop. This means heading over to the **Canal St-Martin,** one of the hottest developing parts of Paris for alternative-style boutiques and for roller-blading Sunday brunches.

The Eleventh (11e)

Not yet ready for prime time. Well, I'm a little bit wrong. It's happening—just don't wear fur.

The Twelfth (12e)

This is the arrondissement of the moment, gathering no moss as it rolls across Paris from the far side of Bastille, past Gare de Lyon, toward **Bercy Village. Le Viaduc des Arts** is a long stretch of street under an elevated train track that has been turned into boutiques and artisans' workshops. Not far away is the **place d'Aligre,** with a great food market and a small, funky flea market. You can walk from Le Viaduc des Arts to place d'Aligre.

The Sixteenth (16e)

Rue de Passy is a terrific find for someone who wants to shop and see the real Paris, as experienced by the BCBG (*bon chic, bon genre*) crowd that hangs out in this district. The well-heeled residents of the 16e have their own park, the Bois de Boulogne, and living close to the park is very chic. More important, the 16e has lots of resale shops. The 8e and the 16e bump heads over couture shopping—*ohlala!*

The Seventeenth (17e)

Another fashionable district, at least in parts. The acceptable neighborhoods for the BCBG set are Péreire, Ternes, and Monceau. This is where I live. The shopping is rather neigborhoody, but we have two great street markets, **rue des Levis** (Métro: Villiers) and **Poncelet** (Métro: Ternes). The flower market at place de Ternes is lovely: I look but don't buy—I think it's expensive. The avenue Niel and the rue des Ternes are the big shopping thoroughfares, although they are not as packed with name brands as, say, avenue Victor Hugo. But wait—this is a great eating district. Also note that the Convention Center at Porte Maillot has a small mall with a great grocery store that is open on Sunday. Nearby, **L'Espace Champeret** (Métro: Champeret) has food and antiques specialty markets that are announced in magazines.

The Eighteenth (18e)

You've heard of the 18e because it includes **Montmartre.** This is a scenic area that tourists like to visit in order to confirm their fantasies of Paris or check up on scenes from the movie

Amélie. It is also the site of some of the fabric markets that design students haunt.

While the 18e was once charming and famous (*Irma la Douce* was shot here), now it abounds with tourists and con men. The **fabric markets of St-Pierre,** near Sacré-Coeur, are wonderful but very funky. In fact, the 18e is funkiness personified. There are some stunning places to live, but do wear sensible shoes and don't mind the hills.

The Nineteenth (19e)

This is really getting out of the swing of things for tourists, except when you get to La Villette park. Although there's no shopping reason to visit here, it is part of the residential renaissance of Eastern Paris; a lot of young people live here.

The Twentieth (20e)

Maurice Chevalier made this area famous when he sang about Ménilmontant, but other than that, there isn't too much shopping action in this booming residential neighborhood. To say you live in **Belleville** tells the rest of the world you are a filmmaker or struggling artiste.

The famous **Père-Lachaise** cemetery is here; the only piece of retailing advice I can offer is to make sure you buy a map of the gravestones; otherwise, you will never find Jim Morrison's. And, yes, shops near the cemetery sell flowers and Doors posters.

THE SHOPPING QUARTIERS

When it comes to shopping in Paris, you must decide if you are just looking or if you actually want to buy something. Do you want a fantasy experience or a real-people experience? Do you mind crowds of tourists, or would you prefer to be surrounded by the people whose home you have invaded? Is your time so limited that you just want the one address that will give you the most value? Please answer these questions for yourself as you read up on my favorite shopping districts and browsing treats. *Allons-y.*

The neighborhoods below are listed in roughly geographic order, starting in the west with the 16e and working to the east.

Passy, 16e

Métro: Passy or La Muette.

Shopping Scene: Rich casual, with a black velvet headband and pearls.

Profile: Passy is the main commercial street of one of the nicest districts of one of the nicest arrondissements. It has a little of everything and is convenient to other neighborhoods. You can visit Passy on your way to the Eiffel Tower, Trocadéro, or the resale shops of the 16e, or you can catch the Métro and be anywhere else in minutes. If possible, visit Passy on a Saturday morning—then you will really be French.

The street has been booming ever since **Passy Plaza,** an American-style mall with that number one American tenant, the Gap, opened. Go to Passy Plaza for a lesson in French yuppie sociology. Shop the supermarket in the lower level, the various branches of American and British big names, and the French candy store.

Franck et Fils, a small department store formerly for blue-haired old ladies with apricot poodles, has been redone. Now, somewhat in the style of a smaller Bon Marché, it is very chic.

Shopper's tip: When you get to the end of Passy (at the **Max Mara** shop), you'll find a back street, rue Paul-Doumer. If you love home furnishings and good design, you'll find a few winners (there's a branch of **Souleiado**) along this tiny street. Forget about shopping this neighborhood on Monday until at least the afternoon.

Victor Hugo, 16e

Métro: Victor Hugo.

Shopping Scene: Chic, French, and rich . . . with dogs.

Profile: This uptown residential neighborhood is still where the big money shops. Victor Hugo is one of the fanciest shopping streets in Paris. Years ago, many big-name international designers had shops here. Most of them have moved, giving the neighborhood an intimate feel. Today most shoppers appear to be regulars who live nearby. This isn't the kind of street tourists normally visit to actually shop; you come here to get a feel for a certain part of Paris, experience a lifestyle that is totally unknown in America, and pretend you are a French aristocrat.

George V, 8e

Métro: George V or Alma Marceau.

Shopping Scene: Between two Métro stops, this area is hidden in plain sight; it's a "secret" district of small boutiques where the staffs know shoppers—and their dogs—by name. There are some name-brand stores, but most are either in the cult league (Creed perfumes) or tiny branches (Hérmes).

Profile: This nugget centers on avenue Pierre Serbie 1er, between Alma Marceau (and av. Montaigne) and the Champs-Elysées. The Hotel George V is the heart of this area and the surrounding shops.

Champs-Elysées, 8e

Métro: F-D-Roosevelt.

Shopping Scene: Outdoor mall.

Profile: The tourist mobs and shopping-cinema-cafe ratio make this one of the most crowded parts of Paris. The stores go from the ridiculous to the sublime. In 1 block are Virgin Megastore, Disney Store, and Monoprix! **Monoprix** is open until midnight in season and 10pm in winter, but closed on Sunday. Along the way you'll see numerous car showrooms, perfume showrooms, drugstores, movie theaters, airline offices, cafes, and change booths. A few big-name designers have stores here. The **Galerie du Claridge** mini-mall has two levels (go downstairs too) and the best selection of the kinds of shops you want to see; most of them are big-name designers.

If time is precious, you might want to make sure you've paid homage at **Monoprix,** 109 rue La Boétie, and pressed your nose (and toes) to the glass at **Charles Jourdan,** 68 av. des Champs-Elysées. While there are some designer shops, mostly this is affordable street fashion from multiples (chain stores). And a lot of cinemas and car showrooms. (Stop by the cafe in the Renault showroom for a snack, lunch, or dinner.) In the past few years the Champs-Elysées has changed a lot, and some of it has been changing for a long time: the **Disney Store, Virgin Megastore,** and flagship **Sephora** brought new life to the most famous street in Paris. Now we have the tearoom **Ladurée,** the new **Louis Vuitton**—where Japanese visitors may beg you to stand in line for them—and the new **Gap** flagship. The latest: branches of French chains like **Lacoste, Petit Bateau,** and the French equivalent of the Gap, **Celio.**

Avenue Montaigne, 8e

Métro: F-D-Roosevelt or Alma Marceau.

Shopping Scene: The rich, the chic, and the bored.

Profile: The avenue Montaigne has become a monument to itself. **Dior** and **Ricci** have always been here. For years, the **Chanel** boutique was a secret jealously guarded by those in the know. Then **Louis Vuitton** built its glitzy flagship store here, and Montaigne became the mega-address it is now. **Escada** has moved in, as has **Inès de la Fressange,** with her oak-leaf logo and preppy clothes in pastel colors (although word has it that Inès was bought out and isn't personally hanging around).

Of course, the Italians also came: **Krizia, Ferragamo, Max Mara,** and **Dolce & Gabbana.** The shopping pace continues to quicken, and the international mix is a crazy salad: from **Jil Sander** (German) to **Calvin Klein** (American). Note that Klein has moved.

One stroll down the short street's 2 blocks of retail will give you a look at those famous names, as well as **Loewe, Thierry**

Mugler, Ungaro, Porthault, Céline, Christian Lacroix, and **Valentino.** Some of the other stores are old-fashioned French shops that deserve a visit just to soak up the atmosphere; try **Au Duc de Praslin** (a candy and nuts store) and **Parfums Caron,** with its giant glass bottles filled with perfumes and its offerings of scents not carried in department stores in Paris, let alone in America.

Rue du Faubourg St-Honoré, 8e

Métro: Concorde.

Shopping Scene: Rich regulars from out of town.

Profile: This used to be the fanciest retail therapy in town. Now there are some multiples (chain stores) and some wannabe big names. **Façonnable** has moved in, but so have **La Perla** (jazzy lingerie and bathing suits), **JP Tod's,** and even **Lolita Lempicka.** Old standbys range from **Hermès** to **Sonia Rykiel,** with international big names (**Versace, Ferragamo**) thrown in.

Department Store Heaven, 9e

Métro: Havre-Caumartin or Chaussée d'Antin.

Shopping Scene: In summer, a zoo. At other times, middle- to upper-middle-class French suburbanites and out-of-towners mixed with an international crowd.

Profile: This 3-block-long, 2-block-deep jumble of merchandise, pushcarts, strollers, and shoppers is a central trading area. If you insist on seeing it, go early (9:30am), when you are strong and crowds aren't in full swing. Winter is far less zoolike than summer.

The two major department stores are reinventing themselves in front of our very eyes. The luxe floor (first floor) of **Au Printemps** has just been revamped, and **Galeries Lafayette** has overhauled its wine and food department, added two new restaurants, and even moved the souvenir department. Furthermore, Galeries has opened a third space (yes, another store) with an English deli across the street from the men's store, where Marks & Spencer once held court.

Check out **Lafayette Gourmet,** the grocery store attached to Galeries Lafayette—it's fabulous, with a new wine library and much more to make you dizzy with delight. Enter the new portion from the rue Provence. Speaking of rue Provence, this is a great street (although it's more like an alley) to know about. Printemps has three buildings in a cluster here and has also opened **Citadium,** an architectural wonder of a French version of the Nike Store.

Where the rue Provence crosses the pedestrian rue Havre Caumartin, you can pop into **Monoprix** (downstairs, below the Citadium) or walk north to **Passage le Havre,** half a block away. This is an American-style mall, with **FNAC, Sephora, Toastissimo,** and many branches of popular midpriced French clothing chains.

Rue de Rivoli, Part One, 1er

Métro: Concorde or Tuileries.

Shopping Scene: International tourists on their way somewhere.

Profile: The rue de Rivoli is the main drag that runs along the back side of the Louvre. The Louvre was once a fortress, which is why it seems to go on forever. They just don't build them like that anymore. Exit the Métro at Concorde and face away from the Eiffel Tower. You are ready to walk. I call this part of the street "Part One" because it is the main tourist area (see p. 93 for the scoop on Part Two). The rue de Rivoli continues after the Louvre, but has an entirely different character. Part One has a few chic shops toward the Hôtel de Crillon end, but soon becomes a good street for bookstores, such as **W. H. Smith & Son.** As you get closer to the Louvre, the stores get more touristy. Here you'll find tons of tourist traps, all in a row.

Madeleine, 8e

Métro: Madeleine.

Shopping Scene: Upscale international, plus foodie heaven.

Profile: Scads of food specialty shops cluster here. The heart of the area is a string of famous food shops almost in a row—**Hédiard, Fauchon, Nicolas** (the wine shop), **Maison de la Truffe,** and more. Fauchon has all but gutted itself and started over, and now has an extremely interesting tea department.

Stretching away from the newly cleaned-up church on rue Royale, look for **Polo/Ralph Lauren** and the glass and porcelain showrooms. There are also a few hidden passages and a brand-new **Christian Dior** shop.

On the Madeleine Métro side of the church, there's a department store for men called **Le Madelois.** Also here are branches of **Kenzo, Weill, Chacok, Body Shop, Marina Rinaldi, Burma, Dorothée Bis, Agatha, Mondi, Georges Rech, Rodier Homme,** and **Stéphane Kelian.**

This area, and the warren of tiny streets between the mall and rue Royale, has become the new headquarters for home design and tabletop shops. **Le Cedre Rouge,** sort of the French version of Pottery Barn, is here, as are other stores that specialize in affordable home style, **Conran** and **Habitat.** The newest arrival is the first freestanding **Le Jacquard Français** store, on rue Richepanse near Le Cedre Rouge.

The New Madeleine, 8e

The newest addition to the Paris "must-do" list is a single block on the Baccarat (west) side of the Madeleine church. Boulevard Malesherbes has long been home to Baccarat and Burberry. Now there are three new stores in a row: **Sia, Shiseido,** and **Resonances.**

Hidden Madeleine, 8e

Métro: Madeleine or Concorde.

Shopping Scene: Secret chic.

Part One: The **rue Boissy d'Anglas** is the narrow street that runs behind the Hôtel de Crillon, from the place de la Concorde, past **Hermès,** down to the place de la Madeleine. It doesn't see many tourists. What it does see are a lot of chic fashion editors and in-the-know types who pop in and out of their favorite stores, secure in the thought that the tourists are on the Faubourg and haven't caught on.

If you cut through the passage de la Madeleine, just off the place de la Madeleine, it leads to the chic part of the rue Boissy d'Anglas. Walk toward Concorde, to your left. Don't stop until you get to the Passage Royale, which will lead you to tea at **Bernardaud.** Along the way there's yet another passage that you have to explore if you are going to see the **Chanel** shoe store, which sells only Chanel shoes.

Part Two: I've nicknamed **rue Vignon** "Honey Street," because it is the home of the **Maison de Miel,** one of the leading specialists in French honey. This street runs on the other side of **Fauchon** (just as the rue Boissy d'Anglas runs behind Hédiard). Vignon holds a few smaller clothing shops as well as other places I like to explore. It's chic without being touristy. This is one of my favorite streets in Paris, and I often use it as my route for cutting over to the *grands magasins.* There are several fast-food places, although I am partial to **Tarte Julie,** where you can sit down or order food to go. There are three plus-size shops on this street, near the far end at rue Tronchet.

Place Vendôme, 1er

Métro: Tuileries or Opéra.

Shopping Scene: Hidden, quiet, discreet.

Profile: Ritzy. The far side of the place Vendôme is the rue de la Paix, which dead-ends 2 blocks later into Opéra. There are more jewelers here (including **Tiffany & Co.**) than on West 47th Street in New York. Well, sort of. It seems Paris is living through the War of the Couture Jewelers. It's not enough that every fancy jewelry shop has always been represented here— **Chanel** decided to move it with its own real-jewelry store (none of that costume stuff, please). To up the ante, **Dior** opened a real-jewelry store nearby. Is it hot here, or what? Maybe these diamonds just make me sweaty. Oy.

Don't confuse **Charvet** (a men's store) with **Chaumet,** a jeweler. There are several men's haberdashers on this street—everyone from **Alain** (Figaret) to **Zegna.** Figaret is not quite as famous as others in the neighborhood, but is a local hero for popular shirt-making for men and women.

Rue St-Honoré, 1er

Métro: Concorde, Tuileries, Madeleine, or Opéra.

Shopping Scene: In the know.

Profile: This is a district I think of as "Behind the Meurice." It includes not only the rue St-Honoré, which begins at the rue Royale, but lots of side streets and hidden shopping venues such as the Marché St-Honoré. The district should properly also include the rue Castiglione. Packed with designer shops of known and unknown reputations (**Jacqueline Peres, Annick Goutal, Guerlain, Payot, Hans Stern**), it's also the connecting street to the place Vendôme and rue de la Paix.

The big-name designer shops do not end when Faubourg changes names and becomes plain old rue St-Honoré. Here are branches or flagship stores of everyone from **Joseph** (British stylemeister, with cafe) to **Gres** (as in Madame), including names we would follow anywhere, like **Longchamp, Hervé Chapelier,** and **Nitya,** and one-off boutiques like **Cerize.** As you move uptown, toward the Palais Royal, you find **Goyard,** a luggage brand that is older than Louis Vuitton; **Lora Lune,** soapmaker to the stars; and the teeny-weeny **Atelier de Vilette.**

Palais Royal, Victoires & Beyond, 1er & 2e

Métro: Palais-Royal.

Shopping Scene: Chic trendsetters.

Profile: If you want your shopping experience very French, upscale, and special, this is it. The **Jardins du Palais Royal** is my single best Paris shopping experience. (It's good for non-shopping husbands because there are a park, history, and much style.) The Jardins du Palais Royal and the area around

Victoires have seen a good bit of turnover. The don't-miss new shop is the gardening shop **Prince Jardiner,** which is next door to **Shiseido's** perfume shop—an older must-do if there ever was one. Note that the brand has launched a dozen new scents.

You'll find the place des Victoires nestled behind the Jardins du Palais Royal, where the 1er and the 2e connect. Facing the place is a circle of hotels; the ground floor of each holds retail space. Wonderful shops fill the streets that radiate from the place.

Rue Etienne Marcel is the major drag, and it has long housed some of the big *créateurs* (designers). You can save this area for last, and depart the neighborhood by browsing this street before heading toward the Forum des Halles or the Beaubourg. Or you can start your stroll from the Etienne-Marcel Métro stop and work backward.

The rue Etienne Marcel is important in the lexicon of high style because so many cutting-edge designers, many of them Japanese, are here. I shop **Yohji,** which has better sales at Galeries Lafayette, where you can use your tourist discount card. There has been an influx of stores for women who wear very tight blue jeans, such as **Diesel Style Lab** (35 rue Etienne Marcel), **Miss Sixty** (49 rue Etienne Marcel), and **Replay** (36 rue Etienne Marcel). Peep into **Kokon to Zai,** 48 rue Tiquetonne, a shop from New York that also has a branch in London.

If you care, note that one side of Etienne Marcel is in the 1er and the other is in the 2e. The extension, rue Tiquetonne (which has a ton of good stores), is also in the 2e. Don't forget to check your trusty map before you leave Victoires—you can continue in any number of directions. You can easily walk to the Forum des Halles or Opéra, or to the boulevard Haussmann and the big department stores, or to the rue de Rivoli and the Louvre. The world starts at Victoires, and it's a magnificent world.

Hidden Passages, 1er

Métro: Palais-Royal.
Shopping Scene: Funky chic.

Profile: This area is hidden in plain sight. You would never find it unless you came upon it by accident or with an insider tip. Between the **Antiquaire des Louvre** and the place des Victoires, this little area includes the old-fashioned *passage* **Vero-Doudat** (where there's a **By Terry** makeup shop) and some retailers who are known by their reputation. They include **Why?**, for funny novelties, and **l'Oeil du Pelican**, 13 rue Jean-Jacques Rousseau, the kind of antiques shop that sells what are called *curiosities*—neat little things. Rue Jean-Jacques Rousseau is only 2 blocks long and leads from the Louvre right to the mall **Forum des Halles.**

For those who have to trade in francs, the main branch of the **Banque de France** is in this area, too.

Sentier, 2e

Métro: Bourse.

Shopping Scene: *Garmento.*

Profile: Some people have printer's ink in their veins; I've got garment center in my blood. If you do, too, you may want to go from Victoires into the Sentier, the wholesale garment district.

From place des Victoires, follow rue d'Aboukir, which leads from the 1er into the 2e. *Warning:* The Sentier may not be your kind of place; it sure ain't fancy. This area is very much like New York's Seventh Avenue—men with pushcarts piled high with fabric, little showrooms that may or may not let you buy, hookers in certain doorways, junk in bins, metal racks and fork-lifts, and mannequins without arms.

There are few big-name designer names here, and there are no guarantees that you will find what you want. Anytime you want to buy something in the Sentier, simply play dumb American: Ask the price and see what happens. For the most part, the area is closed tight on weekends. A few shops are open on Saturday, but Saturday is not the day to tour the neighborhood and see it all. Sunday is totally dead.

Les Halles, 1er/Midtown-Beaubourg, 3e

Métro: Les Halles or Rambuteau.

Shopping Scene: Funky, teen- and tourist-oriented.

Profile: Two landmarks dominate this area: the American-style mall at Les Halles (which replaced the famed food halls), and the Centre Georges Pompidou, the art museum. Surrounding them are all sorts of shopping styles, from museum stores to vintage clothing shops to stores that sell videos and posters and books and faience. (Don't ask me why the **Quimper** people opened a store in this district, 15 rue St-Martin.) While a mall may not be your idea of how you want to shop in Paris, if it's raining, remember that this mall is large and is filled with branch stores of all the big names in international retail. It's mobbed on Saturday.

Rue de Rivoli, Part Two, 1er–4e

Métro: Pont Neuf or Hôtel de Ville.

Shopping Scene: Real, with some emphasis on teens, tweens, and real-people budgets.

Profile: The rue de Rivoli changes names to become the rue St-Antoine, leading directly to the Bastille. Along the way are some junk shops and discounters, as well as the path to the place des Vosges and the Village St-Paul.

I like this part of the rue de Rivoli—a zoo on Saturday, by the way—because it packs in a lot, and the stores are not too expensive. It's changed a lot and now has a lot of well-priced stores. They might not offer couture, but they have stuff to look at and things real people can afford to buy.

Etam, Cite de Femme has made a huge impact by opening an enormous department store, not like the dinky Etam branches all over Europe. It occupies one of the landmark Samaritaine buildings and carries style for kids, women, and the home, as well as a restaurant, spa, and beauty salon. **La Samaritaine,** meanwhile, is in the process of enormous renovations that won't be completed until 2004. The area's Marks & Spencer has become one of the best **Monoprix** stores in town. Also here is the new flagship **1, 2, 3,** a Zara wannabe with lower prices. There's a real **Zara** nearby, as well as stores like **IKKS,** with clothes for the whole family—wearable weekend chic at decent prices.

I like **C&A,** the Dutch department store that is not known for upscale shoppers or chic fashions. It has copies of fashion looks, big sizes (by French standards), and washable clothes (who can afford dry cleaning?), and nothing costs more than 50€ ($54). **Muji,** 99 rue de Rivoli, is always fun to browse—the lifestyle store comes from Japan, has been a huge hit in London, and now conquers Paris.

Marais/Place des Vosges, 3e–4e

Métro: St-Paul.

Shopping Scene: Fabulous, funky fun; Sunday afternoon "in" scene.

Profile: The rebirth of the Marais is no longer news, but new shops continue to open, making it a pleasurable area to explore every time you visit Paris. From the Métro, follow the signs toward place des Vosges. Or take a taxi to the **Musée Picasso** and wander until you end up at the place des Vosges. (This is difficult wandering; you will need a map if you start at the Picasso Museum.)

The area between the church of St-Paul and the Seine holds the **Village St-Paul** (antiques). The Marais lies across rue St-Antoine and is hidden from view as you emerge from the Métro. You may be disoriented; I've gotten lost a number of times. That's why taking a taxi here is a good idea. There's also no hint of charm until you reach the Marais.

While the heart of the neighborhood is the place des Vosges, this is a pretty big neighborhood with lots of tiny, meandering streets to wander. Take in designer shops like **Popy Moreni** and **Issey Miyake** in an arcade that surrounds the place. The side streets are dense with opportunities, from the chic charm of **Romeo Gigli** to the American country looks of

Chevignon. The main shopping drag is rue Francs Bourgeois; look for it on a map when you are at the Picasso Museum, because the medieval streets tend to get you turned around. This street has a few cafes, a few stores that sell used family silverware by weight, and many branches of high-style stores, such as **Ventilo** for ethnic gloss and the newest branch of scent-master **Esteban.**

Between the well-known areas, a bunch of little streets house funky shops that sell everything from high-end hats to vintage clothing. Check out antiques at **Les Deux Orphelines,** 21 place des Vosges, and modern, contemporary housewares and style at **Villa Marais,** 40 rue Francs Bourgeois. Adjacent to all this is the Jewish ghetto with stores that sell Judaica; check out the rue des Rosiers.

Because most stores are open on Sunday afternoon, the entire area is dead on Monday.

Canal St-Martin, 10e

Métro: République.

Shopping Scene: You're wearing black, right?

Profile: Don't look now, but the heretofore déclassé 10e is becoming chic, led by the area surrounding the Canal St-Martin. Overlooking a canal of the Seine, it has plenty of cafes, lots of roller-blading on weekends, and quite a few funky stores, with more along the side streets. The main action is on the quai Valmy and the quai de Jemmapes on the other side—all Paris quais change names every few blocks and on both sides of the water.

When you exit the Métro, use a map to guide you to the canal. Or take a taxi to the **Hotel du Nord,** 102 quai de Jemmapes, 10e, and explore from there. The hottest store is **Antoine et Lilli,** 95 quai de Valmy, which sells fashion and kitsch. There's a cafe, so you can sip and soak up the area while staring at the patrons. Other with-it cafes: Chez Prune and Café Purple.

Operkampf/Charrone, 11e

Métro: Oberkampf.

Shopping Scene: Don't trust anyone over 30.

Profile: This one is hilarious. The neighborhood is divided into two camps: movers and shakers who have decided that the time has come to gentrify and shoppify this area, and locals who want it to stay out of the eyes of tourists and shoppers. If the district were so cute that it would break your heart to see it change, I'd be the first to say so.

As usual, the bars, clubs, and night spots come first, then the stores, so there's not much serious shopping . . . yet. And there is no McDonald's . . . yet.

Bastille, 4e–12e

Métro: St-Paul or Bastille.

Shopping Scene: Hip, moving to mass market.

Profile: Dare I say it? People are losing their heads over this up-and-coming neighborhood. I wanted to move to this part of Paris, but my friend told me I was too old to live here.

Indeed, Bastille is benefiting from the rebirth of the nearby Marais, one arrondissement over, and the ugly but renowned new Opera House. The artists have moved in; so have the Americans (to live, not to set up shop). Long known for its home furnishings stores, the district is gaining some galleries and interior design shops of note. Branch stores of the big names in French retail are here, as is the Gap. Yet it's also still home to the funky Marché Aligre, where I recently took a group of American journalists who all hated it. If you have no ethnic funk in your soul, stick to the rue St-Antoine and maybe the Viaduc des Arts.

The contrasts in the neighborhood are part of the fun. Jean-Paul Gaultier's flagship shop, **Galerie Gaultier,** is at 30 rue St-Antoine. It's a new concept that has all sorts of designs (clothing and products for the home) in one space; there are similar stores in London and Tokyo. The area should be all stores like this, but unfortunately there are a lot of multiples (chain stores). For some more outrageous stuff, look to the fringes. The rue de Reuilly has design ateliers and large decorator showrooms; try **Maison Soubrier,** 14 rue de Reuilly. There's also some funky stuff in what is technically the 11e, on the north side of the rue du Faubourg St-Antoine, along rue Charonne, rue Keller, and rue de la Roquette—these streets form a circle that leads back to the place de la Bastille.

Bercy, 12e

Métro: Cour St-Emilion.

Shopping Scene: Local yuppies.

Profile: This is the new Paris, not anything old-fashioned. I'm not sure if the fun is in riding the new Meteor train (the no. 14 line of the Métro), seeing the rehab of the old wine warehouses, or just laughing at how American this area has become. Bercy was out of it for centuries, before the government moved in with several buildings and Bercy became French slang for the Ministry of Finance. Now there's a terrific mall, **Bercy Village,** a modern high rise with movie theaters, food halls, and *hypermarchés* (giant supermarkets), and everyone wants to hop on board and see what it's all about.

I adore the Bercy Village mall, but then, I like to see American ideas catching on abroad. Nothing could be more charming in my sight than wine warehouses turned into stores. Many retailers tested ideas here and then branched out. They include **Resonances,** a gift shop, and **Truffaut,** a florist and gardening store. Sephora has tested its **White Store** (Sephora Blanc) concept here as well. There's an **Oliviers & Co.,** which carries Mediterranean olive oils. There are branches of this store all over Paris, so this one is more for locals in a part of town that has been late to discover disposable income and designer olive oil.

Montmartre, 18e

Métro: Anvers or Les Abbesses.

Shopping Scene: Uphill, it's touristy as you get into Montmartre and near Sacré-Coeur. Down by the Métro, it's discount heaven, but very déclassé.

Profile: Tourists mixed with locals in search of a bargain at the fabric and discount sources nestled into one side of the hill. The most famous discount icon in Paris, **Tati,** is in this area. You've got to be strong, but this is fun for some.

Warning: Mon Dieu, what a schlep! I investigated the famous place du Tertre in Montmartre, where the artists supposedly hang out, and was royally ripped off—and breathless from the walk up the hill. I'm not certain which facet of the adventure came closer to giving me a heart attack—the number of stairs I climbed to get to the church, or the fact that the portrait artists run price scams. However, the fabric markets are great fun and there are some junk stores that sell overstock from bins. If you can stand the jumble, you might love it here.

Edge of Town/St-Ouen

Métro: Porte de Clignancourt.

Shopping Scene: Largest flea market in Paris.

Profile: Before we get into what's going on in this part of Paris, let me offer a few warnings and explanations so you don't get lost or confused.

Transportation: If you are going to the flea market, you want the Métro stop Porte de Clignancourt, although the market is in the town of St-Ouen. Ignore other addresses, Métros, or bus stops with St-Ouen in their names.

Shopping: From the Métro (or bus) stop, you'll walk through a junky flea market that sells new items and wonder what is going on. No, this is not the famous flea market. You must get to the other side of all this junk.

Lunch: Since you will undoubtedly have a meal out here, note that the market contains several fast-food stalls (crêpes, frites, and the like), as well as bistrots and restaurants. The real talk of the town, however, is a restaurant a block from the market, **Le Soleil,** 109 av. Michelet (☎ **01/40-10-08-08**). It's a terrific bistro, the owner speaks English (and eight other languages), and the crowd has mostly been sent by Patricia Wells, who has written extensively about Le Soleil. Make a reservation, especially for weekend lunch.

Now for the market itself. It consists of many small markets, each with its own personality. For a full description and a map, turn to chapter 7, "Basic Paris Resources from A to Z."

Chapter Six

....

LEFT BANK SHOPPING NEIGHBORHOODS

RIVE GAUCHE

To many, the essence of Paris is the Left Bank. I see it as several villages, all with different personalities. If you're the type who just likes to wander, go to the 6e and spend the day, or even the week. If you're tired of the best-known parts, learn your way around the hidden sections of the district.

LEFT BANK ARRONDISSEMENTS

The Fifth (5e)

Okay, I plead the fifth. I love parts of it (try the market at place de Monge) and I'd like to move there, but I don't think I can afford it. As a tourist, you may not ever make it to my favorite parts and may stay in the more congested areas. The 5e is the famous **Latin Quarter**, or student quarter, also called Panthéon. Filled with little cafes and restaurants, it's also paradise for book hunters. Shops sell *fripes* and jeans, which seem to be all that people around here wear. This is the funkiest part of the Left Bank, just above the chic part of the boulevard St-Germain. There are a few good stores in the 5e—if you're a **Diptyque** candle, soap, and scent freak, you can find the store here (or you can go to Boston).

The Sixth (6e)

Enormous changes in retail have taken place in the 6e, and one of Paris's best shopping districts has simply become better. This is one of the most Parisian arrondissements for tourists and shoppers. It's often called Luxembourg because the Jardin du Luxembourg is here, or St-Germain-des-Prés because of the church and boulevard of the same name. Let's just call it heaven and be done with it.

The district has everything. On the **rue de Buci** and the **rue du Seine** is a street market piled high with fruit, vegetables, and flowers (great for picnic supplies). Prices tend to be higher than at other street markets because of the number of tourists who shop here, but it's so luscious, who cares? The antiques business is also clustered here, and there are a number of one-of-a-kind boutiques. But the area is no longer small and funky. Led by **Sonia Rykiel,** who arrived years ago, a herd of major designers—**Louis Vuitton, Hermès, Christian Dior**—has moved into this prime real estate. Their shops are tasteful (and then some!) and respectful to the soul of the neighborhood. Even the American-style mall at the **Marché St-Germain** is a plus. And, of course, many of Hemingway's favorite cafes and haunts are here. This is a prime place for sitting at a sidewalk cafe, watching all of Paris walk by, and having the time of your life.

The Seventh (7e)

Difficult to get around because of its lack of Métro connections, the 7e is a mostly wealthy residential area, with just a handful of shopping destinations. The real story here is for foodies: the **rue Cler,** a 2-block street filled with food stores, and a street food market on Sunday morning.

The portion of the 7e next to the 6e forms an invisible barrier (much like that between the 1er and the 8e on the Right Bank); it is impossible to know where one begins and the other ends. The closer you get to the 6e, the farther you go in an enclave of hidden good taste.

The Left Bank

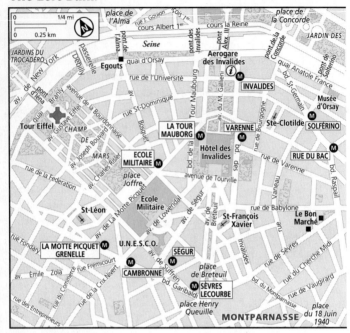

My favorite part is the **rue du Bac,** which lies in the 7e and 6e. It is crammed with wonderful shops for the neighborhood's rich residents—everything from fancy pastry shops and linen shops to fashion boutiques and tabletop temples. More chic still is the 1-block **rue du Pré-aux-Clercs,** which took me years to discover. Some of the best talent in the world lines both sides of the street. Shhh, don't tell the tourists.

The Thirteenth (13e)

One of the largest arrondissements, the 13e is mostly residential and of little interest to tourists. Its districts are Italie, Gobelins, and Austerlitz. Part of it is known as the **French Chinatown,** with a giant Chinese emporium called **Tang Freres.** You can pass.

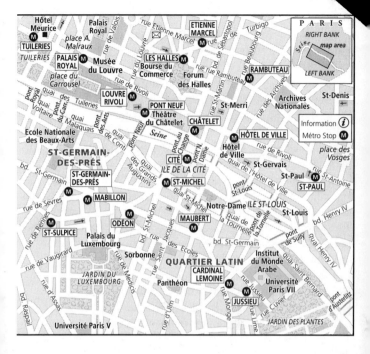

The Fourteenth (14e)

Looking for a Sonia Rykiel outlet store? Step this way. The 14e is home to the **rue d'Alésia,** a street of several bargain shops, including the Sonia Rykiel outlet store, **SR.** There's a great weekend flea market on the other side of the 14e (**porte de Vanves**).

The Fifteenth (15e)

The 15e is the largest arrondissement. A piece of the 15e touches the back of the Eiffel Tower. A small, very chic area forms the boundary between the 15e and the 7e. After that, chic ends rather quickly. Rue de la Convention is a main drag. The Porte de Versailles is just beyond, and there are tons of commercial streets all around this portion of the neighborhood. There are a few outlet stores near porte de Versailles.

THE SHOPPING QUARTIERS

The St-Germain-des-Prés Métro stop works for all the main touristy and tony shopping areas. If you have no particular plan, at least look at a map, pinpoint convenient Métro stops, and decide where you want to be around noon. I often arrange my patterns of exploration so that I end up leaving the Left Bank through the Sèvres-Babylone or the Rue du Bac Métro stop (because then I don't have to change trains). At the end of a hard day's shopping, especially if you are laden with packages, you might want to forgo a long, complicated journey on the Métro. Look at bus route maps to adjust to your own digs. The no. 95 bus goes to the St-Lazare station and makes getting anyplace pretty easy; I also like the no. 84, which goes to my home from the Hôtel Lutétia.

If you prefer a taxi, flagging one can be difficult in this area. Go to the Lutétia or to the taxi rank in front of Café Lipp near Emporio Armani on boulevard St-Germain. Note that the traffic on the boulevard St-Germain moves one way.

Since I think you are most interested in the 6e, I will begin this section there and move in a circular fashion: uptown, then south, then around to the 15e, ending with the 7e. The 6e borders the 7e, so of course you can work backward or start in the 7e. For details about **Alésia** (14e), see the section "Discount Neighborhoods," later in the chapter.

St-Germain-des-Prés, 6e

Métro: St-Germain-des-Prés.

Shopping Scene: Does anyone here speak French? Young, hip, and busy, but very touristy.

Profile: More designer stores move in. This is still the main drag of the Left Bank and the center of the universe. Have a taxi drop you at the church or take the Métro, and you'll be at the center of the action.

You can begin the day with breakfast (coffee and croissants) at any number of famous cafes, like **Les Deux Magots** or **Café**

de Flore. Sure, a cup of coffee costs $5 (4.60€) and continental breakfast is $15 (13.80€), but you can sit for hours and watch the passing parade. Nothing is more French.

Stores that can afford the rent on the boulevard cluster around here. In addition to **Etro, Armani Emporio,** and other big names, there are **Sonia Rykiel** at no. 175 and **Shu Uemura,** a fabulous Japanese cosmetics firm, at no. 176. More than anything, the big names have revitalized the area and made it even more important for you to know what's happening here. Note that the boulevard St-Germain-des-Prés is awfully long. Some of it is somewhat boring, some of it has furniture and lighting showrooms, and some of it marches right into the 5e, which is a fer piece (as we say in Texas) from the church at the heart of it all. Consider the church the center of the shopper's world, then wander into other areas.

Note: On the surface this area is very touristy, but as you get closer to the Seine and into the design showrooms and fancy antiques shops, the air changes—as does the attitude. These stores and dealers are very closed; they prefer their own company or rich French speakers who know their stuff. There are plenty of snobby and status-y places back here that tourists never visit or find.

Behind the Church, 6e

Métro: Odéon or St-Germain-des-Prés.

Shopping Scene: Busy locals; less touristy than the main areas; chic and snobby.

Profile: My favorite part of the 6e is behind the church of St-Germain-des-Prés. Behind the church you'll find place de Furstemberg, rue de Buci, rue Jacob, rue Bonaparte, rue de Seine, rue du Bac, and quai Voltaire. Many of these streets house antiques and decorating shops. The rue de Buci offers a street market (open Sundays!) that sells flowers and food in profusion. This is a must-do Paris stop; those who appreciate a visual scene come to feast their eyes.

These streets are mostly filled with boutiques, bakeries, eateries, markets, and—the fame of the neighborhood—antiques and design showrooms. It is very quaint, and the stores feel different from the ones in the other parts of the Left Bank. This is one of the most charming areas in all of Paris.

Note: The rue Bonaparte is the core of this area. It runs from the Seine alongside the church, with tons of galleries and great shops, then stretches across to the place St-Sulpice for more fun. This one thoroughfare is one of the best just-go-and-wander streets. Treat the rue Jacob with the same esprit.

Rennes Central, 6e–14e

Métro: St-Germain-des-Prés, St-Sulpice, or Montparnasse/ Bienvenüe.

Shopping Scene: Real-people Montparnasse (14e) leads to touristy Left Bank.

Profile: At one of the major intersections of the Left Bank, two streets converge in a V—the rue de Rennes and the rue Bonaparte. Bonaparte runs behind the church as well; rue de Rennes does not.

Rue de Rennes is the central drag of this trading area. It's a pretty big street with a lot of retail; the farther it goes from St-Germain, the less fancy the stores become. Rue de Rennes has a big-city feel, so it isn't exactly the charming Left Bank scene you were expecting.

Closer to boulevard St-Germain, rue de Rennes holds many big-name designer shops, from **Céline** to **Habitat,** as well as the **Gap, Stefanel, Kenzo,** and **Burberrys.** Also here are a number of hotshot boutiques, such as **Loft,** and trendsetters like **Estéban** (home scents).

As you move away from the boulevard St-Germain, there's still plenty to enjoy, but fewer designer stores. Teens can have **Morgan;** I'll take **Geneviève Lethu,** 95 rue de Rennes, for tabletop and fresh fabric ideas. If you are a Monoprix fan, don't bail out of this district until you've shopped at **Inno,** a place that always makes my heart sing—it's a dime store and grocery store right at the Montparnasse station and tower. There are also a lot of commercial stores for teens and tweens, like the Spanish chain **Mango,** at this end.

Little Dragons, 6e

Métro: Sèvres-Babylone or St-Germain-des-Prés.

Shopping Scene: Shoe freaks.

Profile: West of Rennes Central (see previous listing) are several very small, narrow streets crammed with good things to eat and to wear. They are epitomized by the rue du Dragon, which is why I call this neighborhood Little Dragons. You'll also want to check out rue de Grenelle and rue des Sts-Pères. This whole warren of streets abounds with great shops, many belonging to designers of fame and fortune (**Ferragamo, Sonia Rykiel Enfant, Philippe Model**).

This area is sandwiched between the Sèvres-Babylone Métro stop and the neighborhood I call Rennes Central. To one side is **Le Bon Marché,** one of Paris's biggest and most famous department stores. You can also easily walk to St-Placide from here.

St-Sulpice, 6e

Métro: Mabillon, St-Sulpice, or St-Germain-des-Prés.

Shopping Scene: Chic.

Profile: The core of this area lies between rue Bonaparte and the place St-Sulpice. It comes complete with a gorgeous church, a park, several designer shops (**Christian Lacroix, Castelbajac, YSL**), and some postcard places. Also here is the jewel-box pastry shop of Paris's most famous pastry chef, **Pierre Hermé,** at 72 rue Bonaparte. This area stretches behind the park and place, over to the rue Tournon and the rue de Seine, and includes the newish American-style mall **Marché St-Germain.** The side streets are full of small designer shops, some with names you've heard of—like **Souleiado** and **Les Olivades**—but many more that are largely unknown to Americans and exciting to discover.

Although I hated the mall when it first opened, I've gotten used to it. There are several branch stores of English multiples (chain stores), such as **Monsoon** and **The Body Shop;** there are a **Gap** and a few French chain stores, including **Koba,** which sells nice underwear. There's a rather well-stocked *parfumerie* as well. *Note:* This is a great place to use the bathrooms or telephones.

Along the rue St-Sulpice, before you get to the park, you'll find all the kinds of shops you came to Paris to visit. Among them are both a store run by the magazine *Elle* (no. 30), which features items available by mail order from the United States, and the adorable **Maison de Famille** (no. 29), which sells many items imported from the U.S. Both stores have upstairs levels—don't miss any of the nooks or crannies.

Quai to Heaven, 5e

Métro: St-Michel, then walk along the river to the Louvre.

Shopping Scene: Insiderish, quiet, and private.

Profile: Most of the serious antiques dealers on the Left Bank lie between the river and the boulevard St-Germain, from the quai des Augustins to the quai Voltaire. If you continue along the river and just shop the quais, you will pass the stalls that sell old books, ephemera, and junk. This is a tourist scene, and fun to do once or twice as you get to know Paris. The real antiques scene is much more hidden. It's best to make appointments in advance, even. While some browsing occurs, it is generally by locals who continually visit the dealers, know them by name, poke around, chat, pat the dog, and then peek in the back room.

The Islands, 4e

Métro: Pont Neuf or Cité; RER C: St-Michel.

Shopping Scene: Touristy but charming.

Profile: There are two islands out there in the Seine, joined by a little footbridge in the rear of Notre-Dame. Ile St-Louis is the more famous; Notre-Dame is on the Ile de la Cité. There's tourist shopping near Notre-Dame, and a flower and bird market near the police station, but the real fun is on the Ile St-Louis. The rue St-Louis en Ile has many cute shops, which are open on Sunday.

Rue Cler, 7e

Métro: Ecole Militaire.

Shopping Scene: Foodies.

Profile: The Sunday-morning market on the rue Cler, in the 7e adjoining the 15e, is one of my favorite Sunday treats. Some consider it just another Paris food market. I consider it a religious experience.

Paris Hilton, 15e

Métro: La Motte Picquet; RER C: Champs de Mars.

Shopping Scene: Hidden, residential, upper middle class.

Profile: Aside from the obvious **Eiffel Tower** business (very little shopping, even for souvenirs), none of the shopping here is immediately obvious. We come with the car; the Métro connections aren't great. But the highlights are infectious: The **quai Branly** sometimes has an exhibition (an art or antiques show); the **Village Suisse,** a village of antiques shops, is 2 blocks from the Hilton. And 2 blocks from there is a nice street market underneath the elevated rail track. I promise you, there are very few tourists here. It's on the rue Grenelle under the elevated railroad tracks of La Motte Picquet station. This market is on Wednesday and Sunday only, from 8:30am until 1pm. Although it's mostly a food market, there are some sellers of tablecloths from Provence, olive oils, and such.

Orsay, 7e

Métro: Solférino; RER C: Orsay.

Shopping Scene: Urrgh, but then again. . . .

Profile: As shopping districts go, this *quartier* is nothing to write home about. But the Musée d'Orsay has such incredible gift shops that I cannot ignore it. You can get into the shops without going to the museum or paying admission.

Rue du Bac, 7e

Métro: Sèvres-Babylone or Rue du Bac.

Shopping Scene: Left Bank snob.

Profile: As a residential neighborhood, you can't beat the 7e—not even in the 16e. As a shopping neighborhood, you can't beat the rue du Bac, especially if you like looking at the lifestyles of the rich and Parisienne.

You can get here by the easy method or the longer, more complicated but more fun method. For the former, take the Métro to Rue du Bac and walk away from the river on rue du Bac. For the latter, begin on the Right Bank, cross the bridge at the Louvre (see that bright golden statue of Jeanne d'Arc?), and hit the quai at rue du Bac. Walk toward the Métro stop Rue du Bac and away from the river. You get 3 or 4 more blocks of shopping this way. While it's not the best part of the rue du Bac, it's great fun. The street twists a bit, but just wonder and wander, following the street signs. You will quit rue du Bac only when you get to **Le Bon Marché**, so *bon marché* to you.

Secret Seven, 7e

Métro: Rue du Bac.

Shopping Scene: Privately chic. You came with the car and driver, didn't you?

Profile: This is just a 2-block stroll in another world, a world inhabited by very rich and chic women.

This walk takes you along the rue du Pré-aux-Clercs, which lies between boulevard St-Germain and the river.

DISCOUNT NEIGHBORHOODS

....

Alésia, 14e

Métro: Alésia.

Shopping Scene: Discount heaven.

Profile: This is one of the city's major discount districts. Prices in some shops may not be the lowest, but there are a good half-dozen shops to choose from. Not every store in this area is a discount house, so ask if you are confused. Don't make any assumptions!

Most of the discount houses have the word *stock* in their name, which means they sell overruns. Some shops bear a designer's name plus the word *stock;* others have store names, without alluding to what is inside. **Stock 2,** a spacious space at 92 rue d'Alésia, sells men's, women's, and kids' designer clothes at discount prices. Most of it is from **Daniel Hechter,** but there are other brands.

Don't miss **Cacharel Stock** (no. 114), with fabulous baby and kids' clothes. It carries some men's and women's things, but I've never found anything worthwhile here that wasn't for children. **Fabrice Karel,** no. 105, across from Cacharel, makes terrific knits similar to those of Rodier.

The stock shop of **Diapositive,** a big, hip line, is at no. 74. But the highlight of the block is undoubtedly **SR** (no. 64), which stands for—shout it out, folks—**Sonia Rykiel.** The clothes here are old, but they are true-blue Sonia. On my last visit I found a pair of pants I bought at Saks Fifth Avenue for $500 (don't tell my husband) for $125 (115€)!

When you shop this area, keep store hours in mind. Stores generally don't open until 2pm on Monday; many close for the entire month of August. And, again, remember that not all of the stores are discount; they just want you to think they are.

St-Placide, 7e

Métro: St-Placide or Sèvres-Babylone.

Shopping Scene: St-Placide abuts a chichi department store and feeds into fancy rue du Bac, but its style is a million miles away. This is a street of discounters and jobbers—tons of fun, if you like down-market shopping.

Profile: This area is not particularly near Alésia (although you can walk from one to the other), but mentally the two are sisters—homes of the discount shop, the stock shop, the great bargain. St-Placide is a side street alongside **Le Bon Marché,** the department store on the Left Bank. Take the Métro to St-Placide and walk toward Le Bon Marché and the rue des Sèvres. Pass Le Bon Marché, then turn left onto rue St-Placide.

There are maybe 10 stock shops in this 1 block, but they don't do much for me. Every time I visit, about once a year, I come away empty-handed. The best of the bunch is a group of shops owned by **Le Mouton à 5 Pattes.** There are a children's shop, a designer shop, and a real-people shop. There were plenty of big names, like Gaultier and Ferre, in bins the last time I visited.

St-Placide feels a bit seedy and isn't as attractive as Alésia; but there's nothing wrong with the neighborhood, and it is safe. Walk along the street, choosing what interests you, until you come to the rue de Sèvres, a main street of the neighborhood. Because Le Bon Marché is right here, many other retailers have opened branch stores to catch the overflow department-store traffic. There are a **Guerlain,** a **Rodier,** and a **Dorothée Bis,** in addition to a lot of other nice stores. It is not fancy here, but it is quite serviceable. **Zara** just moved in, and there's a Métro station (Sèvres-Babylone) in the square. You can come and go from here, or take the rue de Sèvres for 1 block and hit the neighborhood's really exciting, fancy, expensive stores.

Chapter Seven

....

BASIC PARIS RESOURCES FROM A TO Z

ACCESSORIES

....

The Parisian department stores have very good accessories departments, and buying from them makes good use of your tourist discount card—and the 183€ ($197.65) spending requirement for a détaxe refund, if you plan to stock up on gifts. Note that this chapter includes sections on costume jewelry, shoes, and handbags.

CASTELBAJAC CONCEPT STORE
31 place du Marché St-Honoré, 1er (Métro: Tuileries).

Accessories for everything—fashion and for the home—at this larger-than-life gallery cum boutique from former enfant terrible Jean-Charles de Castelbajac, one of the most imaginative and humor-filled minds in France.

CERIZE
380 rue St-Honoré, 8e (Métro: Concorde).

What fun to gawk in the windows and dream of being the kind of person who wears these items or has someplace to go where you could carry this off—dramatic but really fabulous to outrageous creations. Creative selection of evening bags. Prices are over $100 (92€) but under $1,000 (920€).

FABRICE
33 and 54 rue Bonaparte, 6e (Métro: St-Germain-des-Prés).

Vintage or made with vintage parts, ethnic and faux ethnic, chunky and funky and more, more, more. Fabrice has two stores separated by some other buildings.

JEROME GRUET
9 rue St-Roch, 1e (Métro: Tuileries).

One of several sources on a secret street of up-and-comers, this store makes and sells its own bags and shoes, with a casual chic twist that makes them different from everything else you've seen.

OCTOPUSSY
255 rue St-Honoré, 8e (Métro: Concorde).

Very funky handbags and some accessories; a lot of the stock is created with photo-fashion imagery.

SHADE
63 rue des Sts-Pères, 6e (Métro: Sèvres-Babylone).

Ali Baba and the young *créateurs* of France have teamed up—from kitsch to fantasia.

AMERICAN DESIGNERS IN PARIS

The second American liberation of Paris began quietly enough when Ralph Lauren opened a shop on the place de la Madeleine. Not so subtle was the arrival of the Gap, which now has a store in every major shopping neighborhood in Paris, along with free-standing Gap Kids stores. American style is the latest thing in town, and even French designers are copying it—and American designers (Tom Ford, Michael Kors, Marc Jacobs) are becoming French designers.

You can see much American merchandise at home and p
less for it, but in France there's always the chance you may fin
your favorite items in shades you can't get at home. Still, I don't
suggest you spend too much precious Paris time looking at
American-based designers; these guys are out to win the local
population, and they are selling status to locals, not merchandise that offers value for money. Buy Timberland at home.

You'll also find that American methods of merchandising
and selling are creeping into the French lifestyle, so even the
big department stores are getting a little more American. In
no time at all it will be very hard to find someone in France
to be rude to you. Some Americans in Paris:

BCBG
412 rue St-Honoré, 8e (Métro: Concorde).

CALVIN KLEIN
53 and 56 av. Montaigne, 8e (Métro: Alma Marceau).

CRABTREE & EVELYN
*177 bd. St-Germain, 7e (Métro: Rue du Bac); Passy Plaza,
53 rue de Passy, 16e (Métro: La Muette).*

ESPRIT
9 place des Victoires, 2e (Métro: Bourse).

GAP
Everywhere, including the Champs-Elysées.

OSHKOSH B'GOSH
32 rue de Passy, 16e (Métro: La Muette).

RALPH LAUREN/POLO
2 place de la Madeleine, 8e (Métro: Madeleine).

ANTIQUES

Paris is one of the world's capitals for antiques. One of the pleas-
ures of shopping here is browsing the wide variety of antiques

Worth a Trip

Besides specialty events, there are a few other kinds of antiques events that I really recommend, if you have the strength. They are slightly out of town or on the fringes.

- **Chatou** is a fair in the town of Chatou twice a year (Mar and Sept), on dates announced in the antiques magazines. You take the RER there and walk from the train station (it's well marked). The trick, of course, is to be able to carry your purchases back on the train with you—or to move to Paris and have them delivered. There is a shipping office.
- **Versailles** is known for the palace of the Sun King and even for its hotel, spa, and restaurant, but few people ever talk about the antiques *village* right in the heart of town.
- **Stadium shows** are similar to the Rose Bowl Swap Meet in Pasadena. They take place at various times of the year (weather permitting) at stadiums in the outskirts of Paris and are fabulous for their low prices and huge selection. That's the good news. The bad news is that few of them are served by public transportation. I went with friends from New York who hired a car and driver, which was doubly lucky since we bought so much. The shows usually have shipping offices.

shops. Whether you're buying real antiques or just some "old stuff," remember that U.S. Customs defines an antique as something that is at least 100 years old. If a piece does not come with provenance papers, you must have a receipt or a bill of lading from the dealer that says what the piece is and its origin and age. The French government is rather stringent about what can be taken out of the country; it even tries to keep some designer *fripes* (used clothes) in the country.

Expensive museum-quality antiques are generally sold in the tony shops along the rue du Faubourg St-Honoré and in the 16e, although there are plenty of high-end dealers on the Left Bank. Midpriced antiques are predominantly found in antiques shops on the Left Bank, in the antiques *villages,* and at the markets of St-Ouen. Junk is mostly sold at street markets, fairs, and flea markets.

If you just want to browse and get the feel of the antiques scene, get over to the Left Bank. A grouping of very important dealers sits between the river and the boulevard St-Germain. They may be a tad more expensive than the others in town, but they are the real guys with the real reputations who do not even look up from their newspapers when you walk in. They can tell from your questions just how serious you are, what you know, and, often, whom you know.

If you want to familiarize yourself with the notions and motions of French-style antiques shopping, get to a large news agent and look at the half-dozen magazines devoted to antiques and *brocante.* The most popular is **Alladin,** but all give the schedules of big shows, fairs, specialty antiques events, and such. They cost about 3€ ($3.25) each.

If you are flexible about when you visit Paris and want to maximize your antiques shopping possibilities, you might want to call **Sadema,** one of the leading show organizers (see "*Brocante* Shows," later in the chapter). It books a ton of shows between February and June.

Antiques *Villages*

A *village* in Paris is not a subdivision of an arrondissement but a place for good antiques. *Villages* are buildings that house many antiques dealers under one roof. If you need a rainy-day occupation, a trip to any *village* probably will do it; some are even open Sunday.

Le Bon Marché
38 rue de Sèvres, 6e (Métro: Sèvres-Babylone).

Le Bon Marché is a department store, but it's really three stores in two buildings. One portion is the full department store; the other is a grocery store with a flea market and cafe upstairs. I can't tell you that this is a must-do experience, but it can be fun. It's especially good if you are in the neighborhood or want a taste of a flea market without going to the trouble of getting to one.

LE LOUVRE DES ANTIQUAIRES
2 place du Palais-Royal, 1er (Métro: Palais-Royal).

This is a virtual antiques department store of some 250 dealers. You may have more fun here than at the museum! At least you can shop here. Many mavens claim that this is the single best one-stop source in Paris, because quality is high and the dealers have reputations to protect. You can even bargain a little. There are enough affordable small pieces that you're bound to find something you like without having to pound the pavement. Indoors are a restaurant and a shipping agent. Very sophisticated, very civilized, nothing junky at all. Closed Sunday in August; otherwise, the Sunday scene is from a movie—the other shoppers alone are worth a visit. Clean bathrooms.

LE VILLAGE SUISSE
54 av. de la Motte-Picquet, 15e (Métro: La Motte).

You won't find any gnomes making watches here, or handing out chocolate bars . . . just a lot of dealers in the mid- to high-price range, with some very respectable offerings. There are 150 shops in an area 1 block long and 2 blocks wide—it's sort of like a mall that rambles from building to building.

The Village Suisse is near the Hilton, the Eiffel Tower, and l'Ecole Militaire. Prices are not outrageous, but they aren't low, either; most stores offer shipping. There are no cute or funky stores here, but several shops are theme oriented, selling nautical items or antique jewelry, for example. Sunday is a big day here.

VILLAGE ST-PAUL
Rue St-Paul, 4e (Métro: St-Paul).

This *village,* near a block or more of street stalls selling antiques, can be a little hard to find. It's hidden in a medieval warren of streets between the Seine and the church of St-Paul, close to Marais and Bastille. The *village* is between the rues St-Paul, Charles V, des Jardins St-Paul, and Ave-Maria.

Get off the Métro at St-Paul and walk toward the river. Or walk along the quai going toward the Bastille and take a left when you spy the first antiques shop on the corner of the rue St-Paul. If you are coming from the river, you have the advantage of being able to see the VILLAGE ST-PAUL sign that spans the street across the rooftops.

Hours are generally Thursday to Monday 11am to 7pm. There are many shops. Prices can be steep, but the variety of the merchandise, combined with the charm of the neighborhood, makes this a delightful way to pass the time. A good stop to piggyback with your visit to Marais. Yes, there's life on Sunday afternoons.

Auction Houses

For years, the big name in Paris's auction world was the Hôtel Drouot. But ever since Sotheby's gave up its Monaco offices and moved to Paris, and the government allowed others to play in the big leagues, the scene's become much more competitive. Christies and Sotheby's are trying to take over the town.

When an entire estate is auctioned, there is usually nothing "important" (as the dealers tend to say) for sale. Important works are saved for major auctions. Such big-time auctions are held in the relatively new Hôtel Drouot. (The house took over an existing theater on the av. Montaigne.) Humdrum and average estate sales, where you can still find bargains, are at the main house, not far from Galeries Lafayette.

HÔTEL DROUOT
9 rue Drouot, 9e (Métro: Le Peletier); 15 av. Montaigne, 8e (Métro: Alma Marceau).

Drouot is a weird and fascinating place. At the entrance, an information counter has catalogs and notices of future sales.

Three TV sets on the ground floor show different parts of the building, and there is an appraiser who will tell you, free of charge, if an item you bring in is worthy of auction, and will appraise it for you on the spot. The estimate is done in a small private room. If you agree with the estimate, you can set a date for your auction. The seller pays an 8% to 10% commission to the house.

Auctions take place on weekdays in the summer and daily the rest of the year. They always begin at 2pm and usually end about 6:30pm. Previews are held on Wednesday until 11am. When you read auction catalogs in Paris, note that Hôtel Drouot listings with an "R" after them (for Richelieu) refer to the old location; an "M" refers to the avenue Montaigne location. You can buy Drouot's magazine on newsstands and get an instant look at the auction of the month.

The auction rooms are various sizes; some can be divided or opened according to need. All the rooms are carpeted; art, tapestries, or both hang on the walls. The clients sit on chairs to watch the bidding. Most of the clients are dealers; we have never noticed a very jazzy crowd here, even when we went to a Goya auction. All business is in French. If you are not fluent, bring your own translator or expert, or book a translator (☏ 01/42-46-17-11) ahead of time.

You needn't register to bid; anyone can walk in, sit down, and bid. Paddles are not used. Some dealers occasionally use shills to drive up the price. Auctioneers are familiar with all the dealers and could possibly choose to throw a piece their way. Dealers may even pool in on items. All auctions have catalogs, and the lots are numbered and defined in the catalog. You do not need a catalog to enter a preview or an auction, as you do in New York. The conditions of the sale are plainly printed (in French) inside the first page of the catalog. You can pay in cash up to 1,500€ ($1,620). French people may write local checks; Americans cannot write checks. If you have only American dollars on hand, there is an exchange bureau in the house. If you pay in cash, you can walk out with your item.

Brocante Shows

Brocante is the French word for junk; *brocante* and those who sell it are not antiquers—this is very strict in the French sense of things. An American might not notice the difference.

Brocante is sold everywhere in France, from local markets to fancy shoes. **Sadema,** 86 rue de Lille, 75007 Paris (☎ **01/40-62-95-95;** fax 01/40-62-95-96), is an organization that hosts *brocante* shows. These shows are annual or semiannual, most frequently held at the same time (more or less) and place each year. They are announced in the papers (check *Figaroscope*) and in weekly guides such as *Pariscope*. You can call, write, or fax for their schedule. Some shows are weekend events; others last up to 2 weeks. Sadema charges admission, usually about 5€ ($5.40) per person. It has a registration service, so you can get on their mailing list. I'm waiting for the Web site!

Sadema is not the only game in town; other organizations also sponsor shows. One agency is **Joel Garcia** (☎ **01/56-53-93-93).** Some are fancier and charge even higher admission. In fact, the admission charge is a direct indication of how tony the dealers are: the higher the fee, the more expensive the dealers and their wares.

Annual shows include:

- **Ferraille de Paris:** Held in the Parc Floral de Paris (Bois de Vincennes), this good-sized indoor fair occurs toward the end of February. It includes a lot of affordable merchandise and approachable merchants. Everything from empty perfume bottles to the kitchen sink. The French country kitchen sink. (Métro: Porte Dorée.)
- **Brocante de Printemps:** A March event that usually lasts 10 days; heralds the coming of spring, of course. (Métro: Porte Edgar-Quintet.)
- **Brocante à la Bastille:** You can tell from its title that this event does not take itself or its merchants too seriously. This fair is usually held on both sides of the canal. Pay near the place de la Bastille; there are bridges to the other side. Usually held

for 10 days in April or May, and particularly fabulous in fine weather. I'd fly in just for this event. (Métro: Bastille.)

* **Brocante de Paris:** This huge event is the talk of the town for those who hope to get a designer bargain. Runs for 10 days in May. (Métro: Porte Brochant.)

CHILDREN'S CLOTHING

If you're the kind of mom—or grandma—who likes to drop a bundle on a single outfit for your little darling, Paris welcomes you and your moolah. You'll have no trouble finding expensive shops where you can swoon from the high fashion and the high price.

Note: French clothes don't fit like U.S. clothes—they are smaller and closer to the body. French kids' clothes are usually marked by the age in years just like American clothes: 8A means 8 years (*8 ans*). For an American 8-year-old, buy size 10A. A size chart appears on p. 269.

* Don't forget about the **department stores,** which have rather famous children's departments and much more moderate prices. **Galeries Lafayette** has a large array of designer brands for kiddies, even from American designers like DKNY.

* If you like cheap, fun, throwaway things, try **Monoprix.** Each has a toy department, a good selection of inexpensive basics, and some great ready-to-wear clothing. But wait, sometimes you'll find that prices at one of these "dime stores" are the same as at a department store. Still, if you can get an outfit for $12 to $15 (11€–14€), I think you're doin' good.

* Some of the trendy, fashion-forward boutiques also have a kiddie division. They include **H&M,** 53 bd. Haussmann (Métro: Chaussée d'Antin or Havre Caumartin). I find the quality is not as good as at Monoprix, but some trendy pieces are just so adorable you have to snap them up.

* Couture baby wear is the latest thing—not really made to measure, but from the couture houses. **Christian Dior** sells

a baby bottle (about $20/18€) that is adorable—and a great gift.

- If you're looking for children's shoes, you will need a size chart (p. 269) and some luck. My favorite source is a cheapie chain called **André,** with branch stores everywhere—they have copies of all the hot styles that usually cost well under $20 (18€) a pair. Well-made shoes cost an arm and a leg, no matter how small.

FRENCH CHAINS

BONPOINT
15 rue Royale, 8e (Métro: Madeleine), and others.

BONPOINT SOLDES
82 rue de Grenelle, 7e (Métro: Rue du Bac).

For classic styles, you won't do better than Bonpoint and its perfectly crafted outfits. Parisian women with money and style swear by this resource. You've never seen anything so superbly made in your life. An adorable romper costs $50 (46€); a simple smocked dress starts at $100 (92€), but prices can go to $300 (276€) for the grander stuff. If your child is over age 5, go upstairs.

There are several Bonpoint shops around town. Some specialize in kids' shoes; one has furniture only. There are freestanding stores in New York, London, and Milan. The brand is a French tradition, although Americans may find it way too uptight.

If you're impressed with the clothing but can't hack the prices, you might try the outlet store, where last season's collection (or what's left of it) is sold for a fraction of the uptown price. Here you'll find that $300 (276€) little frock for a mere $60 (55€)! The outlet (closed weekends) is convenient to everything else on the Left Bank.

DU PAREIL AU MÊME
15 rue Mathurins, 8e (Métro: Madeleine), and others.

I consider this best of the mass-market kiddie boutiques. I have been buying for my niece here for a number of years. Most of the line is casual and in strong colors, and the prices are very affordable. There are stores in every shopping district in Paris, and all over France.

PETIT BATEAU
116 Champs-Elysées, 8er (Métro: George V or Etoile).

The famed maker of T-shirts has opened a new flagship. It opened its first U.S. store last year in Manhattan, where prices are twice what they are in Paris. The line is also available in department stores.

TARTINE ET CHOCOLAT
89 rue du Faubourg St-Honoré, 8e (Métro: Concorde).

French-style maternity dresses and layettes, both classic and nouveau. My fave: the big pink hippo in pink and white stripes sitting in a playpen, just begging to be taken home to some-one's child. There are Tartine et Chocolat boutiques in the major department stores.

KIDS' BOUTIQUES & DESIGNER LINES

PETIT FAUNE
33 rue Jacob, 6e (Métro: St-Germain-des-Prés).

Very original baby clothes in the nouveau style. Some even have matching shoes and hats. Everything is very, very small—up to size 2. The clothes are very American, and even the fanci-est isn't in the classic style.

UNE ETOILE EST NÉE
Passage du Havre, 9e (Métro: St-Lazare).

This is a small shop on the ground floor of a mall next door to Printemps; it carries many designer lines, including Kenzo, Catimi, and Baby Dior. I bought Julia a cotton sweatshirt job here that cost an outrageous $60 (55€) but was the cutest thing I had ever seen. It offers a fidelity card to frequent shoppers. And yes, the name is "A Star Is Born."

CHOCOLATES

Who makes better chocolate, the French or the Belgians? You'll just have to keep tasting until you decide. Designer chocolate is not inexpensive. Expect to pay about \$100 (92€) per kilo. Of course, no one could eat a kilo, could they? Hmm. Also remember that once you are home you can order fresh, handmade chocs from Provence at www.zchocolat.com.

CHRISTIAN CONSTANT
37 rue d'Assas, 6e (Métro: St-Placide); 26 rue du Bac, 6e (Métro: Rue du Bac).

The more things change, the more they remain Constant, especially at one of the top *chocolatiers* in town. Constant also sells ice cream and other sweet treats. You'll pass it as you shop the rue du Bac. Open Monday through Saturday 8am to 8pm.

DEBEAUVE & GALLAIS
30 rue des Sts-Pères, 7e (Métro: Sèvres-Babylone).

This shop is between the boulevard St-Germain and the river; many shoppers are more familiar with the other portion of this famous shopping street. This incredibly fancy chocolate shop sells unusual flavors. Note the chocolate postcards (\$7/6.45€).

LA MAISON DU CHOCOLAT
8 bd. de la Madeleine, 9e (Métro: Madeleine); 19 rue de Sèvres, 6e (Métro: Sèvres-Babylone).

If you read American gourmet magazines, you'll find plenty of mentions of this boutique, which wraps its chocolates much as Hermès wraps its goodies. It's famous for its truffles, which are so rich you can't eat more than three a day (breakfast, lunch, dinner). Chocolates are handmade, a rarity these days, and mavens claim you can get no closer to heaven. There are several branch stores, so you shouldn't have trouble getting a fix.

LENÔTRE
49 av. Victor Hugo, 16e (Métro: Victor Hugo).

One of the older, more famous names in candy and sweets, Lenôtre is known for its chocolates and desserts, as well as its tearoom. A nice place to go for a gift for your hostess— Parisian prestige in a box.

MARQUISE DE SÉVIGNÉ
32 place de la Madeleine, 8e (Métro: Madeleine).

Since I like sweet chocolates, I send you here for the hazelnut praline. It has a picture of the marquise herself on the golden foil. There are other divine chocolates here; I'm just addicted to this flavor. There is also candy for diabetics. Those who prefer dark chocolates and headier stuff may pooh-pooh this.

RICHART
258 bd. St-Germain, 7e (Métro: Solférino).

This address is in the chic part of the Left Bank. It serves the local wealthy residents chocolates from Lyon. The most famous ones are filled with crèmes of whiskey or champagne. Open Monday and Saturday 11am to 7pm; Tuesday to Friday 10am to 7pm.

CONTINENTAL BIG NAMES

Despite the fact that the French think French fashion is the best in the world, they have graciously allowed other designers to open in Paris. Of course, the Italians have a good number of shops, representing some of the most famous names in fashion. A handful of the couturiers are British (John Galliano, Alexander McQueen, Stella McCartney); and many of the world's biggest fashion names come from other countries yet show their lines in Paris (Valentino, Hanae Mori, Kenzo, Yohji, and so on), so they have come to be considered French designers. In most cases, nationality doesn't matter—it's the clothes.

The list that follows separates the non-French brands by house, not by designer.

AKRIS
54 rue du Faubourg St-Honoré, 8e (Métro: Concorde); 49 av. Montaigne, 8e (Métro: Alma Marceau).

ARMANI EMPORIO
25 place Vendôme, 1er (Métro: Tuileries); 149 bd. St-Germain, 6e (Métro: St-Germain-des-Prés).

BOTTEGA VENETA
6 rue du Cherche-Midi, 6e (Métro: St-Germain-des-Prés).

BURBERRY
55 rue des Rennes, 6e (Métro: St-Germain-des-Prés); 8 bd. Malesherbes (Métro: Madeleine).

CERRUTI 1881
15 place de la Madeleine, 8e (Métro: Madeleine).

D&G SUPERSTORE (DOLCE & GABBANA)
244 rue de Rivoli, 1er (Métro: Concorde).

DUNHILL
15 rue de la Paix, 2e (Métro: Opéra).

ERMENEGILDO ZEGNA
10 rue de la Paix, 1er (Métro: Opéra).

ESCADA
418 rue St-Honoré, 8e (Métro: Concorde); 51 av. Montaigne, 8e (Métro: F-D-Roosevelt).

ETRO
66 rue du Faubourg St-Honoré, 8e (Métro: Concorde); 177 bd. St-Germain, 6e (Métro: St-Germain-des-Prés).

FENDI
1 av. Francois-1er, 8e (Métro: Alma Marceau).

FERRAGAMO
50 rue du Faubourg St-Honoré, 8e (Métro: Concorde); 68–70 rue des Sts-Pères, 6e (Métro: Sèvres-Babylone).

GIANFRANCO FERRE
38 av. George V, 8e (Métro: George V).

GIANNI VERSACE
62 rue du Faubourg St-Honoré, 8e (Métro: Concorde).

GIORGIO ARMANI (BLACK LABEL)
6 place Vendôme, 1er (Métro: Tuileries).

GUCCI
3 rue du Faubourg St-Honoré, 8e (Métro: Concorde); 23 rue Royale (Métro: Concorde); 350 rue St-Honoré, 1er (Métro: Tuileries).

JOSEPH
44 rue Etienne Marcel, 2e (Métro: Etienne Marcel); 14 av. Montaigne, 8e (Métro: F-D-Roosevelt); 277 rue St-Honoré, 8e (Métro: Concorde).

KRIZIA
48 av. Montaigne, 8e (Métro: Alma Marceau).

LA MAISON SALON VERSACE
41 rue François-1er, 8e (Métro: F-D-Roosevelt).

LAURA ASHLEY
94 rue de Rennes, 6e (Métro: Rennes); 261 rue St-Honoré, 1er (Métro: Concorde); 95 av. Raymond-Poincaré, 16e (Métro: Victor Hugo).

LAUREL
402 rue St-Honoré, 8e (Métro: Tuileries); 52 rue Bonaparte, 6e (Métro: St-Germain-des-Prés).

MARIELLA BURANI
412 rue St-Honoré, 8e (Métro: Concorde).

MARNI
57 av. Montaigne, 8e (Métro: Alma Marceau).

MAX MARA
31 av. Montaigne, 8e (Métro: Alma Marceau); 265 rue St-Honoré, 1er (Métro: Concorde or Tuileries); 100 av. Paul-Doumer, 16e (Métro: La Muette); 37 rue du Four, 6e (Métro: St-Germain-des-Prés).

MISSONI
43 rue du Bac, 7e (Métro: Rue du Bac); 1 rue du Faubourg St-Honoré, 8e (Métro: Concorde).

MIU MIU
16 rue du Grenelle, 7e (Métro: St-Sulpice).

MOSCHINO
68 rue Bonaparte, 6e (Métro: St-Germain-des-Prés).

MULBERRY
14 rue du Cherche Midi, 6e (Métro: St-Germain-des-Prés); 45 rue Croix des Petits Champs, 1er (Métro: Palais-Royal).

PRADA
10 av. Montaigne, 8e (Métro: Alma Marceau).

CYBERCAFES

CLICKTOWN
3 rue de Rome, 8e (Métro: St-Lazare).

Similar to Easy Everything, but closer to the big department stores.

EASY EVERYTHING
31 bd. Sebastopol, 3e (Métro: Châtelet); 6 rue de la Harpe, 5e (Métro: St-Michel).

Open 24Hsur24, as they say in France, this is a fabulous resource, with cyberstations all over Europe and more expected to open in Paris. Clean, neat, bright, easy to use; cafe.

LE WEB BAR
32 rue de Picardie, 3e (Métro: République).

One of the oldest and most established in Paris; young crowd; cafe with DJ.

DEPARTMENT STORES

French department stores have been basically for French people for over 100 years. Recently, however, they have opened their arms to embrace international tourists; **Galeries Lafayette** and **Au Printemps** make a serious attempt to woo American and international tourists. (**Bon Marché** pretends not to care.)

The biggies offer a lot of bang for your time, but they get incredibly crowded on Saturday, especially in summer. If your time in Paris is limited, go to these stores early and use them to your best advantage: Check out the designer fashions and all the ready-to-wear clothing floors, and you will immediately know what's hot and what's not. Don't forget to tour the housewares floors (or building, at Printemps) to see the latest ideas for the home and table.

Also note that there are common-sense reasons to shop at a department store—aside from the obvious time savings. There are financial benefits too. Go to many stores separately, and you'll make many separate purchases; buy it all under one roof and you'll get a détaxe refund if you spend 183€ ($197.65).

Galeries Lafayette has three different buildings, as does Au Printemps. There are also scads of street vendors (with permission from the stores) outside these two stores as well as in a nearby alley. In short, this area is overwhelming. It's not easy to browse, so it won't be fun if you think you are going to tackle it all.

What you need is a plan. I suggest hitting Galeries Lafayette first for fashion, then moving on to the Galeries Lafayette supermarket (Lafayette Gourmet). Afterward, I'd move on to Printemps Maison (a really great store), do only the first two floors of Printemps, and finally end up at Prisunic, which is behind

Printemps. You can do all of this in 3 to 4 hours and have a ball; I think you need to limit your time here to best enjoy it.

However, if you are doing some very serious shopping, and it looks as if you will spend 183€ ($197.65), do not divide your time between two different department stores. Buy everything from one store so that you qualify for the détaxe refund.

Allow at least 15 minutes for the détaxe paperwork, which you must commence in the department store. Expect it to take longer if it's the middle of the tourist season.

GALERIES LAFAYETTE
40 bd. Haussmann, 9e (Métro: Chaussée d'Antin); Commercial Centre Montparnasse, 14e (Métro: Montparnasse/Bienvenüe).

I have come to love Galeries Lafayette in my middle age, mostly because it's easy. It sells everything, and the renovations are astounding. If it's raining or you are in a hurry, you are in good hands. If you want an overview of Paris retail before you begin to shop the streets and small boutiques, this is a good place to educate your eye. If you have children with you, this place is great—there's a kiddie entertainment center. There isn't a more complete department store in France.

Come early in the day and take notes, if need be. Before I learned to love the store, I hated it because I got lost in it and never learned my way around. Don't be intimidated. Trust me, it pays to take some time to familiarize yourself with a reconnaissance trip or by studying the free store maps available on the ground floor. This is one of the largest stores in the world; it is not square, so you need help in learning where everything is.

If you are planning on buying a lot and the thought of all those individual sales slips makes you nuts, you can use a "shopper's card," available at the Welcome Desk.

This is how it works: As you make each purchase, the clerk marks your card with the amount and holds your package at the desk. When you are finished, you pay the grand total. You don't have to keep opening and closing your wallet and signing multiple receipts. It's also one of the easiest ways to get your détaxe, since you pay and claim the credit all at once.

There's only one problem: After you have paid, you must collect all of your packages. It helps if you have marked on the map where you left them.

Foreign visitors get a flat 10% discount on most purchases (except food and red-dot items) with a discount card that's available free from the Welcome Desk. (Be sure to present yours before the sales clerk rings you up.) You can also receive a coupon for this 10% discount from your U.S. travel agent or hotel. The export discount is 12% after an expenditure of 183€ ($197.65); do not confuse the flat 10% discount with the 12% détaxe discount—we are really looking at 10% plus 12%!

When you use the discount card, don't be surprised if you are sent to a main cash register; there are several on each floor, so it's no big deal. It's just annoying if you don't know about it.

Galeries is open until 9pm on Thursday. I don't know about you, but this is my idea of heaven: Shop all day, have tea, then shop into the night. Collapse at your hotel and send for room service, or, better yet, go to Lafayette Gourmet for a take-out *pique-nique*.

Galeries Lafayette offers a fashion show on Wednesday throughout the year, and on Wednesday and Friday from April through October. It's free, but you need reservations (☎ 01/48-74-02-30). The show is in the Salon Opéra. Use the Auber entrance, then the Mogador escalator, and head to the 7th floor. The fashion show is quite jazzy and good and has no commentary, so there's no language problem; free refreshments are served. It's worth doing—it gives you a preview not only of what's available in the store but also of hot looks and trends.

The store also has numerous other services too amazing to mention or explain; there are so many that many people in the store don't know about them. The store doesn't do a great job of telling you all the ways it will take care of you, so ask a lot of questions or just trust me—whatever you need, Galeries has thought of it and provides it; you just have to find where.

The store is very big on philosophy, which explains some of the unusual things hidden within. The store is really a small city. There are a post office, a shoe-repair kiosk, a bank (an ATM that takes U.S. cards is outside on the wall on rue de Chaussée-d'Antin), a penny candy store, two souvenir departments, an exposition space, and a separate museum with real exhibits that have to do with culture, not shopping. The expo space is on the 3rd floor. The store has been famous for its giant expos for the past century—they may amuse you. There are beauty salons, there's a mini-spa, there's everything. When I am asked to categorize this store in terms of an American point of reference, all I can say is: It's Macy's.

Open Monday through Saturday 9:30am to 6:45pm, Thursday until 9pm. Open on the Sundays prior to Christmas and a few other exceptional openings. Closed on French holidays.

Note: The Galeries Lafayette on the Left Bank is a small store catering to locals who work in the area. Its best feature: It opens early in the morning on weekdays. Its second-best feature: It's across the street from **Inno,** my dime-store supermarket. I suggest forgetting it.

Au Printemps, Brummell & Printemps de la maison
64 bd. Haussmann, 9e (Métro: Havre Caumartin).

Printemps Nation
25 cours de Vincennes, 20e (Métro: Porte-de-Vincennes).

Printemps Italie
30 av. d'Italie, 13e (Métro: Italie).

Printemps République
10 place de la République, 11e (Métro: République).

Most people call it merely *Printemps,* which means "spring." The store is much smaller than Galeries Lafayette, so you really cannot compare the two. I'd say Printemps was trying to be Saks; I say "trying," because only the first two floors of the store have been redone. They are fabulous and very Saks-like. The rest of the floors are exactly like Galeries Lafayette, only smaller, with fewer brands.

The Maison store, however, is fabulous—really worth visiting. It doesn't carry only items for the home. It has a huge perfume department on the ground floor and a children's department upstairs. The basement paper goods and crafts are excellent; the store launched this department, *Esprit Libre* (free spirit), which is sensational.

Just like Galeries Lafayette, Printemps has a coupon that entitles foreign visitors to a 10% discount. Mine was in a stack of coupons at the concierge desk at my hotel; I got the coupon during the winter, and it was valid for a full year. You present the card and your passport at the Welcome Service desk on the street floor of the main fashion store, and you receive something resembling a credit card.

The 10% discount offer does not apply to food, books, or discounted merchandise. This has nothing to do with the détaxe refund; if you qualify for détaxe, you get an additional 12% off.

The main store consists of three separate stores: **Brummell,** the men's store, behind the main store; the home store (**Printemps de la Maison**); and the fashion store, **Printemps de la Mode.** Brummell has been renovated and is sensational; there's a great cafe and bar organized by Paul Smith on the top.

Printemps hosts a free fashion show on Tuesday year-round, and on Tuesday and Friday from March through October. The show is at 10am on the 7th floor, under the cupola. Commentary is in English and French; the show lasts 45 minutes.

If this sounds enormously like what you just read about Galeries Lafayette, don't be shocked. I find that the stores are like neighbors who are out to show off to each other. One gets Angelina, so the other gets Ladurée; they are always out to have the same but different ideas, although Printemps does have a few exclusive brands that Galeries Lafayette cannot get. Although the rivalry is intense, to me, the stores are not competitive—they are very different.

Open Monday through Saturday 9:35am to 7pm. On Thursday the store is open until 10pm! Open on the Sundays prior to Christmas and some other exceptional openings.

Bazar de l'Hôtel de Ville (BHV)
52–56 rue de Rivoli, 1er (Métro: Hôtel de Ville).

If you think this is a funny name for a store, you can call it BHV (pronounced *bay*-hache-vay), or remember that the full name of the store tells you just where it is—across from the Hôtel de Ville. The store is famous for its do-it-yourself attitude and housewares. You owe it to yourself to go to the basement (SS) level. If you are at all interested in household gadgets or interior design, you will go nuts.

The upper floors are ordinary enough, and even the basement level can be ordinary (I assure you—I am not sending you to Paris to buy a lawn mower), but there are little nooks and crannies that will delight the most creative shoppers among you. I buy brass lock pieces and string them on necklaces for gifts.

The store has been redone lately and I like it; it's sort of like a nice Kmart in terms of fashion and style statements. I think it should get rid of fashion totally and just do home style, but what do I know? Good crafts and art department; excellent office papers, folders, and paper goods; adorable new Café Brico in the basement. Note that management is bickering over the future of the store and is nervous about the changes going on at La Samaritaine; so in no time at all, everything I have written here could be obsolete and this could be a fashion and big-brand store. I hope not!

Open Monday through Saturday 9:30am to 6:30pm, until 10pm on Wednesday.

Franck et Fils
80 rue de Passy, 16e (Métro: La Muette).

Franck et Fils is a specialty store. It's elegant, easy to shop, uncrowded, and relatively undiscovered by tourists. You can find respectable, classical fashions in an atmosphere geared for madame. You'll feel very French if you browse, although you may get bored if you were expecting something hot or hip. I buy my Chanel-style camellias here; just $10 (9.20€) each!

Open Monday through Saturday 10am to 5:30pm.

La Samaritaine
67 rue de Rivoli, 1er (Métro: Châtelet or Pont Neuf).

I love, love, love this store and hope it doesn't change too much. Finding your way around the separate stores and interconnecting basement can be confusing, but La Samaritaine offers a distinctively French atmosphere, and glorious historical architectural and artistic touches. Of the three buildings, the most important shop is Store 2. The sports department is in Store 3. (Store 1 is now Etam.) In recent years, since being acquired by LVMH, La Samaritaine has made a concerted effort to take its image upscale. These changes will not be completed until 2004, but the basic architecture, painted murals, and wrought-iron interiors hopefully will stay. There is also a roof garden with a great view. I often eat at the restaurant Toupary, which has a view of the Seine and is open for dinner even when the store is closed. It needs a new chef here but the view is grand.

Open Monday through Saturday 9:30am to 7pm; until 8:30pm Tuesday and Friday.

Le Bon Marché
5 rue de Babylone, 6e (Métro: Sèvres-Babylone).

Be still my heart. I get hot flashes when I ponder the changes at Bon Marché and the remarkable joie de vivre that now permeates this store. If I were sending retailing students to Paris to learn about remaking a store, I'd send them straight to Bon Marché. Good-bye old lady; hello Barneys! Bon Marché also has a sensational gourmet grocery store (**Le Grand Epicerie**) next door; look for me there.

Open Monday through Saturday 9:30am to 6:30pm.

FABRICS, NOTIONS & CRAFTS

For those who sew, Paris, the home of fancy seams, offers plenty to get creative with. While fabric may not be less expensive than at home, the selection is so incredible that you will be unable to think about price. Besides couture fabrics, you'll find trendy fabrics—imitations of the hottest looks that Americans are still reading about in *Women's Wear Daily.* When Gianni Versace–style prints went crazy a while back, I bought a washable polyester with a silky hand to make a skirt. The total cost of the project was $25 (23€). No one in the U.S. had anything to compete.

Should you be somewhat interested in fabric, but not interested enough to spend much time tracking it down, stop by **Bouchara** (see listing below). It's moving around a little bit in the next few months due to construction in the area, but you'll find it somewhere near the big department stores in the 9e. Try 35 bd. Haussmann. The store has every imaginable fabric and notion. Most items are moderately priced. I like this store a lot.

If you want a taste of the world of couture or just a silly adventure, you may want to spend a few hours in the Marché St-Pierre area in the 18e, a neighborhood that sells fabrics and notions almost exclusively. Couture ends are for sale; shopkeepers are friendly. Some working knowledge of French will be helpful, and lots of cash. Take the Métro to Anvers, or hail a taxi (a pricey ride) and go directly to **Sympa.** It has three locations, at 1 and 7 rue du Steinkerque and 28 rue d'Orcels.

The couture fabric resources listed below are famous for their selections (Chanel, YSL, Dior): For starters, there are **Artisanat,** which also sells wool and yarn goods, and **Sevilla,** which can be fabulous if you hit it right. Remember that couture fabrics are not inexpensive—often they are $100 (92€) a yard for a silk that may not even be very wide. **Bouchara** carries the good stuff, but is more famous for its wide range of copycat fabrics at good prices. Pascale-Agnés has seen couture fabrics at **Le Stand des Tissus;** there were none when we looked last time. However, there were absolutely gorgeous English wools for about $20 (18.4€) a meter.

The French are not that into crafts, so you will have a hard time finding the basics you crave. There are two bead stores near Les Halles, and Printemps has added a fabulous department, **Esprit Libre,** to the basement level of its Maison store. There you'll find more craft items (and beads) than just about anywhere else in Paris. Galeries Lafayette's fourth floor also sells beads and a few kiddie craft kits. But don't be expecting Michael's in France. Also check out **La Drougerie,** 9 rue du Jour, 1er, near Forum Les Halles (Métro: Les Halles), for trimmings and some beads and crafts fixings.

ARTISANAT TEXTILE
21 rue des Jeûneurs, 2e (Métro: Sentier).

BOUCHARA
54 bd. Haussmann, 9e (Métro: Chaussée d'Antin).

LA SOIE DE PARIS
14 rue d'Uzès, 2e (Métro: Rue Montmartre).

LE STAND DES TISSUS
11 rue de Steinkerque, 18e (Métro: Anvers).

RODIN
36 av. des Champs-Elysées, 8e (Métro: F-D-Roosevelt).

SEVILLA
38 rue de l'Annonciation, off rue de Passy, 16e (Métro: La Muette).

TISSROY
97 av. Victor Hugo, 16e (Métro: Victor Hugo).

FLEA MARKETS

Paris is famous for its flea markets, although I think only two of them are worth getting hot and bothered over. Many people think of the markets in St-Ouen as the only game in town; I think Vanves is better.

PUCES DE VANVES
Av. George Lefenestre, Marc Sangnier and Maurice d'Ocagne, 14e (Métro: Porte de Vanves).

When people tell me they are headed to the flea market in Paris, I always ask, "Which one?" They look at me like I am an idiot, then they stammer and finally say it's "the big one" or "the famous one." That means they are headed to St-Ouen, which is a lot of fun.

However, I think the number one flea market in Paris is Puces des Vanves. This market is not like any other; it's more like a bunch of neighbors went in together on a multifamily garage sale—that just happens to stretch for a mile or so. The market is L-shaped: On the main part of the street are the licensed vendors who pay taxes to the city; on the branch part are the illegal tag-sale vendors, who are, of course, the most fun.

The tag-sale goods are of lesser quality, but together they make for wonderful strolling and browsing. If you don't have much time or can't stand the strain of St-Ouen, this is a neighborhood affair that is perfect for a weekend. Saturday is the best day to shop Vanves. Early birds get the worms, of course; I'm there at 9:30am.

The main part of the market is on the avenue Georges-Lafenestre. With the legal and the illegal guys, there are almost 200 vendors here. A crêpe stand is at the bend in the road; the Sunday food market on avenue Marc Sangnier enhances the experience. *Note:* The basic part of the market closes at noon, but some dealers stay on. In the afternoon (around 1–2pm), a new bunch of dealers moves in to sell new (and cheap) ready-to-wear, shoes, socks, towels, and so on. Open Saturday and Sunday 9am to 1pm.

THE MARKETS OF ST-OUEN
St-Ouen (Métro: Porte de Clignancourt; Bus: PC1).

Also known as the Marché aux Puces, or the famous flea market, St-Ouen comprises several markets, each with its own dealers and each with its own special feel. Before I get into the complexities of the market, I might add that unless your French is good, you may not be properly pronouncing this venue and may have difficulty getting directions or help. Ask your concierge for a lesson before you set out, or use my idiot's guide to speaking French: It's pronounced "San-Twan." Honest.

The St-Ouen markets grew from a series of little streets and alleys. Today, more than 75 acres of flea market sprawl through this suburb. The market most frequently bears the name of the street on which it rests—even though you may be hard-pressed to find the original street sign. The markets themselves are usually well marked; they often have doors on two different streets.

Usually the stalls open onto the street or a walkway but have some covered parts; these are not garage-sale–style street vendors. Even the informal markets are sheltered. There is some street action and selling off makeshift tables, but not a lot. There is, however, plenty of street action in terms of stalls, candy stands, and blue-jeans dealers as you walk from the Métro to the flea market. The first market you see is not the flea market you are looking for; ignore these dealers.

Do remember that there are plenty of places to eat on the premises, not as many places to go to the bathroom as you might like, and more pickpockets and rowdy boys than the French government would like to admit. I was once terrorized with lighted cigarettes and burning matches held by teenage boys who wanted to chase me. While they did burn holes in my clothes, I refused to run—or to surrender my packages. I mention it because if it happened to me, it could happen to you. But hopefully it will not.

If you feel you need a system for working this vast space, try mine. Start with the big guns (Biron, Cambo) and the markets in that area, then walk back, so that Malik is one of your

St-Ouen Markets

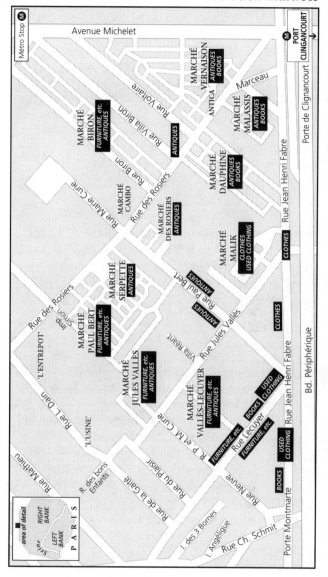

Métro Stop

Avenue Michelet

PORT CLIGNANCOURT

MARCHÉ VERNAISON
ANTIQUES BOOKS

ANTICA

MARCHÉ MALASSIS
ANTIQUES BOOKS

Marceau

Rue Voltaire

MARCHÉ BIRON
FURNITURE, etc. ANTIQUES

Rue Villa Biron

ANTIQUES

MARCHÉ DAUPHINE
ANTIQUES BOOKS

Rue Marie Curie

MARCHÉ CAMBO

Rue Biron

Rue des Rosiers

MARCHÉ DES ROSIERS
ANTIQUES

MARCHÉ MALIK
CLOTHES USED CLOTHING

CLOTHES

Rue Jean Henri Fabre

Porte de Clignancourt

MARCHÉ SERPETTE
ANTIQUES

MARCHÉ PAUL BERT
FURNITURE, etc. ANTIQUES

Rue des Rosiers

Imp. Simon

L'ENTREPOT

Rue Paul Bert

ANTIQUES

Villa Réant

Rue Jules Vallès

CLOTHES

MARCHÉ JULES VALLÈS
FURNITURE, etc. ANTIQUES

MARCHÉ VALLÈS-LECUYER
FURNITURE, etc. ANTIQUES

R. P. et M. Curie

BOOKS

USED CLOTHING

Rue L. Dain

L'USINE

Rue Mathieu

Rue du Plaisir

Rue Lecuyer

FURNITURE etc.

FURNITURE, etc.

USED CLOTHING

Rue Jean Henri Fabre

Bd. Périphérique

R. des bons Enfants

Rue de la Gaîté

Rue Neuve

BOOKS

Porte Montmartre

PARIS
RIGHT BANK
LEFT BANK
Seine
area of detail

I. des 3 Bornes

I. Angélique

Rue Ch. Schmit

last stops. In fact, if you like Marché Malik as little as I do, you'll be happy to run out of there and call it a day.

To do it my way, you'll turn into the market streets on the rue des Rosiers (if your back is to the Métro station you came from, you'll turn left). You'll work this street until the good stuff peters out, and cut to the left by way of the Marché Paul Bert. Then you'll go right on the rue Vallès. At that point, retrace your steps by cutting through Malassis. Note that there are freestanding antiques stores, as well as big (and small) markets. Open Saturday through Monday 8:30am to 7pm.

MARCHÉ ANTICA
99 rue des Rosiers.

Just a little bitty building refinished in the Memphis Milano teal-blue-and-cream look. This market abounds with cute shops selling small collectibles of good quality at pretty good prices. It's a corner of the Marché Vernaison, at rue des Rosiers and rue Voltaire.

MARCHÉ CAMBO
75 rue des Rosiers.

Another serious market, but a little less refined—the dealers are usually busy hobnobbing with each other and may ignore you. You'll see furnishings in various states of refinishing and find dealers in various states of mind—some know what they have and are hard-nosed about it; others want to move the merchandise and will deal with you. They are particularly responsive to genuine dealers who know their stuff and speak some French. The selection is less formal and more eclectic than at Biron (next door), and there are rows of stalls along lanes or aisles.

MARCHÉ DAUPHINE
140 rue des Rosiers.

A newer *village* of some 300 shops opposite the Marché Vernaison, this is one of the first places to hit when you get to the market area. It's enclosed, with a balcony, industrial lighting, and a factory-like high-tech atmosphere under a glass rooftop. There is a shipping agency on hand. Some of the dealers are affordable; I found a button dealer and a specialist in vintage designer clothing that flipped me out for *fripes*.

MARCHÉ DES ROSIERS
3 rue Paul Bert.

A very small market specializing in the period between 1900 and 1930. There are about 13 small stalls in an enclosed horseshoe-shaped building.

MARCHÉ JULES-VALLÈS
7 rue Jules Vallès.

I like this one, although it's small and junky; reproduction brass items for the home mix with real antiques and real repro everything else. Cheap, cheap, cheap.

MARCHÉ LE BIRON
85 rue des Rosiers.

This is the single fanciest market in the place; it's one of the first markets you'll come to on rue des Rosiers. This should be the first stop for dealers who are looking for serious stuff. If you come here first and you are looking for fleas, you may be turned off—it's quite hoity-toity.

MARCHÉ PAUL-BERT
96 rue des Rosiers.

Are we having fun yet? If not, send the husband and the kids for pizza and go for it on your own—this is too good to not enjoy. This market is more outdoorsy than the rest; it surrounds the Marché Serpette in three alleys forming a U. This market is both outside and inside, with lower-end merchandise, including Art Deco, moderne, and country furniture. Most of the items here have not been repaired or refinished. There could be some great buys, but you need to have a good eye and know your stuff. Piles of suitcases, carts, dolls, and buttons in bins. Yummy. If you visit only one market, want to start with the very best, or think the weather may turn on you, start here.

MARCHÉ SERPETTE
110 rue des Rosiers.

This market is in a real building, not a Quonset hut. There is carpet on the floor, and each vendor has a stall number and a metal door. There also are nice, clean bathrooms on the second floor. It's on the edge of the Marché Paul-Bert, but you can tell the difference because this one is totally indoors and is dark and fancy.

MARCHÉ VERNAISON
99 rue des Rosiers.

I like this market a lot, although the new building puts me off a bit. There isn't that much I want to buy; I just like to prowl the various teeny showrooms. There are a few fabric, textile, trim, and needlework mavens who always have things I covet. You may not at first realize that this sprawling market alone constitutes a *village*, with its own streets and byways. This is a good first stop because it has a lot of natural charm and many affordable places; it's also first if you follow my walking path.

PUCES DE MONTREUIL
Avenues André Lemierre and Gallieni, 20e (Métro: Porte de Montreuil).

I have included this market because I want you to know that I know it exists and that I've been there. But it's really only for die-hard flea market shoppers. It's a junk fair of sorts, so there are very few diamonds here—and those are artfully hidden. You could hunt for hours before throwing up your hands in disgust, having found nothing.

This immense market has absorbed three other nearby markets and has a huge path of illegal vendors that stretches from the nearest Métro station all the way across a bridge to the beginning of the market proper. There's a good selection of *fripes,* Victorian bed linens, old hats, new perfumes (look, Mom, who needs détaxe?), work clothes, cheap clothes, records, dishes, junk, junk, and more junk. Did I mention there is a lot of junk? This is a really low-end market without any charm whatsoever. Dealers work this market very thoroughly—it runs a good 10% to 20% cheaper than St-Ouen. But it is 50% harder to find anything good. This is for those with a strong heart and a good eye; princesses and blue-bloods need not apply. Open Saturday and Sunday morning through evening.

FOOD MARKETS

One of the difficulties of shopping in Paris is deciding which markets to visit and which to pass up. Unlike most other cities, which usually have one or two good markets, Paris is crawling with them. There are dozens, and it's impossible to get to them all unless you spend a month doing little else.

Most food markets are closed on Monday mornings; any that open on Sunday are not open on Monday. The rue de Buci gets a slow start on Monday, but the action builds quickly. *Note:* With the exception of the Sunday market at Porte de Vanves and the *brocante* offerings at the place d'Aligre, most flea markets do not have food markets.

Years ago, the major wholesale food markets were in Les Halles; they have since moved to Rungis. This is a wholesale market, and tourists are not particularly welcome. You can go, but you should speak some French and know how to stay out of the way. It's best to sign up for a tour given by a professional, as the market really is "to the trade."

Markets selling organically grown vegetables and fruits, called *marché biologique* or simply *"bio,"* are one of the newer trends. There's one at the intersection of rue de Rennes and boulevard Raspail on the Left Bank on Sunday. My kingdom for a potato latke (called a *galette* here).

When shopping markets, remember:

- Dress simply; the richer you look, the higher the price you'll pay. If you wear an engagement ring or have a wedding band that spells "rich American" in pavé diamonds, leave it in the hotel safe. I like to wear blue jeans and try to fit in with the crowd; I also have a pair of French eyeglasses to complete my costume. Even though my French is atrocious, I speak French or mime my way through it.
- Ask your hotel's concierge about the neighborhood where the market is located. It may not be considered safe for a woman to go there alone or after dark. I don't want to be paranoid, but crime in market areas can be higher than in tourist areas.
- Have a lot of change with you.
- Don't touch the food, especially in the wholesale market. Ask for a taste or let the vendor choose for you. (Try flirting first for a better choice.)
- Food prices are usually fixed; you don't bargain as you might at a flea market. If the vendor likes you, he may throw in something extra.

In Paris, many market areas are so famous that they have no specific street address. Usually it's enough to give the name of a market to a cabbie. Buses usually serve market areas, but the Métro goes everywhere and is usually your best bet. Food markets can be held any or every day of the week; flea markets are usually weekend events. Food markets alternate in various neighborhoods; you can often find a good one any day of the week. All of the food markets listed below are open on Sunday!

Rue Cler
7e (Métro: Latour Maubourg).

My last visit to rue Cler was very upsetting. Although the weather was gorgeous and I was in a happy mood, I was dumbfounded by the number of Americans. Furthermore, the

Americans had the nerve to be speaking English! Still, the rue Cler is a lot more sophisticated than the rue de Buci. A visit here is a special way to spend a Sunday morning. I can't blame all those Americans for visiting; I just want the area to stay French in its soul.

This is in a residential part of the Left Bank, not far from the Paris Hilton and the Eiffel Tower, but not the kind of place you would find on your own without knowing about it.

The rue Cler is only about 2 blocks long, and it overflows with the things that delight foodies. There are two local supermarkets; many small vendors who set up on the street; several branches of famous *chocolatiers,* including **Leonidas** (no. 39); and two famous cheese shops. **Tarte Julie** (no. 28) is a great little place for dessert, tea, coffee, or Sunday brunch; it also has takeout. I'm addicted to the quiche Julie; there are branches of this chain around town.

Almost every store on the 2-block stretch is open on Sunday and closed all day Monday. Stores open between 8:30 and 9am Sunday, then close at 1pm for the day. You can buy many things, not just food items. This is a fabulous "we are French" adventure.

If it's a Sunday and you are looking for a nice stroll, you can leave the rue Cler on the rue St-Dominique, window-shopping as you stroll (sorry, the shops in and around here will be closed), and find yourself at the Eiffel Tower in no time.

RUE DE BUCI
6e (Métro: St-Germain-des-Prés).

If you go to only one street market in Paris, this should be the one. This is everyone's fantasy of Paris. The rue de Buci is behind the church of St-Germain-des-Prés. This colorful, quaint flower and food market is on rue de Buci and rue de Seine. Although it's in a neighborhood with a number of antiques shops, the market does not sell *brocante.*

There are fresh fruits and vegetables piled high on tables, buckets and buckets of brightly colored flowers, rotisserie chickens, even seashells and sponges. There are a few grocery stores and take-out food joints as well. Come hungry; leave very satisfied. If possible, avoid Monday morning, when not much is open. Sunday here is a special treat.

PLACE D'ALIGRE
12e (Métro: Ledru-Rollin).

The place d'Aligre has a covered indoor meat market, an open flower and vegetable market, several tables devoted to *brocante* dealers, and even a few shops. Furthermore, few tourists come here, so you get a true picture of real-life Paris. There is a lot of ethnic diversity in the shoppers and some of the wares.

Betty, a discount source that hasn't impressed me for a few years, is right here, so if you're curious, you can stop by (open Sun). This used to be a great place to buy Léonard at discount; lately it has a lot of career clothes that don't do much for me. There is still some Léonard, but not enough for me to suggest a special trip.

The *brocante* is yard-sale quality; you may be annoyed that you came so far if you expect much more. This market is open Tuesday through Sunday, and closes at about 1pm. While ready-to-wear is sold here, it is exactly what Grandma Jessie would call dreck, if you'll pardon her French. The yard goods are worthy buys from nearby factories.

This area used to be in the boonies. Now, thanks to **Le Viaduc des Arts,** a new shopping attraction only a block and a half away, this is no longer the case. However, the stores here are not open on Sunday, which is a big mistake. The two can be combined Tuesday through Saturday.

PRESIDENT WILSON
Av. du President Wilson, 16e (Métro: Iéna or Trocadéro).

This is my new favorite market; it's not small like some of the others. While it's held in the street, it doesn't so much feel like a street market because it's so dignified. This is a very up-market street market; the Museum of Modern Art is across the way. The market is open Wednesday and Saturday morning. It is long and quite complete, which means there's even cooked food. Once before you die.

Raspail
Bd. Raspail, 6e (Métro: Sèvres-Babylone).

This street venture runs just 1 long block. The regular market days are Tuesday and Friday morning, but the regular market is nothing to write home about. I adore the Sunday morning *bio* market, although it's small and everything is very expensive. That includes farm chickens (22€/$23.75 each!) and made-while-you-wait potato pancakes, for 2€ ($2.15) each.

FOODSTUFFS

If you are looking for an inexpensive gift to bring home, consider taking a small but tasty treat or even putting together your own food basket. Foodstuffs are not necessarily easy to pack or lightweight, but they can be rather cheap and look like a lot once you get home and put them in your own basket or wrap them in a clever fashion.

My single best gift in this category is a jar of Maille's Provençale mustard. You can purchase a selection of four Maille's mustards (total cost $6/5.50€), which makes a great hostess or housewarming gift.

The easiest, and probably the cheapest, place for foodstuff shopping is **Monoprix.** I've become a convert to **Inno,** place Juin 18, 14e, and usually go there immediately after checking into my hotel. It's a direct shot on the Métro and a good job for someone with jet lag. There's a **Monoprix** on the Champs-Elysées, another behind Printemps on boulevard Haussmann, and yet another at St-Augustin; all of these locations are central to most hotels on the Right Bank.

If your palate or your pocketbook is advanced, Paris has no shortage of food palaces. As far as I'm concerned, the grocery stores next to Le Bon Marché (**La Grande Epicerie**) and on boulevard Haussmann (**Lafayette Gourmet**) are more reasonably priced than the more famous houses, and more fun to shop. Don't forget the entire rue du Buci, with two grocery stores and many small shops, including a branch of **O & Co.,** an olive-oil specialty shop.

The circle of stores surrounding the place Madeleine is almost entirely food specialty shops, including **Maille** and **Maison de la Truffe,** as well as some of the food palaces such as **Fauchon** and **Hédiard.** One block over on rue Vignon is the **Maison de Miel,** the honey shop. You will not starve in Paris, or lack for gifts to bring home.

You cannot bring back any fresh foods; processed hard cheeses are legal, all others are not. Dried items (such as mushrooms) are legal; fresh fruits and vegetables are not. Foie gras in a tin is legal; fresh is not.

If you plan on buying foodstuffs, save your plastic bags from your shopping adventures, or bring a boxful of plastic bags with you. Wrap each jar or bottle in plastic and tie the top of the bag with a twist tie before you pack the item. If the cushion provided by your clothes doesn't protect the jar, at least you won't get mustard all over your new suede shoes. Many of the big food stores will ship for you, but beware: Foodstuffs usually are very heavy.

Augé
116 bd. Haussmann, 8e (Métro: Madeleine).

It's not hard to find a great wine shop in Paris; but this one is special, so try to pop in. This immediate neighborhood has enough of interest that it's worth a trip; see the Boulangerie St-Ouen listing below.

Barthélemy
51 rue de Grenelle, 7e (Métro: Sèvres-Babylone).

This is a shop the size of a large closet, but it smells like cheese heaven and is one of the most famous cheesemongers in France. Everything is fresh and ready to go; if you love cheeses, you will be so happy here that you'll never want to leave.

Boulangerie St-Ouen
111 bd. Haussmann, 8e (Métro: Madeleine).

Paris has plenty of good bread shops. You wonder what is wrong with me to send you to one slightly out-of-the-way address. Do you trust me? This shop makes bread in shapes, including the Eiffel Tower! Furthermore, you can get it with an egg wash, which preserves it (the staff will ask you if you want the bread for eating or for display). So we're really talking about a super souvenir for under $10 (9.20€).

The store is about 2 blocks past Madeleine and near the new Monoprix flagship store, so you're going to like it here. It's also near Augé, so look at that listing (above). Finally, a pronunciation lesson—if your French isn't that great, you may not know how to say the name. It's just like the flea market in Clingancourt: "San-Twan." Trust me on this.

Dernier Goutte
6 rue de Bourbon le Chateau, 6e (Métro: St-Germain-des-Prés).

There is only one Juan in Paris, and he is half of the team that owns this small wine shop—an American in Paris by way of Puerto Rico. He is the mentor to just about everyone with good taste on the Left Bank. You can buy by the region, by the price, or by trust.

Fauchon
26 place de la Madeleine, 8e (Métro: Madeleine).

Prices are high here, and many of these items are available elsewhere (have you been to a Monoprix or Inno lately?), but it's a privilege just to stare in the windows or check out the renovation and all the new ideas. The salespeople are extraordinarily nice. There are three parts to the store: fruits and dry goods in a mini–department store; prepared foods next door; and the cafeteria, across the street. You buy a ticket, then pick up your purchases. Don't forget to check out the new tearoom.

FOUQUET
22 rue François-1er, 8e (Métro: F-D-Roosevelt).

Asked to pick the single best gift item in Paris, I just might say it's a Fouquet gift box. As heavy as they are famous, they are nonetheless wonderful. Too heavy to carry home with you? Not to worry: The store will ship. There's no problem finding lovely gifts in the $25 to $50 (23€–46€) range; just bear in mind that the cost of shipping may double the price. Still, the boxes are so extravagant that it does seem worth it. Jars are filled with chocolates, jams, gingered fruits, nuts, and other assorted edibles.

GARGANTUA
284 rue St-Honoré, 1er (Métro: Tuileries).

Another of my regulars between the Hôtel du Louvre and Hôtel Meurice, Gargantua has cooked foods, wines, jars, and cans of fine eats. It's only a block from the Tuileries, so you can picnic in the garden. Because this is a full-line shop, you can get everything at one stop. They'll happily throw in free plastic knives and forks.

HÉDIARD
21 place de la Madeleine, 8e (Métro: Madeleine).

Conveniently located around the bend from Fauchon and Marquise de Sévigné (where I buy my favorite chocolate candies), Hédiard competes handily with Paris's other world-class food stores. It's been in the food biz since the mid-1800s, and there is little you cannot buy in this shop. It also delivers, but room service may not be amused.

LENÔTRE
44 rue d'Auteuil, 16e (Métro: Michel-Ange Auteuil); 49 av. Victor Hugo, 16e (Métro: Victor Hugo); 5 rue du Havre, 8e (Métro: Havre Caumartin).

Lenôtre will always mean chocolate and dessert to me, but the store is a full-fledged deli. Pick up a picnic here. It's open on Sunday (quite unusual) and will gladly guide you through any pig-out. For a price, Lenôtre will deliver to your hotel.

O & Co.
28 rue de Buci (Métro: St-Germain-des-Prés); 81 rue St-Louis en l'Isle, 4e (Métro: St-Michel, then walk across bridges).

This is a small chain that will no doubt become a famous chain; it was begun by the people who created the soap manufacturer L'Occitane, which they sold before going on into the olive business. The store in Cannes is better than either of the Paris stores because it's larger, but either of these stores will do the trick, and both are open on Sunday.

The firm specializes in olive products—everything from designer tapenade (an olive spread) to olive oils from different parts of the Mediterranean basin. There are French, Spanish, Italian, and even Greek oils, all of which you can taste. The small can of oil costs about 15€ ($16.20), but some cost a little more; and every now and then one is special—there was a big sale on Serbian olive oil last time I was in the store, no joke.

If you are looking for a great $5 gift, there's a 4€ bottle of flavored olive oil. Be sure it doesn't leak into your clothes, though.

There are also soaps, beauty treatments, olive-wood products, and much more. One of the best new stores in France.

Tchin-Tchin
9 rue Montorgueil, 1er (Métro: Les Halles).

I've included this special shop because I adore it, but also because I love the entire block, which is in a convenient part of Paris where you will undoubtedly be prowling. This is a wine and champagne shop that specializes in small and unknown labels and specialty champagnes.

FRENCH DESIGNERS

....

AGNÈS B.
3 and 6 rue de Jour, 1er (Métro: Etienne Marcel); 6 rue Vieux-Colombier (Métro: St-Germain-des-Prés). Men's store: 22 rue St-Sulpice (Métro: St-Germain-des-Prés). Sportswear: 1 rue Dieu, 10e (Métro: République).

An international chain of ready-to-wear shops selling casual clothes with enough of a fashion look to make them appropriate for big-city wearing. Jazzier than the Ann Taylor look, with lifestyle stores branching out to feature art galleries, makeup, men's clothing, kiddie clothes, and more. Travel gear too.

ANDRÉ COURRÈGES
46 rue du Faubourg St-Honoré, 8e (Métro: Concorde); 40 rue François-1er, 8e (Métro: F-D-Roosevelt); 49 rue de Rennes, 6e (Métro: St-Germain-des-Prés); 50 av. Victor Hugo, 16e (Métro: Victor Hugo).

ANDRÉ COURRÈGES STOCK
7 rue de Turbigo, 1er, first floor (Métro: Etienne Marcel).

Courrèges invented the miniskirt and gave us white patent leather boots. Despite his past excesses, he has a very traditional basic line, some dynamite skiwear, and very little that is weird or wacky. You still can find some stuff so reminiscent of the 1970s that you don't know if it's new or old merchandise.

The upstairs stock outlet is closed on Monday and opens at 10:15am otherwise.

AZZEDINE ALAÏA
7 rue de Moussy, 4e (Métro: St-Paul).

ALAÏA STOCK
18 rue de la Verrerie, 4e (Métro: Hôtel-de-Ville).

Tunisian-born Alaïa shocked Paris fashion with his skin-tight high-fashion clothes and his first boutique in the then–up-and-coming Marais neighborhood. Now people expect the unusual from him; get a look at the architecture of this place and you know he'll never disappoint.

The clothes are only for the young and those with figures like movie stars, but the man is on the cutting edge of fashion and retail. Like many shops in the Marais, this one opens at 11am.

The outlet shop is in the headquarters of the firm and not inconvenient to tourist haunts. You'll find end-of-season clothing, samples, pieces of this and that, all at 50% to 60% off regular retail. Even with last season's garments, you're looking at prices that begin around $200 (184€).

BARBARA BUI
50 av. Montaigne, 8e (Métro: Alma Marceau).

Barbara Bui is not well known to Americans, but has done so well in Paris lately that she now has four shops. There are also stores in New York's SoHo and in Milan. The stores are sparse in design and chic in simplicity; there are new boutiques in a row on avenue Etienne Marcel, as well as a cafe (no. 23). If you like Prada, test the waters.

CACHAREL
5 place des Victoires, 1er (Métro: Bourse).

CACHAREL STOCK
114 rue d'Alésia, 14e (Métro: Alésia).

Jean Cacharel made his name in America when he introduced charming clothes in precious prints. Thankfully, he has graduated from sweet; an English design team (Clements & Ribiero) took over the ailing line a few years ago, and the results have been spectacular. This is the line to watch.

CÉLINE
38 av. Montaigne, 8e (Métro: F-D-Roosevelt or Alma Marceau); 24 rue François-1er, 8e (Métro: F-D-Roosevelt);

*26 rue Cambon, 1er (Métro: Tuileries); 58 rue de Rennes, 6e
(Métro: St-Germain-des-Prés).*

An old French name that was born right after World War II
and reborn when Michael Kors took over the design of the line.
Céline makes clothes and leather goods; nothing smacks of hot
more than this current line. The stores—there are 83 around
the world—sell out of many of the models.

Céline has pretty much lost the horsey motif and the idea
of going after Hermès; now it's all sleek, sophisticated, and
casual, yet rich, rich, rich—scarves, bags, and ready-to-wear
are the specialties, with an emphasis on creativity in materials, such as string knits. Prices are lower than at Hermès, but
they are not modest; the cowl-neck sleeveless cashmere shell
costs $650 (598€) (after détaxe!); a ribbon-knit cardigan costs
$1,200 (1,104€).

Chanel
*31 rue Cambon, 1er (Métro: Tuileries); 42 av. Montaigne,
8e (Métro: F-D-Roosevelt or Alma Marceau).*

What becomes a legend most? The mother house, as it's known
in French, which holds both couture and a boutique at the famed
rue Cambon address, tucked behind the Ritz.

Two smaller boutiques are open across town on the tony
avenue Montaigne; they are expanding, because rue Cambon
is mobbed with tourists. There are also specialty boutiques,
such as one that sells only fine jewelry and another that sells
only shoes.

There aren't a lot of bargains here, even on sale. You may
be hard-pressed to find sales help that is pleasant. But prices
are less than regular retail in the U.S., and serious shoppers
will undoubtedly qualify for a détaxe refund. Sale prices in the
U.S. may be surprisingly competitive.

A lot of the accessories—which are the only things that mor-
tals can hope to embrace—are put away in black cases, so you
have to ask to be shown the earrings and chains, which is no
fun and puts a lot of pressure on you. However, the sales help

in this department is usually nice, and the selection is fun. I try to treat myself to a pair of earrings whenever I am flush. At $150 (138€) per pair for simple ones, I have a lasting souvenir of Paris.

If you're game, try a used Chanel suit. A classic is a classic is a classic, no? Check with **Réciproque, Dépôts-vent de Passy,** or **Didier Ludot.** Used suits are not cheap (this is not a new trick): you'll pay around $2,500 to $3,000 (2,300€–2,760€). Ludot usually sells the blouse with the suit, but that raises the price of the suit; at Chanel the blouse is another purchase. Expect to pay $3,500 (3,220€) or more for a new suit at Chanel. *Note:* Used Chanel is less expensive in New York and in London.

If by any chance you expect to find faux Chanel in French flea markets, you can forget it right now. France is very strict about copyright laws; Chanel is even stricter. You want a pair of imitation earrings for $20? Go to Manhattan.

CHARVET
8 place Vendôme, 1er (Métro: Opéra or Tuileries).

Although Charvet sells both men's and women's clothing, this is known as one of the grandest resources for men in continental Europe. Elegant men have been having shirts tailored here for centuries. You may buy off-the-rack or bespoke. Off-the-rack comes in only one sleeve length, so big American men may need bespoke. The look is Brooks Brothers meets the Continent: traditional yet sophisticated. American men like to come here for status appeal. The shop's mini–department store is filled with *boiserie* and the look of old money. A man's shirt, like all quality men's shirts these days, costs well over $100 (92€).

CHRISTIAN DIOR
30 av. Montaigne, 8e (Métro: Alma Marceau).

Ohlala, totally renovated and rejuvenated to make room for all that Dior has become since its reinvention with John Galliano, this is a showplace that you just have to visit, if only to *lechez les vitrines* (window shop). This large house fills many floors—you can get ready-to-wear, costume jewelry, cosmetics, scarves, menswear, baby items, and wedding gifts, as well as couture. In fact, several little shops cluster around the main "house," and you wander as if you were in Bergdorf's.

I give Dior high marks for merchandising its famous name to make everyone happy; I give its salespeople high marks for the stereotypical haughty behavior that offends many. Okay, I give the $1,000 (920€) necklace I loved high marks, too—for high prices. And that was costume jewelry; imagine the new line with precious gemstones! There are very small branch stores at 16 rue d'Abbaye, 6e (Métro: St-Germain-des-Prés), and 35 rue Royale (Métro: Madeleine).

CHRISTIAN LACROIX
26 av. Montaigne, 8e (Métro: Alma Marceau); 73 rue du Faubourg St-Honoré, 8e (Métro: Concorde).

You no longer need to be a couture customer to buy a little something from Christian Lacroix. I found a pin for under $100 (92€) that was worth writing home about. The Bazaar line is less expensive than the regular line, although I did pay $450 (414€) for a skirt—we are not talking bargains here. Clothes may be dramatic and expensive, but the accessories are wearable and affordable. Walk in to examine everything; the Montaigne space is a visual feast. For color and sheer delight, this place should be on everyone's must-see list.

DOROTHÉE BIS
46 rue Etienne Marcel, 2e (Métro: Etienne Marcel); 33 rue de Sèvres, 6e (Métro: Sèvres-Babylone).

The woman responsible for getting this business off the ground was none other than the duchess of Windsor. Sweaters and knits always have been the house specialty. Prices are moderate to those of us used to outrageously high designer prices. There are several retail outlets: for men, for women, for sportswear, for discount.

Emanuel Ungaro
*2 av. Montaigne, 8e (Métro: Alma Marceau); 2 rue
Gribeauval, 7e (Métro: Rue du Bac).*

If you were to translate the colors of the rainbow through the
eyes of a resident of Provence, you'd get the palette Ungaro is
famous for. The couture house is a series of three connecting
chambers, so you can see many aspects of the line in one large
space. Don't be afraid to walk in and take a look.

The Ferragamo family now owns Ungaro; their factories
in Italy make the shoes.

Façonnable
9 rue du Faubourg St-Honoré, 8e (Métro: Concorde).

Façonnable has taken over the high street of every French city
and moved into vacant space on the Faubourg St-Honoré. Under
the auspices of Nordstrom, it has also come to the U.S. and
even opened a store on Fifth Avenue in New York.

The clothes are simply preppy menswear. Navy blazers. Navy
and white stripes for summer. Khaki trousers. Gray flannel
trousers. Topsider shoes. You get the picture. The Faubourg
store is sort of like a fancy version of "Gap goes BCBG"; the
stores in Nice are nicer, if you'll excuse the expression. Maybe
preppy just plays better at the beach.

Gerard Darel
22 rue Royale, 8e (Métro: Concorde).

This mid-level designer has numerous freestanding stores all
over France and representation in major department stores; he
also advertises heavily in women's magazines, so you may fall
for the ads first. The clothes are simple and tasteful; the ads
are evocative of Jacqueline Kennedy Onassis and actually have
more flair than the current collection. Still, the clothes are tailored, excellent for the office, and not outrageously expensive.
I paid $125 (115€) for a pair of silk trousers.

GIVENCHY
3 av. George V, 8e (Métro: George V); 66 av. Victor Hugo, 16e (Métro: Victor Hugo).

Hubert de Givenchy retired, and Julian MacDonald, who has yet to do anything shocking, now designs Givenchy's couture. The couture house is upstairs at 29–31 av. Victor Hugo. The men's store takes up three floors and sells everything. Women's accessories and ready-to-wear are in two separate shops.

HERMÈS
24 rue du Faubourg St-Honoré, 8e (Métro: Concorde); Hermès Hilton Hotel, 18 av. de Suffren, 15e (Métro: Bir-Hakeim).

Perhaps the best-known French luxury status symbol comes from Hermès. The Hermès scarf is universally known and coveted; the handbags often have waiting lists. I've personally gone nuts for the enamel bangle bracelets, which are much less expensive in Paris than elsewhere in the world. Since they cost about the same as a scarf, you may want to reprogram your mind for a new collectible. And the tie? It's a power tie with a sense of humor; that's all I can say.

Remember, in order to get the best price at Hermès, you need to qualify for the détaxe refund. Plan to buy at least two of anything, or four ties. (Unless, of course, you buy a saddle.)

If you can't buy anything but want the thrill of your life, wander the store to educate your eye, then show your copy of this book at the scarf counter, where they will give you a free copy of a gorgeous booklet called *Comment Nouer Un Carré Hermès* ("How to Tie an Hermès Scarf") if they have it in stock. It's all pictures, so don't worry if you can't read French. They often run out of this booklet, so don't pout (or write me a nasty letter).

There are thousands and thousands of choices in this store, from the traditional to the downright silly. The ready-to-wear collection is so hot it will leave you panting. You'll also have trouble breathing as you battle through the throngs who gather at the scarf counter and the tie racks. If you are claustrophobic, go to the Paris Hilton and shop in peace.

Final tips: Don't forget to see if your airline sells Hermès scarves and ties in its on-plane shop; they usually cost slightly less than at Hermès (although the selection is often limited). I recently flew both Air France and Delta, and Hermès was less expensive on Air France than on Delta. If you want used Hermès, **Didier Ludot** is the most famous specialist.

Jean-Paul Gaultier
30 rue Faubourg St-Antoine, 12e (Métro: Bastille).

Junior Gaultier
7 rue du Jour, 1er (Métro: Les Halles).

A mini–department store and tribute to a huge talent. Despite his wackiness, Gaultier is getting a reputation for wearable style. Take in the high-tech shock appeal of Gaultier's unique mix of video tech, fashion, and architecture. The younger line (Junior) is less expensive and not appropriate for anyone over 40. Make that 30. Discount shops on rue St-Placide sometimes sell it.

Kenzo
3 place des Victoires, 1er (Métro: Bourse); 16 bd. Raspail, 7e (Métro: Rue du Bac); 23 rue de la Madeleine, 8e (Métro: Concorde); 60–62 rue de Rennes, 6e (Métro: St-Germain-des-Prés).

Yes, Kenzo does have a last name: Takada. Yes, Kenzo is Japanese, but he's a French designer. Yes, Kenzo has retired, but the line lives on. The clothes are showcased in big, high-tech stores designed to knock your socks off. The line isn't inexpensive, but there are great sales. If you're looking to make one moderate designer purchase, you can get a T-shirt for $30 (27.60€) that will make you feel like a million.

LACOSTE
372 rue St-Honoré, 8e (Métro: Concorde).

Lacoste is often called *le crocodile* in France, which is confusing for those of us who consider it an alligator! This is one of those tricky status symbols that you assume will be cheaper here—after all, it is a French brand. But it isn't. You can pay $85 (78€) for a short-sleeve shirt in France; the same shirt costs $65 at Saks Fifth Avenue in the U.S.

LANVIN
15 rue du Faubourg St-Honoré, 8e (Métro: Concorde).

The House of Lanvin is one of the oldest and best-known French couturiers, due mostly to its successful American advertising campaigns for the fragrances My Sin and Arpège ("promise her anything"). In recent years, the line has been in transition as the house tries to find its place in the modern world. I have no idea how it has stayed in business.

The men's store has a fabulous cafe on the basement level that is a must for any weary shopper. You can get a burger for less than $10 (9.20€), and some of the best scrambled eggs I've ever eaten.

LÉONARD
36 av. Pierre 1er de Serbie, 16e (Métro: Iéna).

Léonard is a design house that makes clothes but is perhaps more famous for the prints the clothes are made of. Many pieces are made from knitted silk; the prints are sophisticated, often floral, and incorporated in ties and dresses. A men's tie costs about $100 (92€), but it makes a subtle statement to those who recognize the print. I can get it for you cheaper if you come to Italy with me; I've been to the factory shop.

The last time I was in Paris, Pascale-Agnés and I were walking past Léonard and admitted a terrible secret to each other: We now like Léonard. I don't know if we're getting older or the line is getting better (or both), but I do think this is a very chic, very French way to spend some money making a splashy entrance at just the right place.

A discounter named Betty at the place d'Aligre sells Léonard stock.

LOLITA LEMPICKA

14 rue du Faubourg St-Honoré, 8e (Métro: Concorde); 3 bis, rue des Rosiers, 4e (Métro: St-Paul).

Although she sounds like a Polish union leader straight from the docks, Lolita Lempicka is the darling of the hot set in Paris— and has been for several years.

The Marais location sells the Lolita Bis line; it's a less expensive (and less wacky) line than her signature collection, with jackets in the neighborhood of $350 (322€). Accessories are extremely affordable and may even come in around $25 (23€). Anything from this designer has to be considered collectible by fashion mavens. Fashions are sexy, sometimes suggestive, and always close to the body.

LOUIS VUITTON

101 av. des Champs-Elysées, 8e (Métro: George V); 6 place St-Germain, 6e (Métro: St-Germain-des-Prés); 57 av. Montaigne, 8e (Métro: Alma Marceau or F-D-Roosevelt).

Mamma mia, what has Bernard Arnault brought us? Paris is totally changed, and the Champs-Elysées is energized by this new shop, this new push, and the arrival of Marc Jacobs. Swarms of people stand in line, waiting to get in.

Louis Vuitton opened his first shop in 1854 and didn't become famous for his initials until 1896, when his son came out with a new line of trunks. Things haven't been the same since. Nor will you ever be the same after you've seen what's been going on for the past 5 years or so: The Left Bank store, designed by Anoushka Hemphill, and the newer Champs-Elysées store, built to showcase the ready-to-wear line designed by Marc Jacobs, are two of the most impressive new additions to Parisian style.

On the Left Bank, the front door alone is worthy of a half-hour of silent, stunned appreciation. The store is on different levels, and you weave up, down, and around. Toward the front of the store is the house collection of restored but older LV luggage and steamer trunks; these are for sale. You may also bring in your old ones for repair or renovation.

MARITHÉ ET FRANÇOIS GIRBAUD
38 rue Etienne Marcel, 1er (Métro: Etienne Marcel).

Masters of the unisex look, the Girbauds are still making the only clothes that make sense on either sex with equal style. They have many lines, and you may never see everything these designers can do. The main store is a must because of the architecture. Le Mouton à 5 Pattes sometimes carries discounted jeans.

NINA RICCI
39 av. Montaigne, 8e (Métro: Alma Marceau).

I think we can cut to the chase here. Nina Ricci is a couture house. Downstairs is where the samples are sold. There is a large, incredible selection of evening gowns, and a few day dresses and suits. If you don't need a ball gown but are looking for a gift to give someone you want to impress, consider the gift department, which is small enough to consider with one big glance. This store is closed Saturday and from 1 to 2pm daily.

RODIER ETOILE
15 av. Victor Hugo, 16e (Métro: Victor Hugo).

RODIER RIVE-GAUCHE
35 rue de Sèvres, 6e (Métro: Sèvres-Babylone).

RODIER FORUM DES HALLES
1er (Métro: Châtelet).

RODIER PASSY
75 rue de Passy, 16e (Métro: La Muette).

RODIER KASHA
27 rue Tronchet, 8e (Métro: Madeleine).

Rodier's knits are ideal for travel. I wear a lot of their clothes on the road. Regular retail prices in Paris are no bargain, but can be good during sales. However, prices at French sales may not be as good as U.S. sale prices! Know your stuff before you pounce. Also note that some pieces in France are not available in the U.S.

There are 16 boutiques in Paris; the big news is the new home for the Kasha line, near place de la Madeleine.

SONIA RYKIEL
70 rue du Faubourg St-Honoré, 8e (Métro: Concorde);
175 bd. St-Germain, 6e (Métro: St-Germain-des-Prés).

SONIA RYKIEL ENFANT
4 rue de Grenelle, 6e (Métro: Sèvres-Babylone).

SR STOCK
64 rue d'Alésia, 14e (Métro: Alésia).

Sonia Rykiel began rewriting fashion history when she was pregnant and couldn't find a thing to wear; her children's line was born when she became a grandmother. I say, forget the expensive kiddie things and save up for the expensive grown-up clothes. Also visit the outlet if you are a true fan, because you might get lucky. I've been there when it was great and when it was lonely; you simply never know. Sonia's things are unique—they are classics and stay in style forever; in fact, the 20- and 30-year-old sweaters have a cult following.

THIERRY MUGLER
49 av. Montaigne, 8e (Métro: Alma Marceau); 10 place des Victoires, 2e (Métro: Bourse); 6 rue Boissy d'Anglas, 83 (Métro: Concorde).

Count on Mugler for a certain look—both pure and outrageous. The shops' selling space could put a museum to shame.

A longish entry leads into a salon of selling space. Along the way you'll pass blue lights, modern art, and a few spare articles of clothing.

VALENTINO
17–19 av. Montaigne, 8e (Métro: Alma Marceau); 27 rue du Faubourg St-Honoré, 8e (Métro: Concorde); Valentino Homme, 376 rue St-Honoré, 1er (Métro: Concorde).

Valentino shows in Paris and takes his fashion very seriously here. He renovated the shop in order to hold his place of esteem among his couture neighbors. The shop also sells the Oliver line, but you won't find V or Night in this palace of beige marble and glass.

VENTILO
267 rue St-Honoré, 1er (Métro: Concorde): 2 rue Louvre, 1er (Métro: Etienne Marcel).

Paris has half a dozen Ventilo shops; I have been to most of them, and each one feels different. It's a good lesson in the use of space and how it reflects the customer's reaction to the clothes. My favorite, on the rue Louvre, has a tearoom and carries the home furnishings line.

Ventilo was once a famed name in couture; now it's a bridge line with slightly exotic touches and some ethnic inspirations that make it fashionable yet memorable. I'm a huge fan, although the past few years have not driven me as wild as the collections before that. I also like the fragrances.

YVES SAINT LAURENT
Rive Gauche, 19–21 av. Victor Hugo, 16e (Métro: Victor Hugo); 38 rue du Faubourg St-Honoré, 8e (Métro: Concorde).

YSL COUTURE
43 av. Marceau, 16e (Métro: Alma Marceau).

YSL COUTURE ACCESSORIES
32 rue du Faubourg St-Honoré, 8e (Métro: Concorde).

L'INSTITUT BEAUTÉ YVES SAINT LAURENT
32 rue du Faubourg St-Honoré, 8e (Métro: Concorde).

What becomes a legend most? These days that's hard to answer. With Gucci's buying YSL and Tom Ford's taking over the YSL Rive Gauche line, there was so much tension that YSL quit his couture line.

Don't forget that Saint Laurent is also in the perfume and beauty biz—we are talking empire here. A beauty institute that does skin care (but not hair) is next to the accessories shop on the Faubourg. More affordable than clothes. If you must be up on the newest, shop nowhere else but the Victor Hugo store, which is the model for the upcoming renovation of all the branch stores. I didn't find it so shockingly different, but *tout* Paris is impressed.

HANDBAGS (EVERYDAY)

No one does handbags like the French; *non*, not even the Italians. If you want to splurge on only one thing, a handbag is a great notion—especially a brand that isn't well known in the U.S., so you can get a style that few others will have. Also note that the banana war could very well raise the price of French handbags made with plastic in the U.S., making them an excellent purchase in France.

Most department stores have enormous handbag departments, usually on the ground floor. It makes more sense to buy a handbag at a department store if you can use the tourist discount card.

DIDIER LAMARTHE
19 rue Danou, 2e (Métro: Opéra).

Lamarthe is worth knowing about, saving for, splurging on, or even loading up on. If you are looking for something drop-dead

French, this brand is elegant, sportif, and totally different from the other big names. In the U.S., it's available only through Nordstrom.

HERVÉ CHAPELIER
1 bis, rue du Vieux-Colombier, 6e (Métro: St-Germain-des-Prés); 390 rue St-Honoré, 8e (Métro: Concorde).

Smack in the middle of the great shopping on the Left Bank is the mother shop of designer Hervé Chapelier. He made his mark on the Paris handbag scene over 10 years ago, but is just beginning to be known in America. I suggest you make a bee-line as soon as possible, and maybe go back every day. This could be the stock-up gift and indulgence resource of your trip. While I have not been especially moved by Kate Spade's work, I have gone nuts for Hervé—who is not even as clever as Kate Spade and yet has a very similar look, always in nylon.

I'm not the only one who is impressed; these bags are a cult status symbol and the must-have accessory in Paris, especially in summer as a weekend tote, beach bag, or carry-on. Both Printemps and Galeries Lafayette sell a few bags, but ignore that and go only to one of the stores, where you can see the wide range of yummy colors—that's what does you in. The lines are sleek, sturdy, and sometimes boxy, just like, uh, Kate Spade.

For some reason, there are also cashmere sweaters, but forget them. You came for the tote bags. Almost all styles cost less than $100 (92€); the average price is $40 to $50 (37€–46€), and you will be chic for years to come. There are two other shops, but they aren't in high-traffic shopping districts for tourists.

LANCEL
8 place de la Opéra, 9e (Métro: Opéra), and many other locations.

Another French brand that many Americans don't know too well. These make excellent travel bags because they're not real leather, and some models have an outside flap pocket that is perfect for the plane ticket and passport. I have five versions of the same bag in assorted colors and sizes. Again, buy at a department store so you can use the discount card.

LONGCHAMP
404 rue St-Honoré, 1er (Métro: Concorde).

Totally renovated and rejuvenated new flagship with tons of fabulous bags, totes, and luggage. Many leather items are coated to withstand the weather. Available at department stores too.

MANDARIANA DUCK
219 rue St-Honoré, 1er (Métro: Tuileries).

An Italian brand of nylon and industrial luggage, handbags, and even fashion—very hip, sleek, and avant-garde.

JEWELRY (COSTUME)

The essence of French fashion, aside from couture, is simplicity—consider the basic black skirt and white silk blouse, a staple of every stylish Frenchwoman's wardrobe. Of course, the way to spruce up these basics has always been accessories. Hence the importance of the Hermès silk scarf.

Should you care to go for something glitzier, these sources offer some of Paris's boldest statements. Their specialty is either copies of more serious jewelry or originals that will have value in the marketplace for years to come. The originals reach beyond the basic definition of "costume jewelry." Coco Chanel invented costume jewelry; designer costume jewelry, whether new or vintage, remains a solid investment—although it can be pricey.

The major designer brands now make their own costume jewelry, so they are not listed below. The sources here give you the range from fabulous fakes to boldest bangles.

ANEMONE
7 rue de Castiglione, 1er (Métro: Tuileries or Concorde).

Year after year, a reliable resource for costume jewelry and earrings. Anemone is across from the Meurice and near Catherine. Earrings begin around $50 (46€)—this is Paris, you know. Prices are not give-away, but sometimes you can find some good pieces; I bought a YSL gold-tone collar here that I still live in, and it was worth every bit of its $350 (322€) price tag. Fun to look in the window even if you don't buy.

BURMA
249 rue St-Honoré, 8e (Métro: Concorde).

If the real thing is beyond you, try Burma. Serious copies, created to fool Mother Nature.

GAS
44 rue Etienne Marcel, 2e (Métro: Etienne Marcel).

This is a small store with very inventive pieces, often made from odds and ends. More fun than couture in terms of a look; possibly a good investment as a collectible. They use faux gemstones in copper settings; I collect the bees. The earrings don't pinch!

LESAGE
21 place Vendôme, 1er (Métro: Tuileries).

In the Schiaparelli space on the place Vendôme, Lesage announces itself with discreet lettering in the window (just below the pink SCHIAPARELLI sign). You could easily walk by without ever noticing, but designer mavens have known for years that Lesage is the house that does all the beading for the couture houses.

MICHAELA FREY
9 rue Castiglione, 1er (Métro: Concorde); 167 rue St-Honoré, 1er (Métro: Tuileries).

This Viennese design firm has stores in most European capital cities but none in the U.S., so you may not know the brand. If you are familiar with the enamel bracelets from Hermès, you are unwittingly familiar with Frey's work. Frey did this enamel work long before Hermès put its distinctive twist on it.

NEREIDES
23 rue du Four, 6e (Métro: St-Germain-des-Prés).

This shop sells a very south-of-France look, casual and resorty, but with bigger pieces than you might wear to work. You'll find various sizes and shapes, a touch of brushed gold, and Etruscan influence.

SWAROVSKI
7 rue Royale, 8e (Métro: Concorde).

Over the years, this crystal maker has provided much of the glitter to Lesage and Chanel. Now, its own brand has an international reputation and a line of jewelry and handbags. Everything is made from the top-of-the-line crystals.

JEWELRY (IMPORTANT)

Traditionally, all of the important Parisian jewelers are on the place Vendôme, with a few moving away from the obelisk and stretching toward Opéra.

Two couture houses, both of which made costume jewelry for decades, have launched stores selling the real thing, and I don't mean Coca-Cola. **Chanel** started a few years ago, and **Christian Dior** has come on board.

If you want name-brand real jewelry and don't care if it's used, go to the string of specialty boutiques just outside the place Vendôme on the rue St-Honoré. Family heirlooms cram their windows; prices in cash may be juggled slightly.

LINGERIE & BATHING SUITS

....

Most French specialty stores that sell underwear also sell bathing suits. The department stores have enormous "festivals," selling masses of bathing suits in a designated area (the same space that will sell coats in late summer). For the largest selection of bathing suits in Paris, try Galeries Lafayette from May through August. You can even buy some suits a la carte—top and bottom in different sizes, as needed.

There are also a number of multiples (chain stores) that sell underwear and bathing suits (in season). These shops sell either one brand (such as Etam) or many, and aim to serve the mid-market, and they are much more expensive than similar stores in the U.S.

Not only was the brassiere invented in Paris, but France has always made the latest in industrial equipment for manufacturing modern underwear. Prices are high, but the technology is unsurpassed. I buy most of my lingerie at **Monoprix.**

ERES
2 rue Tronchet, 8e (Métro: Madeleine).

Eres is perhaps the most famous name in bathing suits in France—we're talking high end, almost couture bathing suits. It has branched into lingerie too. Some department stores also sell the line; it is extremely chic and expensive. And wonderful. There are boutiques around town, but this is the main shop. It's next door to Fauchon on the place de la Madeleine.

IZKA
140 rue du Faubourg St-Honoré, 8e (Métro: Champs Elysées Clemenceau).

This tiny store is known for its seamless lingerie and use of modern French technology from Lyon.

MALLS & SHOPPING CENTERS

Slowly, Paris has been going mall mad. The shopping center of your teen years does not exist in great abundance in Europe, but Paris is trying out every kind of mall you can imagine. The larger mall structures are often called "commercial centers." The success of **Les Trois Quartiers** has brought about the *intime* mall—sort of American in feel, but smaller and therefore less intimidating. There are new entries constantly, all with very good addresses. Don't forget that the French had the original version of the mall, 150 years ago, with their *passages* and *galeries* (see "*Passages*," below). For discount outlet malls, see chapter 10, "Paris Bargains."

FORUM DES HALLES
11 bis, rue de l'Arc-en-Ciel, 1er (Métro: Les Halles or Châtelet).

The Forum des Halles, built to rejuvenate a slum, serves as an exciting monument to youth, style, and shopping. It's a huge square with a courtyard. The atmosphere is rather American and sterile, and it's easy to get lost once you are inside. You'll find it conveniently located directly above a Métro stop, Les Halles, and down the street from the YSL discount store, Mendès. It's also a stone's throw from the Beaubourg, which you may want to visit. There are fast-food joints in the Métro part of the complex, and real restaurants among the shops in the regular complex.

A series of escalators connects the floors; there are master maps throughout the mall to help you find your way. Although a number of designers and bridge lines have stores here, the stores are often not as charming as the boutiques on the street can be. The Forum was built in stages; be sure to see the newest part of the mall, which stretches underground. Most of the stores in the Forum des Halles open Tuesday through

Saturday between 10 and 10:30am and close between 7 and 7:30pm. All stores are closed all day Sunday and until noon Monday. All stores take credit cards.

LE CARROUSEL DU LOUVRE
99 rue de Rivoli, 1er (Métro: Palais-Royal).

This is an American-style shopping mall. While it isn't very big, its construction revolutionized Paris retail and brought on a new surge of mall building within landmark sites. The mall is attached to the Louvre and has many entrances and exits.

For the easiest access, enter from the rue de Rivoli, where a small banner announces the space. This entrance is not particularly prominent, so you may have trouble finding it. The mall is on two subterranean levels; enter and take the escalator down one flight to the food court. Go down another level and you are in a mall like any other in your neighborhood, except that this one has **Lalique, Sephora,** and **Virgin Megastore.** There are just over a dozen stores, as well as a branch of the French Government Tourist Office; there are some excellent museum shops too.

LES TROIS QUARTIERS
23 bd. de la Madeleine, 1er (Métro: Madeleine).

This is what I'd call a mini-mall. It's nothing to write home about, despite the fact that locals love it and find it very American. The stores are small (with the exception of **Silver Moon**) and well integrated. I like the mix of designers and upscale suppliers. This is a good way to see a lot of shops fast. Designer shops range from **Kenzo** to **Chacok;** there's a newish department store just for men (**Le Madelois**) and a few multiples (chain stores).

The success of this mall has made the surrounding area one of the hottest in Paris retail; there's a new mall-like structure next door, **Le Cedre Rouge,** and a rehabbed passage across the place de la Madeleine.

Plaza Passy
53 rue de Passy, 16e (Métro: La Muette).

It looks like a redone Deco-style apartment complex in South Beach, without the blue stucco, but this new mall helps you get a lot done in one neighborhood. It has an upper-class feel to it, especially when you glance around at your fellow shoppers. It's not a big mall or a very special one. It's just that it's easy and still French. Many of the retail tenants are French chains or American ones, including the Gap.

I am not embarrassed to tell you that I think it's super here; it's not terribly French, but it is very much a part of the new French retail scene—global, man, global! I also like the grocery store, **Champion,** on the lower level. Boutiques are open daily 10am to 7:30pm; the grocery store is open Monday through Saturday 8:30am to 8:30pm.

A Suburban Mall

Quatre Temps
La Defense (Métro: La Defense; RER A: Grande Arche).

I realize that you didn't come to Paris to go to a mall in the 'burbs. If you are staying at a hotel in La Defense, staying in town a long time, or even moving to Paris, this is a great source. I go out here once a month for a big haul at the *hypermarché* **Auchan,** and then go to the other stores. Auchan delivers to some parts of Paris (but not all) for a charge of about \$15 (14€).

MUSEUM SHOPS

Almost all Paris museums have gift shops, and there are about 50 museums in Paris. That's a lot of museum gift shops. Some even have their own chains, with branches in various museums; the Louvre has special shopping bags for all its gift shops. Some shops just sell slides, prints, and a few high-minded books or postcards. But several are really with it.

Centre Georges Pompidou
Centre Georges Pompidou, 4e (Métro: Châtelet).

The main gift shop at the entry level is mostly a bookstore, so don't get confused. There are more gifts on the mezzanine, and sales areas after certain exhibits. The department store Au Printemps runs the shops.

Musée Carnavalet
29 rue de Sévigné, 3e (Métro: St-Paul).

This museum in the heart of the Marais documents the history of the city of Paris; the gift shop sells reproductions of antique items, many owned by famous people. I have the Georges Sand stemware. Closed Monday.

Musée des Arts Décoratifs
107 rue de Rivoli, 1er (Métro: Musée-du-Louvre).

Don't miss the salon in the far rear of this shop, which has books. The store sells a mix of books and gift items, all with a wonderful eye toward design. Prices aren't low, but you'll find unique gift items—even a copy of the very first scarf Hermès ever created. Some of the merchandise is tied to traveling exhibits and changes regularly. There are books on design in several languages.

Closed Monday and Tuesday; open Sunday noon to 5pm.

Musée d'Orsay
Gare d'Orsay, 7e (Métro: Orsay).

The gift shop isn't as wonderful as the architecture, but it's damn good; you can buy prints and some reproductions, as well as a scarf or two. Good selection of postcards and gifts (including wonderful art books) for kids. There are also small sales areas near specialty exhibits.

Musée du Louvre
Palais du Louvre, 1er (Métro: Musée-du-Louvre).

There's a gift shop under that glass pyramid, and it is a beauty, with two levels of shopping space. The store sells books, postcards, and repro gifts. *Beaucoup* fun! You do not have to pay admission to the museum to gain entrance. After walking into the pyramid, take the escalator down, and you will be in a lobby reminiscent of a train station. Glance around, read a few signs, and you'll soon see the gift shop—it's straight ahead.

MUSIC

I've gone nuts for Johnny Hallyday and have bought a number of his tapes and CDs. There are zillions of them (the man's career spans decades), but they can be pricey. In fact, CDs in France (and all of Europe) are much more expensive than in

Jean-Louis Ginibre's Jazz Picks

Paris is my friend Jean-Louis's hometown. He's American now, but he still goes to Paris to buy jazz. His fave, for LPs and secondhand jazz and blues recordings, is **Paris Jazz Corner.** He also suggests that fans check out the stalls at the **Marché Malik** in the flea markets at St-Ouen (p. 140), which are open only Saturday, Sunday, and Monday. Call ahead before visiting these shops to make sure they're open.

CROCODISC
64 rue de la Montagne Ste-Geneviève, 5e (Métro: Luxembourg); ☏ *01/46-34-78-38.*

LIBRARIE GILDA
36 rue des Bourdonnais, 1er (Métro: Châtelet); ☏ *01/42-33-60-00.*

PARIS JAZZ CORNER
5 rue de Navarre, 5e (Métro: Monge); ☏ *01/43-36-78-92.*

the U.S., so buy only must-have items you can't get elsewhere. I list some small specialty stores below; the larger electronic palaces, which sell cassettes, CDs, DVDs, books, tickets, telephones, videos, and sound equipment, have branch stores in all major shopping areas. They include **FNAC** and **Virgin Megastore.**

PASSAGES

A *passage* (it rhymes with "massage") is a shopping area, like an arcade in London. Today, *passages* are the French equivalent of American mini-malls; they cut into building lobbies like throughways. In the early 1800s, new buildings were large, often taking up a block. To get from one side of a building to another, pedestrians used a *passage.* It's inside the building, so it's totally covered. Doorways lead through the original structure.

There are *passages* all over Paris. One of the most famous is the **Galerie Vivienne.** One doorway is on the rue Vivienne, the other on the rue des Petits-Champs. The *passage* is not surrounded by a greater building but is directly across from the National Library and near the Palais-Royal; it holds a number of cute shops.

Also check out **Cour du Commerce St-Anne** (59–61 rue St-André-des-Arts, 6e; Métro: St-Germain-des-Prés or Odéon), on the Left Bank. The famous restaurant Le Procope is in this tiny alley. Also here are a tea salon that I suggest for shoppers, **Cour de Rohan,** and a few shops. It's not that the shopping is so great; it's that the charm is heart-stopping.

Others to see, if only for the architecture and not the stores: **Galerie Véro-Dodat,** 19 rue Jean-Jacques Rousseau, 1er (Métro: Palais-Royal); **Passage des Panorama,** rue St-Marc, 2e (Métro: Grands Boulevards); and **Passage Verdeau,** 31 bis, rue du Faubourg Montmartre, 9e (Métro: Grands Boulevards).

Le Passage du Havre, 109 rue St-Lazare, 8e (Métro: St-Lazare), is a charmless modern *passage,* like a U.S. mall, that has a number of useful shops and a nice, big branch of **FNAC.**

PLUS SIZES

Galeries Lafayette has one of the best selections of large sizes in Paris, and there are specialty stores for *les rondes*. Note that **H&M** has a line called BIB (big is beautiful). I shop at C&A, which has inexpensive clothes but tends to go up to size 50, which is a size 20 in the U.S.

CLUB AUTEUIL
4 rue Marignan, 8e (Métro: F-D-Roosevelt).

A one-off boutique with mostly fancy clothes for work or dress-up. This street is between avenue Montaigne and the Champs-Elysées.

HELENA MIRO
195 rue St-Honoré, 8e (Métro: Tuileries).

This Spanish designer specializes in colorful, somewhat funky but not over-the-top clothes. Sizes go up to size 60.

MARINA RINALDI
7 av. Victor Hugo, 16e (Métro: Etoile or Victor Hugo); and many other shops.

The large-size division of the Italian brand Max Mara, this is one of the best made of the plus-size garment brands. Styles tend to be classics, with a selection of dress-up, weekend, and office clothing.

SHOES (FASHION)

Shoe freaks will find the Little Dragons neighborhood on the Left Bank (see chapter 6, "Left Bank Shopping Neighborhoods") a treasure trove of little stores belonging to famous designers and hoping-to-be-famous designers. Weave along these streets and you can't go wrong. Be sure to stop at the many shops on the rue des Sts-Pères, then make your way onto rue du Four, where there are more shops for teens. Don't forget to shop rue de Grenelle as well.

The department stores all have enormous shoe departments; Au Printemps is trying to make a reputation for its selection.

For something truly French, try some of these resources.

FRANÇOIS VILLON
58 rue Bonaparte, 6e (Métro: St-Germain-des-Prés).

This store is not well marked, and it looks rather ordinary. Very little prepares you for the fact that this local shoemaker fits the stars, from Brigitte Bardot to Catherine Deneuve. I got the address from Princess Grace. (Honest.) Aside from the custom work, it carries regular shoes in classic styles.

HAREL
7 rue Tournon, 6e (Métro: Odéon); 8 av. Montaigne, 16e (Métro: Alma Marceau); 64 rue François-1er, 8e (Métro: F-D-Roosevelt).

In style, color, skins, and workmanship, these are among the most exquisite shoes I have ever seen in my life. The prices match. Flats begin around $500 (460€), while heels are more like $700 (644€). Still, press your nose to the glass just to understand it all.

KARENA SCHUESSLER
264 rue St-Honoré, 1er (Métro: Concorde).

This German shoe designer worked her way up through many big brands, including Stephan Kelian and Maud Frizon, to have her own line. Very trendy.

RODOLPHE MENUDIER
14 rue Castiglione, 1er (Métro: Concorde).

I don't care if you buy here; I don't really even care if you enter. The windows are enough to knock you out.

SHOES (SENSIBLE)

....

MEPHISTO
78 rue des Sts-Pères, 6e (Métro: Sèvres-Babylone).

Sensible shoe folks consider this brand of walking shoe for men and women one of the best in the world. You'll pay about half the U.S. price. Also sold in department stores.

MODA
79 rue Victoires, 9e (Métro: Chaussée d'Antin).

This is a discount shoe store selling major brands; there's more about it in chapter 10. I have bought many versions of chic bowling or running shoes here from major names like Prada, MuiMui, and Jil Sander. One block from Galeries Lafayette, it carries shoes for men, women, and even children. Not all are sensible shoes, but the prices are.

REPETTO
22 rue de la Paix, 2e (Métro: Opéra).

This is basically a supply house for ballerinas, but it offers much in terms of fashion, including dresses that would be great for black-tie events. This is the firm that introduced "le ballet" into fashion as a shoe rather than a dance item.

WESTON
1 bd. de la Madeleine, 1er (Métro: Madeleine).

Weston has been known for ages for its men's shoes. Its first women's boutique stocks classic styles; also handbags.

SOUVENIRS

....

Paris abounds with souvenir shops. I often call them TTs (tourist traps). They cluster around the obvious tourist haunts

(Notre-Dame, the Champs-Elysées) and line the rue de Rivoli from the Hotel Meurice to the front gate of the Louvre.

They all sell more or less the same junk at exactly the same non-negotiable prices. The only way you can get a break is to deal on the amount you buy. If you buy a few T-shirts, you may get a discount. The price of T-shirts fluctuates with the dollar: The price varies in euros (note the handwritten signs).

Some of my favorite things to buy at souvenir stands include a toothbrush with your (or a similar) name in French; a breakfast bowl sponged in blue and white, also with your name in French; boxer shorts with Parisian motifs; T-shirts from French universities; key chains with miniature Eiffel Towers, street signs, Napoleon, and more; and scarves with kitschy tourist-haunt designs that are so bad they are fabulous.

None of the department-store souvenir departments is very good. Most of the stores also sell souvenirs from kiosks in front of the department stores on boulevard Haussmann. Galeries Lafayette has moved its souvenir department several times; right now it's on the ground floor in the far rear, behind the makeup department. It is the best of the department-store souvenir spaces, but it doesn't have the right kind of energy.

SPECIALTY LOOKS

ANNE FONTAINE
66 rue des Sts-Pères, 6e (Métro: St-Germain-des-Prés).

This is a chain of stores with about a dozen shops in Paris alone—I simply chose the first address on the business card. You can go online for more info and addresses (www.anne fontaine.com) for this firm that sells only white and black shirts for women. Most cost less than $50 (46€).

COMPAGNIE FRANÇAISE DE L'ORIENT ET DE LA CHINE
163 and 167 bd. St-Germain, 6e (Métro: St-Germain-des-Prés).

A chain with stores all over, even in Brussels. Some branches carry the entire line, and some have just clothes or just home style. Ignore the boutique in Galeries Lafayette; it doesn't do the line or the look justice.

As you can guess from the name, the clothes are inspired by the Orient. I have a jacket made of Scottish tweed in a Chinese style—such a brilliant combination of ideas that I wear it all the time. While the clothes are somewhat ethnic, they are not costumey.

FAVOURBROOK
Le Village Royal, 25 rue Royale, 1er (Métro: Madeleine).

This is an English firm that has moved into the French fabric trend and gone wild for Regency. The wares include men's vests, accessories for men and women, and all sorts of sumptuous creations. With a business suit, one of these ties would make a powerful statement.

L'ESCALIER D'ARGENT
42 Galerie de Montpensier, Jardin du Palais-Royal, 1er (Métro: Palais-Royal).

I found this shop because it's close to the vintage clothing store Didier Ludot. It's also close spiritually—it specializes in 18th-century textiles. It mostly makes ties and vests; ties cost about $60 (55€). The location only reinforces the magic of the goods; this is Paris at its best.

LITTLE BLACK DRESS
125 Galeries de Valois, Jardin du Palais Royal, 1er (Métro: Palais-Royal).

Vintage king Didier Ludot has created a line of new dresses—black only, my dear—inspired by famous vintage choices. Prices average around $200 (184€).

TEENS & TWEENS

Teens will have no trouble spending their allowances, and all future allowances, in Paris. Many will like the tourist traps along the rue de Rivoli, with sweatshirts and boxer shorts; others will go for the *fripes* and vintage clothing. Any young woman will be mad for **Monoprix,** the big chain of dime stores—all have tons of fashion at pretty fair prices, but they are best for accessories, grooming items, and small items.

Most of the Left Bank is awash with stores that cater to students, some more fashionable than others. American-style clothes are in vogue with the French, so be careful—those Levi's could cost twice what you'd pay at home. For hot, body-revealing looks, check out **Kookai,** 1 rue St-Denis, 1er (Métro: Châtelet), and 15 rue St-Placide, 7e (Métro: Sèvres-Babylone); and **Morgan,** 165 rue des Rennes, 6e (Métro: St-Sulpice), on the Left Bank, and 81 rue de Passy, 16e (Métro: La Muette), on the Right Bank. **H&M** (see chapter 1, "Paris *Vite*") is my best suggestion—this is one of my favorite stores in the world.

Major global chains that cater to teens, such as the Swedish giant **H&M,** the Spanish firm **Mango,** and the French chain **Pimkie,** have stores all over town. Many mothers prefer to take their teenagers to the major department stores, because the *grands magasins* carry so many different lines in one place.

AU VRAI CHIC PARISIEN
8–10 rue Montmartre, 1er (Métro: Etienne Marcel); 47 rue du Four, 6e (Métro: St-Germain-des-Prés).

The Left Bank shop is tiny, but exactly what you want in a Left Bank store: cozy, with great stuff at moderate prices. On sale, you'll want to buy armloads of these quasi-teen/quasi-adult fashions.

ETAM, CITE DE LA FEMME
73 rue de Rivoli, 1er (Métro: Pont Neuf).

Etam is a gigantic chain—do not confuse this flagship store with the zillions of little Etams all over Paris, France, and the rest of the EU. There is only one City of Women, and this is it.

Etam bought one of the landmark buildings from Samaritaine and turned it into a five-floor department store with an entire lifestyle worth of design, including a cafe, hair stylist, spa, and beauty department. The Tammy clothing line was created specifically for hip 9- to 15-year-olds. Prices are low to moderate; high-fashion looks are everywhere.

The cafe is quite good and offers a wonderful view of Paris rooftops, as well as a chance to sip "perfumed" (flavored) iced tea—try rose, the hottest (coolest) taste in town.

KILIWATCH
84 rue Tiquetonne, 2e (Métro: Etienne Marcel or Les Halles).

Near the hottest shops on rue Etienne Marcel and not far from the Forum Les Halles mall, this store is very deep and stocked with the most amazing combination of new clothes and vintage. The whole look is pulled together for you under one roof, and you finally understand what being a teen is all about, at least fashion-wise. A marvelous mix that includes jeans, shoes, outerwear—everything you need to be trendy.

LE SHOP
3 rue d'Argout, 2e (Métro: Etienne Marcel).

Don't let the address frighten you—this is easy to find and worth doing, possibly right after you check into your hotel. The store is huge, has loud music blaring at all hours, and hosts quite the teen scene. The clothes are cutting edge; this is where you'll find what's coming up next, as well as the crowd that wears it. Plenty of giveaways about clubs and concerts as well. This is one of the most important stores in French fashion.

MANGO
6 bd. des Capucines, 9e (Métro: Madeleine).

Mango has many shops around town; it is a low-cost brand of fashions mostly for teens and tweens. Very popular with the French.

PRO MOD
67 rue de Sèvres, 6e (Métro: Sèvres-Babylone).

This French chain is somewhere between the Gap and Ann Taylor. It is not that teen-oriented unless your look is BCBG; it's for all female members of the family. In summer, the clothes are perfect for any beach destination. In fall, they are more serious and businesslike, copies of current styles. Everything is priced so you can wear it one season and forget about it the next year. Many branches.

ZARA
2 rue Halevy, 9e (Métro: Opéra); 44 av. des Champs-Elysées, 8e (Métro: F-D-Roosevelt).

Zara makes well-priced, chic clothes for work and weekend without being silly and cheap. They copycat the latest jacket shape or skirt silhouette or whatever fashion gimmick is cutting edge, so you can look of-the-minute without going broke.

VINTAGE

Also see the "Resale & Vintage" listings in chapter 10.

DIDIER LUDOT
Jardins du Palais Royal, 1er (Métro: Palais-Royal);
Au Printemps, 9e (Métro: Havre-Caumartin).

The most famous name in designer vintage in Paris, with a boutique in the Au Printemps department store and a series of spaces in the Jardins du Palais Royal. The house specialties are Chanel and Hermès; now that YSL has retired, there's a growing cache of the master's work. Also shoes, handbags, scarves, costume jewelry, luggage, and more.

E2
15 rue Martel, 10e (Métro: Gare de l'Est).

This showroom specializes in making new clothes from pieces of vintage works, mixing and matching decades and periods of fashion history. It is made to measure; prices begin around $350 (322€).

RAG
85 rue St-Martin, 4e (Métro: Hôtel de Ville).

This looks like a head shop, but I have found some great stuff here at good prices. Furthermore, it's in a string of vintage clothing shops, and just a few meters from the Centre Pompidou. I've found everything here, much of it American, but the Hermès scarves for $80 (73.60€) are French.

Chapter Eight

....

PARIS BEAUTY

Perfume and makeup are possibly the best buys in Paris these days. I'm talking French brands; not all wrinkle creams cost less than in the U.S. (or elsewhere). If you understand the ins and outs of the system and are willing to do some homework, you can score gigantic savings. There will be a quiz next Friday.

Don't underestimate the power of novelty, new launches, or experience as a souvenir: You may want to invest in some Parisian spa time, certain to be somewhat different from treatments back home. There's a huge trend toward hotel spas (even for nonguests), day spas, and in-store spa treatments at department stores. You can shop and drop. You'll also find perfumes and beauty products in France that are not available elsewhere, so it may not matter what they cost—that they exist is reason enough to test them or share them with your friends back home.

VIVE LA DIFFERENCE

....

Makeup in France is different from French makeup in the U.S. This is because makeup (even French brands) sold in the United States must be made according to FDA regulations, regardless of where it's manufactured. When you get to France, the names of your favorite products may be the same or different, and even makeup with the same name may not be identical in shade.

In addition, some products available in France are not sold in the U.S. at all. This may be because they haven't been launched yet or because the FDA has not approved them.

French perfume is also different in France than in the U.S., mainly because it is made with potato alcohol (yes, you can drink it—just like Scarlett O'Hara), while Anglo-Saxon countries use cereal alcohol. Potato alcohol increases the staying power of the fragrance, as well as the actual fragrance—to some small degree. If you've ever shopped for perfume in the Caribbean, you know that certain stores make a big brouhaha over the fact that they import directly from France. Now you know why that's important. The French version is considered the best or most authentic version.

Many American brands you see in France, such as Estée Lauder and Elizabeth Arden, are made in France (or Europe) for the European market. You may save on these items after the détaxe refund, but generally you do not save on American brands in Europe.

French perfumes are always introduced in France before they come out internationally. This lead time may be as much as a year. If you want to keep up with the newest fragrances, go to your favorite duty-free store and ask specifically for the newest. If you are stumped for a gift for the person who has everything, consider one of these new fragrances. The biggest spring launch comes in time for Mother's Day in France, which is usually a different day than in the U.S., but always in spring (May or early June).

The converse of this rule also applies. Some older scents are taken off the market in the U.S. and U.K. because sales aren't strong enough. These fragrances are still for sale in France. I saw an American woman at Catherine doing a gangbusters business in Fidji, which she says is no longer sold in the U.S.

Finally, some scents never come to the U.S. at all. Guerlain is big on this, as are many other design houses when it comes to their ephemeral scents—the ones that come and go for a season or a promotion.

ALL BEAUTY ALL DAY

··

SEPHORA
*70 av. des Champs-Elysées, 8e (Métro: F-D-Roosevelt);
Forum des Halles, 2e (Métro: Châtelet or Les Halles); 50
rue de Passy, 16e (Métro: La Muette); 66 rue de la Chausée
d'Antin, 9e (Métro: Trinité); 38 av. du Général Leclerc, 14e
(Métro: Alésia); Carrousel du Louvre, 1er (Métro: Louvre).*

This is a large chain of cosmetics and beauty-products shops with
stores all over France, in most major Euro capital cities, and now
in the U.S. as well. The flagship Champs-Elysées store, which
is open daily, is the best one to visit. The store in the mall at the
Carrousel du Louvre is open Sunday and closed Monday.

Sephora is not a discounter, but it offers instant détaxe and
a very, very large selection of brands. You may do better price-
wise in a department store (with your discount card), but
you'll have more fun at a branch of Sephora.

Those are the facts; the emotions are harder to explain. This
is simply a shrine to the beauty industry, and a makeup junkie's
best fix. The helpful salespeople wear cute uniforms; if you ask
for extra samples, you may get them (samples are not automatically given; you must ask); and this is a great source for
inexpensive—and inventive—gifts. You can buy prepackaged
gift boxes of the house brand, or build your own box. The animal-shaped bath gels are great for kids. There is also a small
bookshop with books and reference materials related to beauty
and fragrance. I bought my niece a perfume-making kit here.

BATH & SOAP

··

Since medieval times, the French have been known for their interest in the bathing arts (don't snicker—it's dry cleaning that's
expensive in France, not bathwater). It was the French who first
learned how to mass-produce soap (in Marseilles), and they still
make some of the best soap and bath products in the world.

Products from other countries inspired some stores' newer gimmicks, but many are totally original. My favorite is from **Lora Lune,** who offers an aromatherapy bath liquid that comes with a small sac of semiprecious stones (another stone is in the bottle)—you put the stones into the tub and they ionize the water. Everybody must get stoned. This is similar to the theory of the healing power of crystals and is the last word in Paris. It makes a great gift for anyone who has almost everything, for about $65 (60€).

A less expensive gift gimmick to package together a *gant de toilette,* the French version of a washcloth, with a bar of designer soap or a soap that has a cute story, like one of the new salad soaps (lettuce and tomato with basilic, for instance). The total cost is about $10 (9.20€).

Below I have listed some French brands that are known for their bath products and have their own stores; some of them also have U.S. distribution. I also threw is a few secret one-off boutiques.

L'OCCITANE
1 rue du 29 Juillet, 1er (Métro: Tuileries).

This is a huge chain. There is a store in almost every shopping area; this branch (close to the Louvre and around the corner from Lora Lune) and the one at 18 place des Vosges are open Sunday. You'll have many chances to shop this brand in Paris and at French department stores. L'Occitane not only is home of the best 3€ ($3.25) gift in France (scented soap), but makes scented water to pour into your iron—truly the silliest item ever. The candles are heaven scent.

L'Occitane is a soap manufacturer from Provence that has hundreds of shops around France and is growing globally. It is not only a line—it's a mood, a statement, and always a good source for a well-priced gift.

There are numerous scented products for men, women, and children and for body, bath, and home; L'Occitane launched color makeup and is beginning a spa business.

Lora Lune
199 rue St-Honoré, 1er (Métro: Tuileries).

At first glance, you might think this is an ordinary bath and soap shop, maybe a French version of Origins (just a block away). But you'd be wrong. This is a creative creature with much interest in environment and ecological issues: You can bring containers to be refilled, and the makeup is all natural. The street level of the two-floor shop stocks soaps, bath salts, and beauty cures. This is where I buy the aromatherapy liquid with semiprecious stones in it (see above). I also buy small gifts; minicontainers with a single dose of bath salts make wonderful party favors.

Octée
18 rue des Quatre-Vents, 6e (Métro: St-Germain-des-Prés).

Known for its fragrance line, this small shop also sells color-coded perfume and soap. The gimmick is that the colors you prefer (no names) indicate your personality type. If you are a regular, note that the store has moved.

Perlier
8 rue de Sèvres, 7e (Métro: Sèvres-Babylone).

This beauty line, which uses honey in many of its products, is widely sold in the U.S. In fact, sometimes I can buy it at Marshall's and save on French prices. The nicest thing about the line is its large number of small items that make adorable gifts (like the honey bath balls). There are all sorts of beauty products, though—shampoos, bath gels, body lotions, night creams, morning creams—you get the idea. I'm addicted to the vanilla-scented line.

Saponifère
16 rue Vignon, 8e (Métro: Madeleine); 59 rue Bonaparte, 6e (Métro: St-Germain-des-Prés).

This gift shop-towel shop-bath shop sells tons of soaps. It has a chic, Provençal, beachy feel.

INTERNATIONAL BEAUTY BRANDS

ARMANI
Armani stores, including 25 place Vendôme, 1er (Métro: Tuileries), and department stores.

Armani makeup is available in the U.S. in limited distribution.

DR. HAUSCHKA
Sunday only, Marché Biologique, bd. Raspail at rue du Cherche-Midi, 6e (Métro: Sèvres-Babylone).

This German brand of natural products is a cult brand, not well known in France or in the U.S. For some reason it's available—at excellent prices—from a stand in this Sunday market. It's a fun market to begin with, and the chance to load up on the rose oil (Bodyoilie Rozen) can turn my Sunday into paradise.

SANTA MARIA NOVELLA
2 rue Guisarde, 6e (Métro: Mabillon).

This very famous (to the point of cult worship for some) Italian pharmacy has begun to expand into international shopping cities. The Paris shop does not compare to the mother ship in a former convent in Florence, but if you can't get to Italy, stop in here. I buy the weekend soap, divided into three small bars for Friday, Saturday, and Sunday.

SHISEIDO
3 bd. Malesherbes, 8e (Métro: Madeleine).

Don't confuse this listing with the Shiseido-owned perfume shop in the Jardins du Palais Royal—this is a brand-new building in a brand-new location, part of a stretch of new installations that have turned this into one of the city's most interesting retail corners. Shiseido is known for pricey but well-made beauty treatments and many innovations in beauty and anti-aging products.

SHU UEMURA
176 bd. St-Germain, 6e (Métro: St-Germain-des-Prés).

If you consider yourself an aficionado of cosmetics, to be in Paris and not go to Shu Uemura is a sin. Yes, it's even better than Bourjois; more expensive too. He's one of the most famous makeup artists in the world, and a cult hero in his native Japan. You can buy his makeup and skin-care products in every world capital.

In makeup, color is the name of the game here. The hues are spectacular. A single square of color costs about $16 (15€). Splurge.

Samples, mirrors, and brushes fill this high-tech shop, just encouraging you to come in and make up your face again and again.

Most of the department stores also carry the brand. There is a new Shu Uemura Nail Bar in Bon Marché.

BRITISH BEAUTY BRANDS

Every now and then you get a British brand that has turned French, such as the perfume house **Creed,** which made the switcheroo about a hundred years ago (p. 199).

BODY SHOP
Le Carrousel du Louvre, 99 rue de Rivoli, 1er (Métro: Louvre).

This British icon, despite hard financial times, still has several stores in Paris. Look for them in major trading areas, especially where there are teen and tween fashions.

Mary Quant
49 rue Bonaparte, 6e (Métro: St-Germain-des-Prés).

The woman who brought us mod back in the 1960s has several new shops in London and freestanding stores in other shopping capitals, such as New York and Paris. Mostly she sells makeup.

AMERICAN BRANDS

You'll find American beauty brands in the major department stores and at Sephora; they are always more expensive in France than in the U.S.

FRENCH FACE & BODY

Darphin
97 rue du Bac, 7e (Métro: Rue du Bac).

This is a chic, almost secret beauty salon that does facials and treatments (French skin salons never do hair). It sells its own line of natural bath and beauty products, which have made it to America in limited doses—only the rich and with-it know about this line. They're big on body shaping and have many hydroplus (water-added) products to moisturize and balance. Their products are sold in department stores and *parapharmacies* and are known as "the poor man's Sisley."

Decleor
Department stores and parapharmacies.

A line of treatments created around the concept of therapeutic oils. This large line treats everything from dry skin to aging. I'm not sure if I am addicted to the benefits or just the scents, but I keep buying.

LECLERC
Department stores and parapharmacies.

This brand, known for makeup for years, has closed its shop and concentrated on department-store distribution and research and development. The latest launch is a complete line of face and beauty treatments.

PHYTOMER
There is a Phytologie hair treatment center at 33 rue des Arcades (Métro: St-Augustin or Madeleine), but no free-standing shop. *Parapharmacies* carry the firm's beauty products. Prices for the Vie line (with gold foil on the box) sometimes top 200€ ($216), but the products are worth the money.

SEPHORA BLANC
Bercy Village, 12e (Métro: Cour St-Emilion).

This is a division of the famous beauty source Sephora, with a different subtext—the stores and the products are white (*blanc*). The store doesn't sell color makeup or perfumes, just face and body treatments from all over the world.

SISLEY
Department stores and duty-free shops.

Perhaps the most famous name in French skin care, this line added makeup a few years ago and is a favorite for Americans who adore the fact that the line is about half price in France. Sisleya, the most famous of Sisley's ritzy wrinkle creams, retails for $300 in the U.S. It's $130 (119.60€) in France if you take advantage of all possible deductions. Be sure to buy at a department store with a discount card or at Catherine (p. 202).

PARAPHARMACIES

These stores specialize in French pharmaceutical brands of makeup and beauty treatments, usually discounted 20%. These are wonderful places to research new products and things you never see in the U.S. All department stores have a *parapharmacie* section, usually adjacent to the makeup department.

Euro Santé Beauté
37 rue de la Boetie, 8e (Métro: St-Augustin), and other locations.

More than 200 brands are on sale here; I consider it one of the better *parapharmacies* in town. I love this chain; I visit one in every French city that has one. Most of the stores are relatively large by French standards. Ask for a price list, which you can pocket and use to comparison shop. This is a large chain; there is also a branch next door to the Hotel Concorde St-Lazare (Métro: St-Lazare).

Select Beauté Santé
4 rue Duphot, 1er (Métro: Madeleine).

This large shop is easy for most shoppers because of the location—it's not far from the Hôtel de Crillon, The Ritz, and Chanel's main store.

FRENCH MAKEUP SECRETS
....

By Terry
21 Galerie Vérot-Dodat, 1er (Métro: Palais-Royale); 6 rue Jacob, 6e (Métro: St-Germain-des-Prés).

Makeup addicts, search no more: This is the "in" place to visit and test and swoon for.

Terry de Gunzberg gained fame when she created all the colors and makeup for Yves Saint Laurent's beauty line, for which she still consults. After years in the big-time beauty biz, Terry created her own line, which is known for the density of the pigment. Because she uses so much pigment, the color is said to last longer than normal makeup. Her itsy-bitsy salon

About Bourjois

You've heard of Chanel, but Bourjois? Bourjois is the name of the company that owns the Chanel line of makeup and perfume; it makes a lower-priced line of makeup under the Bourjois name—at the same factories where Chanel is manufactured! This doesn't mean that the lines are identical, but if you can't afford Chanel and want to give this line a whirl, you may be pleased with the investment (about 50% to 75% less than Chanel).

Bourjois is hard to find in the U.S., but it's not hard to find in Paris—if you know where to look. You can buy it at any branch of **Monoprix** or **Sephora,** or at any big French department store. What makes the line so special? For starters: many, many, many shades of eyeshadow sold in big containers that can last forever. The nail polishes and lipsticks are also good. The rouge colors are excellent.

is not far from the place des Victoires and the Palais Royale in an old *passage*. She also has a small shop on the Left Bank.

You get "made over" in the salon and then pick the choices for your palette (a small plastic container that is fitted to hold assorted color pots). The palette is free if you fill it, but you can also buy a la carte. Absolutely great item for someone who travels.

The shops also create custom colors; this is pricey but makes a status statement.

STEPHANE MARAIS
217 rue St-Honoré, 1er (Métro: Tuileries).

This makeup artist, the latest Shiseido protégé, works with a line of 188 products. He also does fashion shows in Paris, and private faces for civilians.

PERFUME & SCENT

ANNICK GOUTAL

*14 rue de Castiglione, 1er (Métro: Tuileries or Concorde),
and other shops around town.*

The tiny shop on the rue de Castiglione is a Paris landmark,
but Annick Goutal has a number of outlets in Paris and elsewhere in the world. For example, Bergdorf's in New York and
Harrods in London sell it. Just step into the Belle Epoque–style
salon and sniff the house brands, which include perfumes,
lotions, and house scents. Be sure to look at the firm's logo,
in a mosaic on the sidewalk in front of the store. I'm addicted
to the soap called l'Hadrien, the house soap for hotels in the
Concorde chain. I like it so much I've been known to pay cash
for it.

CREED

38 rue Pierre Serbie 1er, 8e (Métro: Alma Marceau).

This was a British perfume house when it was founded in
1760; during Victorian times the firm moved to France. It is
now a cult brand that makes scent for royalty and rich people. Prince Rainer asked the house to create a little something
for Grace Kelly to wear on their wedding day. Now you can
buy it—or any of the other scents worn by celebs, kings, and
queens. You can commission a custom-made scent or choose
from the ready-made fragrances.

GUERLAIN

*68 av. des Champs-Elysées, 8e (Métro: F-D-Roosevelt); 2
place Vendôme, 1er (Métro: Opéra); 93 rue de Passy, 16e
(Métro: La Muette); 29 rue de Sèvres, 6e (Métro: Sèvres-
Babylone); 35 rue Tronchet, 8e (Métro: Madeleine).*

GUERLAIN INSTITUTS DE BEAUTÉ

68 av. des Champs-Elysées, 8e (Métro: F-D-Roosevelt);
29 rue de Sèvres, 6e (Métro: Sèvres-Babylone); Hôtel de
Crillon, 10 place Concorde, 1er (Métro: Concorde).

Perhaps the most famous name in fragrance in France, Guerlain has two types of boutiques in Paris. Some sell products only, while others have salons on the premises.

Perfumes are sold only through Guerlain stores and are not discounted; the brand is rarely found at duty-free stores. If you see it at a duty-free, chances are there is no discount. Some Guerlain fragrances you'll see in France are not sold in the U.S. There is a brand-new Guerlain spa in the Hôtel de Crillon (p. 57).

PATRICIA DE NICOLAI

80 rue Grenelle, 7e (Métro: Rue du Bac).

A nose is a nose is a nose; this is the granddaughter of the Guerlain family. Fragrance, candles, potpourri, and more. Note the odd hours: It's closed from 2 to 2:30pm daily.

SALON SHISEIDO

142 Galerie de Valois, Jardin du Palais-Royal, 1er (Métro: Palais-Royal).

If you think this store caters to Japanese tourists, you can forget it right now. This happens to be not only one of Paris's best-kept secrets, but one of the must-do addresses any serious shopper (I mean, sociologist) should seek out, merely from an academic standpoint.

First, a quick history lesson: Shiseido is a Japanese makeup firm. A million years ago it hired the most famous makeup artist in Paris, Serge Lutens, and let him explore his creativity. This tiny shop, with the most glorious decor in Paris, sells his private inventions and designs. It is best known for his custom-made perfumes. And note that everything is a perfume—there are no derivatives. A bottle of scent costs about 90€ ($97). Beware the stopper; it's not set in too well, so you must pack your fragrance carefully or hand-carry it onto the plane.

To find the shop, walk behind the Comédie-Française (next to the Palais-Royal Métro) into the garden of the Palais-Royal. Past the creative modern sculpture are the centuries-old gardens. On both sides of the gardens is an arcade crammed with shops. The Shiseido salon is in the far arcade across the garden.

DISCOUNTERS

....

Discount is a dirty word in France, and *duty-free* has become confusing. Even a source that discounts, and has done so for years, suddenly is terrified of mix-ups.

Here's the deal: Discount is one thing, détaxe is another, and duty-free is still another.

The big beauty firms do not approve of **discounting,** but they tolerate it up to 15% or 20%. The percentage varies by brand; at an honest store, the staff will explain that the amount of the discount varies.

Détaxe is the tax refund that any non-EU passport holder qualifies for after spending 183€ ($197.65) at any one store in 1 day; for a full explanation, see "Détaxe Details" (p. 41).

Duty-free sold at the airport is a flat 13% off—you qualify to buy duty-free when you are departing the EU only.

A quick overview:

- At Sephora you get no discount, but you get instant détaxe (if you qualify).
- At a major specialty *maison,* such as Guerlain, Creed, or Caron, you get no discount, but you do get 13% détaxe (if you qualify).
- At a major department store, you get a 10% discount with the store's tourist discount card (you obtain it free at the store's Welcome Desk), and you also get 12% détaxe (when and if you qualify).
- At the airport you pay exactly 13% less than the department-store full price.

- At the few so-called duty-free shops in central Paris, you get the maximum discount that they allow, which ranges from 13% to 20%, plus the détaxe refund of 19.6% (if and when you qualify). If you do not spend enough (183€/ $197.65) to get the détaxe refund, you get the upfront discount—even if you buy only one mascara.

CATHERINE
7 rue de Castiglione, 1er (Métro: Concorde or Tuileries).

If you've never been to Paris before, listen up. Catherine (☎ 01/42-61-02-89; fax 01/42-61-02-35) is my duty-free shop of choice. This is where I do the bulk of my shopping, because of the selection and the way it handles discounting and détaxe.

Catherine is one of the few duty-free shops that not only will give you the discount but also will advance you the détaxe up front. It works this way: Let's say you have spent 183€ (I have no trouble doing it; I think I can count on you). Now you qualify for a 19% + 20% discount. Your credit card will be charged with the discount in place—a highly unusual practice. A second imprint is made with the tax difference written on it. Should you fail to file the proper papers, you will be charged the détaxe amount. If you do file the papers as you leave the EU, Catherine will destroy your second chit when it receives your paperwork.

The store also carries some accessories; I got one of the best handbags of my life there for about $125 (78€)—it's a copy of an Hermès bag, sort of a drawstring pouch with Kelly straps. They have copies of all the latest styles from the big brands.

A few other details about Catherine:

- The store moved several years ago; the new store is across the street from the old one. The old store still exists, so don't get confused.
- I always work with Patricia, a member of the Levy family, which runs the store. She and her sister Fanny and their

mother, Mme. Levy, all speak perfect English. M. Levy makes me speak French so that he can laugh.

- There is a flat 15% to 20% discount if you don't reach the 183€ ($197.65) level on all brands except Chanel and Christian Dior, which allow only a 15% discount. If you show your copy of *Born to Shop*, you will get a 20% discount on those two big names.
- Mail orders are taken by fax or phone, but require a $100 (92€) minimum purchase.

Parfumerie Rayon d'Or
94 rue St-Lazare, 8e (Métro: St-Lazare).

I recently got an angry letter from a reader who had shopped at Catherine and wanted to know why I didn't mention the other discounters in town. Well, the ones I have found aren't as good. However, this store has very low prices and a large selection that may strike your fancy. I must also say that the saleswomen were more than a little rude. Still, the selection and price are excellent. This is a small chain; its Web site is www.aurayondor.fr. Good luck.

HAIRSTYLISTS

I now have a hairstyle I can do myself, but for years I was a slave to someone clever enough to take the curly kink out and give me a coif of merit. I have been to just about all the major salons in Paris and many of the not-so-major ones; usually there is someone who speaks English.

Going to the hairstylist in Paris is fun if you have the time and the patience. While the fanciest salons are expensive, they offer not only a chance to pamper yourself but also a social history lesson and a look at a way of life that you can't be part of on any other level unless you marry into it. I'd give up a few hours in the Louvre in order to visit Carita.

ALEXANDRE DE PARIS
3 av. Matignon, 8e (Métro: Matignon); Les Trois Quartiers, place de la Madeleine, 1er (Métro: Madeleine).

Alexandre is legend, perhaps the most famous of the old-school hairdressers. The name is so well known that there's a separate hair-accessories business, with shops all over the world and products sold in major department stores. Avenue Matignon location: ☎ 1/43-59-40-09; place de la Madeleine location: ☎ 01/49-26-04-59.

CARITA
11 rue du Faubourg St-Honoré, 8e (Métro: Concorde).

Perhaps the most famous name in beauty in all of Paris, Carita offers an entire town house devoted to putting madame's best foot forward. The entrance is on the Faubourg, off the street and inset a little bit.

The great thing about this place, aside from the fact that the reception staff speaks English, is that it's so organized that you can be assured you'll be taken care of. Just walk to the appointment clerk (on street level to your left once you've parted the waves) and make an appointment. You can also call or fax ahead for an appointment. You can, of course, ask for a particular stylist, but if you don't, not to worry. You'll be in good hands regardless.

The stylists wear white uniforms; the patrons wear expensive clothes and carry the best handbags in Paris. You receive a paper number when you check your belongings and pick up your smock; don't lose it. This is your client number, which stays with you until you pay the bill.

Note: Patrons do not take off their clothes here; the smock goes over what you are wearing.

The cost of this pampering is the going rate for ultra-fancy in Paris; you can do better price-wise, but never experience-wise. I consider each trip to Carita a souvenir for myself. I come away with a memory and a good do. A shampoo and blow-dry, which includes service (meaning you do not tip), costs about

$60 (55€), or more if you add hair-care products. In France you pay for each ingredient they put in your hair when they wash it.

Carita added beauty and skin-care products a few years ago and now offers spa services—a natural extension of what they have always done, and done so well. The back desk at street level sells beauty products and accessories. ☎ **01/44-94-11-00;** fax 01/47-42-94-98.

Charlie en Particulier
1 rue Goethe, 16e (Métro: Alma Marceau).

There is only one Charlie in Paris, the hair stylist who rose to fame at Alexandre and is now off on her own. I hear that she charges $400 to $500 (368€–460€) for a haircut. I even hear that she's worth it. I hear that regulars fly in from Geneva just for a trim. I hear so much that I'm saving up. I have also heard that on Wednesday you can get a cut by a junior stylist for 30€ ($32.40); ask! ☎ **01/47-20-94-01.**

Christine Boulben
115 av. Villiers, 17e (Métro: Péreire).

This salon is the opposite of Carita; it is a tiny neighborhood place where I go when I am in town (I have my color done at Michaeljohn in London). Christine gives me the best haircuts of my life. She does not speak English, but she copies a photo with brilliant style. The cost is about $50 (46€) for a wash, cut, and blow-dry. Closed Monday. Call ☎ **01/42-61-49-48.**

Jean-Marc Maniatis
35 rue de Sèvres, 6e (Métro: Sèvres-Babylone); 18 rue Marbeuf, 8e (Métro: F-D-Roosevelt); Galeries Lafayette Haussmann, 9e (Métro: Chaussée d'Antin). Beauty school, Forum des Halles, 2e (Métro: Les Halles).

Still one of the hot shops for models and runway stars, Maniatis has salons in Paris (one is in Galeries Lafayette) and a beauty school. The beauty school has a service that offers free haircuts to clients who are willing to let a student practice on them. Men, women, and teens may participate; the stylists make all the choices—you are the guinea pig.

If you want to go for a regular Maniatis session, note that the Right Bank salon is open on Monday; the Left Bank salon is not. Rue de Sèvres location: ☎ 01/45-44-16-39; rue Marbeuf location: ☎ 01/47-23-30-14; Galeries Lafayette location: ☎ 01/42-82-07-09. Beauty school: ☎ 01/47-20-00-05.

L'Oréal Centre Technique
14 rue Royale, 1er (Métro: Tuileries or Concorde).

Right in the heart of things, L'Oreal has its offices and technical center, which is reserved for testing models and VIPs. If you feel like a hair fling but are watching your budget, you can sometimes volunteer—it costs about $25 (23€) for color or a cut. The center closes from noon to 2pm, but otherwise you can drop in or phone to ask. The location couldn't be better. ☎ 01/40-20-97-30.

HAIR SALON CHAINS

Jacques Dessange (see below) is a chain of salons with shops all over France. The latest trend is toward less expensive and less formal chains. Many of them do not require appointments, and some have salons in the U.S. Check out **Jean Louis David, Camille Albane,** and **Jean-Claude Biguine.** All three have convenient salons; your hotel concierge will tell you which is nearest. They are all relatively inexpensive (by Paris standards), but do not expect the same quality of work or service that you get at a big-name salon. If you are having a number of services performed and price is an issue, go over a price list with someone who speaks English before you begin. Most Paris salons charge a la carte, which means you can be charged for each shampooing. The price includes service; only regulars top off the bill.

Note: Most of the chains have training sessions when you can get a free or a cheap (usually under $10/9.20€) do. The best of the bunch is **Centre Camille Albane,** 114 rue de la Boetie, 8e (Métro: F-D-Roosevelt). For reservations and availability, women aged 20 to 50 can call ☎ **01/43-59-31-32**). Dessange (☎ **01/44-70-08-08**) also does training sessions and imposes similar age restrictions. It charges a mere 10€ ($10.80); you must make a reservation at least 1 week in advance.

JACQUES DESSANGE
37 bd. Franklin D. Roosevelt, 8e (Métro: F-D-Roosevelt).

Still famous after all these years, Dessange has a number of shops in Paris and other locations, including the U.S. The clientele is younger and not as fancy as Carita's, but Dessange has a big-time reputation nonetheless. Hollywood's José Eber started here. Sometimes you can find a promotional package of shampoo, cut, and dry for 35€ ($37.80). They may also give you a free makeup consultation. The beauty and makeup line is available at the salon and at pharmacies. Call ☎ **01/43-59-31-31** for the salon nearest you (there are hundreds in France).

JEAN LOUIS DAVID
38 av. Wagram, 8e (Métro: Etoile).

This hairstylist revolutionized the business about 30 years ago when he opened no-appointment salons with fixed prices that are fair to low. Jean Louis David has salons in many countries around the world, but the bulk of the business is in France, with a lot of salons in Paris. For the location nearest you, call ☎ **01/58-05-06-03.**

LUCIE SAINT CLAIR
4 av. Pierre 1er de Serbie, 16e (Métro: Alma Marceau).

This location is the chain's flagship, also called Top International. There's a special that includes a cut, *balayage* (streaks), and blow-dry for about $100 (92€). The salon also offers some spa services. ☎ **01/47-20-53-54.**

Colorists

I experimented with a few colorists when I first moved here. Like many Parisian women, I ended up going to London for my color. But there is one colorist who is so famous I often think that if I had gone to him, I might have a happier story to tell.

CHRISTOPHE ROBIN
7 rue Mont-Thabor, 1er (Métro: Concorde or Tuileries).

Every fashion magazine I read raves about this guy, whom I can't help but think of as Christopher Robin from Winnie the Pooh. Shame on me! Prices start at about $300 (276€); there is a product line to help keep the color between treatments. ☎ **01/42-60-99-15.**

SPA ME

Water, water everywhere and not a drop to drink: of course not, this is Paris. You drink wine; bathe in water; and celebrate beauty, health, and science in saltwater, mud, algae, scented oils, honey, and wine.

Spas have been around France since the Romans marched through, and *maman* trains every French girl to visit the *esthetique* regularly for *les soins* (the cures). The beauty "cures" are not considered a luxury, but a necessity. What has changed in France, especially in Paris, is the idea of the day spa—borrowed from New York and translated with French style, as well as French prices. Because *les soins* are part of everyday life in Paris, they are very affordable. Even the fanciest spas and salons in Paris are a bargain compared to U.S. prices for same or similar treatments.

While French families may still sign up for a 1-week cure at the famous spas all over the country (mostly in coastal destinations like La Baule, Biarritz, and Monte Carlo), more and more of the working public is taking advantage of the day spa.

SPA THOUGHTS

Whatever spa you choose, remember some basics:

- In France, body treatments are likely to be done on your naked body. No paper panties.
- Although prices include service, you do tip.
- Most spas will try to sell you their products; some will be rather aggressive about it. The products may be less expensive at Monoprix or a *parapharmacie*.
- Sometimes a spa will take a walk-in, but it's usually best to book ahead. If you want a jet-lag treatment on arrival, book before you travel to France.
- Smaller spas may not have English-speaking personnel; ask your hotel concierge for help if you do not speak French.

The customers are almost equally men and women—in France there is nothing sissy about a guy having a spa treatment, especially when he's traveling.

There is a difference between an *Institut de Beauté* and a spa. One is a fancy beauty salon with a few treatments; the other is full-service, with many treatments and often a gym. Parisian hotels have the best selection of day spas in Paris; many of them are open to nonguests.

Hotel Spas

ANNE SEMONIN
Hotel Bristol, 112 rue du Faubourg St-Honoré, 8e (Métro: Champs Elysées Clemenceau).

This luxury hotel has the best of all worlds—the Anne Semonin spa, next door but in the same building; an Anne Semonin treatment room adjoining the pool and health club; and Anne Semonin products in the rooms.

Semonin is an international cult figure; she does not advertise, but is known for her all-natural products and treatments.

The best is a jet-lag cure, which consists of a wrap that eliminates toxins. Prices begin at 50€ ($54).

There is a men's spa in Madelois, a men's department store. Barney's and Bergdorf Goodman carry her products in the U.S. ☎ 01/42-66-63-98.

FOUR SEASONS GEORGE V
31 av. George V, 8e (Métro: Alma Marceau or George V).

If you want swanky, nothing in Paris compares to this spa, with its neoclassical decorations and swimming pool. It looks like something out of a decorating magazine. Treatments are currently for hotel guests only, but the Four Seasons also offers VIP spa rooms (available by the hour) for small groups, such as a bridal party or a family. The hotel also offers a package that includes room, breakfast, and a spa treatment. ☎ 01/49-52-70-00.

GUERLAIN
Hôtel de Crillon, 10 place Concorde, 1er (Métro: Concorde).

Not to be confused with the Guerlain retail spaces all over Paris. This is the last word, a spa unique to this hotel. Nonguests may book the services or even join the gym. ☎ 01/40-07-90-44.

LES SOURCES DE CAUDALIE
Hotel Meurice, 228 rue de Rivoli, 1er (Métro: Tuileries or Concorde).

The Hotel Meurice's Espace Bien-Etre (Space of Well-Being) is a relatively new branch of the Bordeaux wine spa Les Sources de Caudalie. All treatments are made with grape products, proven to have anti-aging affects. You can buy the products at the hotel, any *parapharmacie,* and the nearby Monoprix Opéra.

For your treatment, try a Sauvignon wrap, a California grape massage, or a crushed Cabernet scrub. Red-wine spa products offer relaxing, slimming, or anti-aging properties. There are also facial treatments, and special treatments for jet lag, dry skin, and vitality. I do the 1½-hour facial lifting, since I am at that age. I try to go once a month, and I do use some of the products in between (along with scads of others as well!). Prices begin at 50€ ($54), but most wraps and massages are around 110€ ($118.80). ☎ **01/44-58-10-77.**

LES THERMES DU ROYAL MONCEAU
Hotel Royal Monceau, 37 av. Hoche, 8e (Métro: Etoile).

The spa craze began at this hotel spa, which offers the most luxury for the money in Paris and perhaps the largest spa space, with 1-day cures priced at just over $100 (92€). Most deliciously, you need not be a guest at the Royal Monceau to enjoy the spa; you may also buy multiple treatments for use over a 6-month period at a discounted rate.

Royal Monceau is the only spa in town to offer the added boost of daylight: an outdoor Zen garden surrounds the exercise and spa rooms. The spa is more like a country club than anything else. ☎ **01/42-99-88-00.**

THE SPA AT THE RITZ
The Hotel Ritz, Place Vendôme, 1er (Métro: Opéra).

This spa is actually called a health club; you can join for a day or a year, or just sign up for beauty or spa services. The treatments are from La Prairie of Switzerland. ☎ **01/43-16-30-30.**

SPA GIVENCHY
Hotel Trianon, 1 bd. de la Reine, Versailles.

If you prefer a French brand name, a few couturiers have beauty and spa services. This is perhaps the most famous. Guests are equally divided between those staying at the hotel and those who come specifically from Paris just for the treatments and the luxuries. A day at the spa with two treatments costs a mere 80€ ($86.40). ☎ **01/30-84-38-00.**

Secret Spas

BLEU COMME BLEU

2 rue Castiglione, 1er (Métro: Concorde or Tuileries).

One of the best ideas to hit Paris, Bleu Comme Bleu does hair, makeup, and spa treatments. No wonder it's a secret find—passersby could hardly know what this is by peering in the windows. A facial costs about 60€ ($65), and a body wrap is 110€ ($119). It's next door to the Hotel Meurice, a block from the Catherine perfume shop. It also has a cafe and a boutique. Great fun. ☎ 01/58-62-54-54.

DANIEL JOUVANCE, ESPACE MER

91 av. des Champs-Elysées, 8e (Métro: F-D-Roosevelt or George V).

You don't need to go to a hotel to enjoy a spa day: Daniel Jouvance, who operates a spa in La Baule, the French Atlantic center for thalassotherapy, also has Espace Mer, right on the Champs-Elysées. You can test and choose from his wide range of products on the ground level, or go upstairs for traditional Brittany-style treatments, most of which involve the use of water.

The spa offers cures broken down into types (serenity, kinestherapy, skin and beauty). Thirty-minute treatments cost about 30€ ($32), a 70-minute toning treatment costs about 50€ ($54), and half-day combination packages are available. My idea of heaven? Stroll (and shop, of course) the Champs-Elysées, spa for part of the day, then a movie. ☎ 01/47-23-48-00.

SOTHY'S

128 rue du Faubourg St-Honoré, 8e (Métro: Champs Elysées Clemenceau).

Not far from the Hotel Bristol at the far end of this famous street, the tiny Sothy's shop and spa is an insider's delight. Prices for anti-age treatments begin at 75€ ($81). Although the product line is not well known in the U.S., the full-service spa is perhaps the best destination for a combination of makeup, beauty, and body treatments. ☎ **01/53-93-91-53.**

Hairstylists with Spas

Bleu Comme Bleu (see "Secret Spas," above) and **Carita** (see "Hairstylists," earlier in the chapter) offer both hair and spa services.

JEAN-CLAUDE BIGUINE
10 rue Marbeuf, 8e (Métro: F-D-Roosevelt).

The treatment business has become so hot that beauty brands are not the only ones that want a piece of the action. Enter the big-name French hairdressers. Jean-Claude Biguine has expanded his empire from hair to makeup to spas, and offers a full program to rehabilitate you. The daylong treatment costs 200€ ($216) and includes treatments for body and hair, as well as manicure, pedicure, waxing, haircut, and blow-dry. ☎ **01/53-67-81-90.**

Department Store Spas

The department stores are always at war with each other, seeking out the latest brand names or supporting the classic French brands. Be sure to check for spa news at each Information Desk.

Galeries Lafayette has the **Ingrid Millet Spa;** the old, prestigious line of products and services is well thought of in France. Printemps has **Yves Rocher** (see below). I myself plan to open **Le Doggy Spa** at one of the department stores. I think it's a howl.

Mass Market Spas

L' OCCITANE
This maker of oils, soaps, makeup, and body products from Provence is slowly adding spa services to some of its spaces around the world, offering pampering and quick-fix solutions

in body care. The first one was in London, and now Paris is getting into the rub. Ask at your local boutique for the nearest spa.

YVES ROCHER
92 av. des Champs-Elysées, 8e (Métro: F-D-Roosevelt).

This makeup, beauty, and hair-care brand has zillions of salons across France. Prices are low; rates for spa services are in keeping with the prices of products—awfully fair. This is the line that many teens begin with; as they gain disposable income, they move on to bigger brands. ☎ **01/45-62-78-27.**

NAIL BARS

The nail bar concept is one of the many American retail ideas to take Paris. It's no longer hard to find a storefront that *posez les ongles* (puts on nails) or claims to do American-style manicures. That doesn't mean you will get the kind of manicure you are used to—or even a decent manicure. It took me a year of heartbreak to find a regular nail salon, which I consider the best in Paris (below). If you need a quickie repair, most **department stores** also have a nail bar.

INSTITUT LAUGIER
39 bis, rue Laugier, 17e (Métro: Péreire).

This is near where I live—the middle of nowhere if you are a tourist on a short trip. However, I think it is the best in town. It does gels, silk wraps, tips, and repairs almost as well as in the U.S.—which is otherwise impossible to find in Paris. Fadia speaks English. Appointment needed. ☎ **01/42-27-25-03.**

FINAL BEAUTY TIP

If you are not interested in any of the specialty listings, the smartest way to buy beauty products is at a duty-free shop, or at a department store where you can get a détaxe refund by buying 183€ ($197.65) worth of merchandise on the same day. Since soap is only about 4€ ($4.30) a bar, that's a lot of soap. On the other hand, department stores have a much larger selection of makeup, beauty treatments, soap, and bath and body products than anyone else. Don't forget to get your tourist discount card (p. 201).

Chapter Nine

....

PARIS HOME STYLE

FRENCH STYLE

....

Over the years, American home design has been tremendously influenced by French style. Guess what? Now Americans are influencing French style. Actually, Americans are influencing French everything, even marketing and store layout.

While country French is now considered classic, my grandmother's idea of decorating had to do with draped silk swags, watered silk, and reproduction Louis. Maybe she knew which Louis it was; surely I did not. Today I live with a jumble of her Louis and my Souleiado mixed with flea-market finds from all over France. I'm not alone.

The young French prefer a more streamlined look; those with money want their lines from or in the style of Jacques-Emile Ruhlman. Minimalism is still working here, partly because of the lack of space in apartments and partly because the arrival of **Armani Casa** has reinforced the Euro-Japanese chic simple look and made it more French than looks from history or the countryside. In fact, the new food trends often look best served in the popular Zen tableware.

Those going to Paris in search of home furnishings and accessories not only can choose among many styles, but also can check out French antiques, *brocante*, table linens, or merely candles (wait till you see what the French can do with candles).

For listings of antiques shops, antiques events, *brocante* fairs, and even flea markets, see chapter 7, "Basic Paris Resources from A to Z." It is against the law to transport paint on an air carrier, so I don't list specialty stores that sell French and English house paints. For everything else, flip this way. You need not do over the house or change your personal style, but please, make room for one lasting souvenir.

SMELLING FRENCH STYLE

French home scents are so affordable and come in so many formats that they make perfect souvenirs. New methods of scent distribution are invented all the time: You'll find everything from perfumed powder for the vacuum cleaner to devices that sweeten the air.

Home Scent Resources

CHRISTIAN TORTU
17 rue des Quatre-Vents, 6e (Métro: Odéon).

Tortu is one of the most famous florists in Paris, sort of the Robert Isabell of the City of Light. He has gone the product route—which makes sense in his line of work—with a wide range of candles and home scents. His brand does not have very good distribution. The shop is in the Left Bank, very close to Souleiado.

DIPTYQUE
34 bd. St-Germain, 5e (Métro: Maubert).

If you are not seriously into Diptyque, you can buy the candles at Printemps and save yourself a trip. This shop is not in the heart of the Left Bank shopping. In fact, it's sort of in the middle of nowhere, and you must make a special trip. So taxi right here and giggle right back to your hotel with a suitcase filled with gifts and goodies. The tiny store sells candles, soaps, and scents. Candles are a deal at $25 (23€) each, almost half the U.S. price. Closed Monday.

ESTÈBAN
49 rue de Rennes, 6e (Métro: St-Germain-des-Prés); 20 rue Francs-Bourgeois, 3e (Métro: St-Paul).

One of my favorite scent suppliers is Estèban, which is distributed all over Europe. The store carries diffusers, burners, incense, sprays, scented rocks, and so on. The Marais store is open Sunday.

LAMPES BERGER
At department stores.

Lampes Berger makes fashionable oil-burning lanterns, not unlike genie lamps. They come in dozens of styles and cost $40 (36.80€) to approximately $100 (92€). You buy the scented liquid oil separately for approximately $15 (13.80€) per bottle. There are more than a dozen scents. The process of using this product is more complicated than lighting an aromatherapy candle—but then, this one works.

If you smoke, look into this product immediately. Your colleagues at work will be much more fond of you after you set one up in your office.

Carrying flammable goods on airplanes is technically illegal (bringing on the lamp itself is not), so you may need to use the toll-free number in the U.S. to get the liquid.

MARIAGE FRÈRES
30 rue du Bourg-Tibourg, 4e (Métro: St-Paul); 13 rue des Grands-Augustins, 6e (Métro: Grands Augustins).

Mariage Frères is one of the most sophisticated and expensive teahouses in Paris; it has its own line of tea-scented candles, which are in demand by those willing to spend about $50 (46€) for a candle. Also sold in department stores. Very chic gift.

SMART SHOPPERS' HOME STYLE

Let's face it, very few people with any smarts at all go to Paris to buy fine antiques. Okay, maybe you're Lord Rothschild and you go to Paris for a few finishing touches for Spencer House. If you're playing in the big leagues, ignore this paragraph. There's no question that Paris has top-of-the-line resources; but the truth is, if you have ever cast a wary eye at the bottom line, you know that Paris has top-of-the-line prices as well. Even Parisians leave town to buy antiques.

People who have price in mind work the wide network of antiques shows, *brocante* fairs, auctions, flea markets, and weekends in the country that provide not only wonderful entertainment but also far better prices than you'll ever find on the Faubourg St-Honoré. Note that there are a number of annual events that charge admission (about 5€/$5.40, sometimes more).

If you're a serious shopper and plan on some big-time buying, keep the following tips in mind:

- Buy from a dealer with an international reputation.
- Prices are usually quoted in dollars once they top $5,000.
- There is now a value-added tax on some antiques; ask for a détaxe form.
- Make sure you receive the appropriate paperwork so that your purchase can leave the country. The French are not going to let any national treasures slip through their fingers.
- Insure for replacement value, not cost.

LE LOOK

Paris has its share of home-style shops, similar to Pottery Barn, that sell a Euro look at a fair to moderate price. Prices might not be any better than at home (in fact, they could be higher), but you'll find style galore, not to mention items you can't find elsewhere. I am constantly amazed by this look—it was first mastered by the Englishman Sir Terence Conran and owes its success to many American retailing methods.

BOUCHARA
1 rue LaFayette, 9e (Métro: Chaussée d'Antin).

In terms of home style, this is the low end, but worth visiting if you have a good eye or are in search of fabrics by the meter. Dress fabrics are upstairs; the home style is on the ground floor. Good place around Christmas for ornaments and decorative touches. You can also get pillows in the usual French sizes, which are hard to find in the U.S. This store is next door to Galeries Lafayette's main store.

THE CONRAN SHOP
8 bd. Madeleine, 2e (Métro: Madeleine); 117 rue du Bac, 7e (Métro: Sèvres-Babylone).

This is a British shop, but Sir Terence Conran is an expert on French design. The Madeleine store is even more exciting than the Left Bank store; it's newer and has a cafe. Both stores are filled with tons of whimsy and charm. Just browse and breathe the magic: There are books, luggage, foodstuffs, gifts, home style, housewares, pens, paper goods, and more.

FLAMANT
8 place de Furstenberg, 6e (Métro: St-Germain-des-Prés).

Long a brand name in French home style, Flamant recently opened stores in all the major French cities. It makes its own furniture, but also has gift and tabletop items. There's a touch of the English in the look, but it is a dream style for many French families.

GENEVIÈVE LETHU
95 rue de Rennes, 6e (Métro: St-Germain-des-Prés); 12 rue de Passy, 16e (Métro: La Muette).

This designer has boutiques in Printemps Maison, Galeries Lafayette, and Bon Marché, and several freestanding stores in Paris. Did I say several? There are about a dozen shops in Paris and maybe 50 across France. There are also shops in the Far East and much of Italy. The only one in North America is in Montreal. So shop in Paris or buy a franchise of this tabletop and kitchen shop and bring her to America.

Lethu designs some of the most refreshing (and affordable) tabletop items in Paris: Her use of color is bold and extravagant, and her prints are exotic without being beyond the pale. She mixes contemporary tabletop and country looks so elegantly that even a formal setting will work. The tablecloths are my favorite, but there's much more to choose from.

HABITAT
8 rue pont de Neuf, 1er (Métro: Pont Neuf); 45 rue de Rennes, 6e (Métro: St-Germain-des-Prés); 12 bd. de la Madeleine, 9e (Métro: Madeleine); CC Montparnasse, 14e (Métro: Montparnasse); 35 av. Wagram, 17e (Métro: Ternes or Etoile).

Although Sir Terence Conran developed both, Conran and Habitat are not the same store. In fact, these days they are not even similar: Habitat sells lower-end goods and is not my idea of something you'll want to plan your trip to Paris around.

LE CEDRE ROUGE
5 rue de Médicis, 6e (Métro: Odéon); 25 rue Duphot, 8e (Métro: Madeleine).

A chain with shops outside Paris, Le Cedre Rouge tends to focus on a country garden look. Affordable style for the masses, but quite classy. Everything is beautifully displayed. This is not just for those who are looking to stock the house; the tote bags and other small items also make good gifts.

MAISONS DU MONDE

Centre Commercial Les Halles, 1er (Métro: Les Halles);
Centre Commercial Quatre Temps (Métro: Grande Arche).

This mass merchant may not interest you—the look isn't that different from Pier One, and you can do well with this sort of thing (Indian and Asian imports) in the U.S. Living in Paris, I have found this chain a godsend for getting funky looks and high style at a moderate price. I have bought candles, picture frames, cutlery, and many table accessories here.

MIS EN DEMEURE

27 rue du Cherche-Midi, 6e (Métro: Sèvres-Babylone);
66 av. Victor Hugo, 16e (Métro: Victor Hugo).

Sort of a hipper, more French Conran's. On my last visit, there were lots of country tabletop looks (items made with twigs) and papier-mâché Christmas ornaments. Some items border on the fabulous; others are ordinary. But when you first step inside and see all the glassware, linens, furniture, and lamps displayed together, you will think it's quite *extraordinaire*.

SPECIALTY LOOKS

A number of chic-er-than-thou shops are so fabulously French that you have to visit them, if only to browse.

AGNÈS COMAR

7 av. George V, 8e (Métro: Alma Marceau or George V).

The small shop is very "in" with local ladies; they buy unique gift items here and try to outdo each other with the latest thing. It's a small town.

ARMANI CASA

195 bd. St-Germain, 6e (Métro: Rue du Bac).

Beyond the superstore in Milan, Armani now has a handful of home furnishings stores in world capitals. The Paris store is especially well positioned near other designer showrooms, many of them Italian, and not far from the designer shops clustered around St-Germain-des-Prés. The store sells tabletop and gift items, as well as furniture. There are no bargains here, but at least it doesn't look like expensive Conran (as it does in Milan).

ASTIER DE VILLATTE
173 rue St-Honoré, 1er (Métro: Palais-Royal).

Blink and you miss this small shop. It is deep, but from the front you could pass it and not know that it is one of the most special spaces in France. It sells a look and a way of being and a mishmash of objects displayed to thrill your heart. The business revolves around hand-thrown whiteware (dishes), but there are sweaters, gloves, socks, gifts, and objets d'art. The dishes are not inexpensive—a large piece can easily cost $150 (138€)—but this is the chic look of the moment.

CATHERINE MEMMI
32 rue St-Sulpice, 6e (Métro: Odéon) and 11 rue St-Sulpice, 6e (Métro: Odéon).

The look is minimalist, which isn't my thing, but the influence is from Kyoto and the designer's motto is "humble but beautiful." There are clean lines, luxury fabrics, and neutral tones galore; even Galeries Lafayette has a Memmi space. The shop at no. 11 sells more of what Memmi calls "Les Basiques."

GRANGE
5 place St-Augustin, 8e (Métro: St-Augustin).

Grange has been a famous name in French design and home style for over 100 years; its first freestanding boutique is large and filled with two levels of room sets, furniture, and tabletop accessories. Mostly, it's large items that won't fit in your luggage, but you might get inspired. And there is a Monoprix across the street.

LA TUILE LOUP
35 rue Daubenton, 5e (Métro: Monge).

Just trust me on this one. This shop brims with country French charm. It's in a slightly out-of-the-way location, but you can easily wander into the 6e from here. If it's a market day (Wed or Fri), stop by place Monge, too.

LE PRINCE JARDINER
117–121 Arcade Vallois, 37 rue de Valois, Jardins du Palais Royal, 1er (Métro: Palais-Royal).

In the far corner of the arcade of shops in the Palais Royal, this store specializes in gardening and country looks. A prince owns it; hence the name. The gardening bags have become the weekend tote of the BCBG chic.

MAISON DE FAMILLE
29 rue St-Sulpice, 6e (Métro: St-Sulpice or Mabillon); place Madeleine, 8e (Métro: Madeleine).

This is almost a multiple (chain store), since there are now a few in Paris and several in the provinces. And why not? This is a terrific store with a wonderful look. The soothing blend of English, Euro, and chinoiserie will seduce you.

I love the look and feel of these stores, but a shopper might pay high prices for British, American, or imported goods from elsewhere. I can easily find similar things in the U.S. for less— yet put it all together, and you have a serious browse with some drooling.

ROSEMARIE SCHULZ
30 rue Boissy d'Anglas, 8e (Métro: Madeleine).

If you check out only one new address this trip, this is it. It's near Territoire, inside the Galeries de la Madeleine. Be sure to see them both. Emotionally, the two shops are worlds apart. Schultz is a German designer and possibly a florist—her shop sells fabrics, pillows, sachets, and flowers. This is one of the most imaginative shops I've ever been in. Its "dream pillows," which are silken and almost medieval in look and feel, cost $30 to $50 (27.60€–46€) apiece. Everything in the shop excites multiple senses: touch, smell, and sight. There are even items for under $10 (9.20€), including potpourri.

SIA
5 bd. Malesherbes, 1er (Métro: Madeleine).

Sia is a mass merchant of style and class; this is its first shop, across from the Madeleine. It is known for fake flowers, and sells all sorts of tabletop items and home style (in department stores too) at very good prices. I like the plastic container filled with silk rose petals, which you can throw at the bride or across your dinner table, or scent with a home ambience spray.

TERRITOIRE
30 rue Boissy d'Anglas, 8e (Métro: Madeleine).

I'm not certain how to categorize this shop. The look evokes English breeziness, lighthouses along the French Atlantic coast (where many Parisians summer), and American summer cottages with Adirondack chairs on the lawn. There are books, gifts, and some tabletop items. Also tote bags, fireplace equipment, and even toys. It's a jumble of log-cabin chic.

FABRIC SHOWROOMS

If you are a member of the trade or simply want inspiration, you are welcome to browse in decorator showrooms. Don't be surprised if many of the home-furnishings fabric suppliers want nothing to do with you unless you quickly brandish a business card that proves you are a designer. Most showrooms have U.S. representatives or distributors, and they do not want to undercut their own agents.

This leads to an even more important point: You may find that these same items are the same price (or even less) in the U.S. If you are a member of the trade and present a business card, you can ask for a 10% trade discount.

You may also want to negotiate for the détaxe refund, for which you must qualify when you arrange to ship outside the country. Many firms will not ship to the U.S. at the risk of offending their American agents.

Finally, remember that a huge amount of "French style" is actually British. Some of the best fabric showrooms in Paris showcase British goods! If you discover that your favorite item is British, save money by buying it in the U.K.

If you're just looking, check out the fabric showrooms tucked behind the place des Victoires, not far from the Palais Royal. Walk along the rue du Mail to the place des Victoires. This area borders the Sentier, or garment district (Métro: Sentier or Bourse). **Brunswig & Fils,** 8 rue du Mail, originally a French firm, is now owned by an American family, so it's hard to know where to buy and when you will save.

PASSEMENTERIE & RIBBON

I buy bits of *passementerie*—fringe and braid—at the flea markets, but if you are decorating your home and willing to splurge on the best, Paris has several serious sources.

AU BON GOUT
1 rue Guisarde, 16e (Métro: La Muette).

This store's name means "With Good Taste"; they aren't kidding. It sells braids, buttons, and all the things I love. It's at the low end of the Passy district, so combine a visit here with a trip to the neighborhood. It sells couture buttons, but no CC buttons.

CLAUDE DECLERQ
15 rue Etienne Marcel, 2e (Métro: Etienne Marcel).

This designer makes new *passementerie* following old color schemes and methods; he will do custom work to match.

MARIE-PIERRE BOITARD
8 place du Palais-Bourbon, 7e (Métro: Invalides).

A good resource for simple *passementerie* in a chic, totally Parisian environment.

PASSEMENTERIE DE L'ILE DE FRANCE
11 rue Trousseau, 4e (Métro: Ledru-Rollin).

This is just past Bastille, but right on Napoleon in terms of style. It opens at 9am; closed weekends.

TABLETOP & GIFTS

Every place you look in Paris, there's another adorable shop selling gifts or tabletop items. No one sets a table like the French. The department stores often have exhibits or even classes in table arts; you can take notes—or pictures.

DINERS EN VILLE
27 rue de Varenne, 7e (Métro: Rue du Bac).

If you take my advice and stroll the rue du Bac, you will find this store on your own and congratulate yourself for being such a clever bunny. This is a small, cramped, crowded two-room store filled with the kind of French tabletop merchandise you and I adore. There isn't anything in this store I wouldn't buy.

EN ATTENDANT LES BARBARES
50 rue Etienne Marcel (at Victoires), 2e (Métro: Etienne Marcel or Palais-Royal).

Great shop for cutting-edge chic gifts. I'm most impressed with the items (especially candlesticks) made from resin. Stop by, if only to gawk.

LA DAME BLANCHE
186 rue de Rivoli, 1er (Métro: Tuileries).

Nestled between the tourist traps on the rue de Rivoli is this tiny shop selling reproduction faience, Limoges boxes, and Louis-style porcelain.

MURIEL GRATEAU
Galerie de Valois, Jardins du Palais-Royal, 1er (Métro: Palais-Royal).

Muriel once designed ready-to-wear for Charles Jourdan; now she has her own place. There are linens in more colors than the rainbow, and beautiful textiles. Her linen napkins come in 36 colors.

RESONANCES
3 bd. Malesherbes, 1er (Métro: Madeleine).

I find this store very American (part of the New Paris), but because it's easy enough to get to and next door to the Sia store, you may want to pop in. It sells gifts, tabletop design, office design, cards, and novelties.

KITCHEN STYLE

Paris is rightfully renowned for its table arts; luckily for tourists, there are a number of kitchen supply houses within a block or two of each other, so you can see a lot without going out of your way. Price is not the object here; selection is everything. Note that most of the kitchen shops open at 9am (sometimes earlier), so you can extend your shopping day by beginning with these resources. The "kitchen neighborhood" is a block and a cross street; you can easily start at one and walk to the others. Remember, rue Montmartre is not in Montmartre; it is near Forum des Halles. And Etienne Marcel is a great shopping street.

A. Simon
48 rue Montmarte, 2e (Métro: Etienne Marcel or Les Halles).

Note to regulars: A. Simon has moved. There's a blue-jeans store in the old space, across the street. A major supplier of kitchen and cooking supplies for over 100 years, this store is conveniently located down the street from the Forum Les Halles mall. You can buy everything from dishes to menus here; I buy white paper doilies by the gross—many of these sizes and shapes not available in the U.S.—at fair prices. Touch everything; this is a wonderland of gadgets and goodies.

Dehillerin
18–20 rue Coquillière, 1er (Métro: Musée-du-Louvre or Les Halles).

Perhaps the most famous cookware shop in Paris, Dehillerin has been selling cookware for over 150 years. It sells mostly to the trade, but you can poke around and touch the copper, cast iron, tools, gadgets, and more. Or someone may even help you—try out your French; it goes a long way here. The store opens at 8am and closes for lunch.

Duthilleul & Minart
14 rue de Turbigo, 1er (Métro: Etienne Marcel).

This shop sells professional clothing for chefs, kitchen staff, waiters, and so forth. It's a great resource for creative fashion freaks or teens. You can buy anything from kitchen clogs to aprons; a *toque* costs $12 (11.05€), and the *veste chef* (chef's jacket) is $30 (27.60€). There are various styles of aprons (which make good gifts) and many wine-related items. You'll find it around the corner from the other kitchen shops, right at the Métro stop.

LA CORPO
*19 rue Montmartre, 1er (Métro: Etienne Marcel or
Les Halles).*

This one isn't my favorite, but it, too, has a vast selection of
kitchenware, including much equipment. While you may be
tempted, remember that electric gadgets are a no-no. Still there
are lots of enticing pots, pans, and supplies.

MORA
*13 rue Montmartre, 1er (Métro: Etienne Marcel or
Les Halles).*

Similar to A. Simon, but with more utensils (more than 5,000
in stock), Mora has a salon for bakery goods that sells *fèves*
(charms that go into the *gâteau de roi*, or king's cake, for
Epiphany) in small and large packages. It has a huge paper-
goods section as well.

CANDLES

One of the first stores in Paris that bowled me over with just
how clever the French can be was a candle shop, **Point à la
Ligne.** Now that line is available at any French department store
and in the U.S. Still, when you wander Paris, you will find
extravagance and wit, often at an affordable price, at shops
selling candles.

I now travel with my own candles, which I light in the bathroom while I soak in the tub or place by my bedside while I
read. Do remember to snuff out the candle before you go to
sleep! I used to buy **Rigaud** candles at my favorite duty-free
shop, Catherine, but I now use other brands—I am always testing what's new.

Rigaud was the leading brand of scented candles when no
one else was into them, and it is still at the top of the market
in terms of status and quality. Most of the big fragrance houses
(**Guerlain, Manuel Canovas, L'Occitane, Roger & Gallet**) sell

scented candles in addition to perfume or soaps. For more home scent resources, see "Smelling French Style," earlier in this chapter. Point à la Ligne specializes in novelty candles, not scented candles.

POINT À LA LIGNE
67 av. Victor Hugo, 16e (Métro: Victor Hugo); 25 rue de Varenne, 7e (Métro: Rue du Bac).

Probably the most famous of the contemporary candle makers in Paris, Point à la Ligne has candle sculptures as well as ultra-skinny, enormously chic long tapers that make sensational birthday or celebration candles on a cake. In sum, all sorts of fabulous things. The products are available in all French department stores.

DELUXE LOGO STYLE
....

Want a chic souvenir? Purchase something from a famous French address. Several shops, cafes, and even tourist attractions sell attractive logo merchandise.

BOUTIQUE CRILLON
Hôtel de Crillon, 10 place de la Concorde, 8e (Métro: Concorde).

The Crillon is one of the most famous hotels in Paris. Even if you aren't staying here, you may want to visit for tea or to shop. Because the hotel is part of the Concorde chain, which is owned by a famous French family (heard the name Taittinger?), the gift shop sells products made by other companies in which the Taittinger family has an interest. Accordingly, you'll find an amazing array of French luxury goods—Annick Goutal and Baccarat, to name just a few. Also here are Crillon logo goods that you wouldn't dare steal from your room—robes, slippers, note cards, and such.

Even without its association with the Hôtel de Crillon, this would be a good group of shops. Better yet, the hotel gift shop is open Sunday and stays open late during the week.

BOUTIQUE DU CAFÉ DE FLORE
26 rue St-Benoît, 6e (Métro: St-Germain-des-Prés).

The Café de Flore is one of the three famous Paris bistros on the Left Bank (the other two are Les Deux Magots and Brasserie Lipp), and so far it's the only one that has opened its own gift shop. The tiny store, around the corner from the cafe, is just adorable. You get a free chocolate when you wander in (you may buy a box), and you can choose from dishes, serving pieces, paper goods, and all sorts of gift items. Rumor has it that this store may close because of the value of the real estate; but you will be in the neighborhood anyway, so have a look.

COMPTOIR DE LA TOUR D'ARGENT
2 rue du Cardinal Lemoine, 5e (Métro: Maubert-Mutualité).

La Tour d'Argent, one of the most famous restaurants in Paris, has withstood the comings and goings of new rivals. Whether you eat there or not, you may want to shop next door, where you can get a picnic to go or a gift basket to take home. There are also ashtrays, crystal, china, and more.

SALON DU THÉ BERNARDAUD
11 rue Royale, 8e (Métro: Concorde).

This is tricky, because there's an entire Bernardaud china shop at this address. What I'm suggesting are the porcelain logo souvenirs sold at the front counter of the tea shop.

CHINA, CRYSTAL & SILVER

French crystal and porcelain have been the backbone of French luxe for centuries. Prices can be fair in France, but the shipping will kill you. Come with a price list from home, because a sale in the U.S. may wipe out any French savings.

BACCARAT
30 bis, rue de Paradis, 10e (Métro: Château d'Eau);
11 place de la Madeleine, 8e (Métro: Concorde); 10 rue de la Paix, 2e (Métro: Opéra).

Baccarat's headquarters, shipping office, showroom, and museum are in the 10e, where it has a gigantic shop (no seconds, sorry); the flagship boutique is in the high-rent district of the 8e. Prices are the same at either venue. There's also a new, small shop, which seems to hint at more to come.

Finding the shop at the factory can be confusing—you must walk through the offices and up some stairs. Once you're up the stairs, the shop is to your left. It's hard to distinguish it from the museum that sprawls in front of you. In both, long tables hold merchandise laid out in rows—you may touch. You can even try on the earrings. Whether or not you can walk out with your choice is up to the gods. Baccarat is often 6 to 7 months behind in its orders, so if what you want is not in the shop, it will be shipped . . . someday. Prices are not negotiable. If something breaks in your package, Baccarat will replace the item. It ships anywhere in the world and accepts mail orders. The selection in the sublimely located place de la Madeleine shop is not as overwhelming and not as much fun.

BERNARDAUD
11 rue Royale, 8e (Métro: Concorde).

If you're making the rounds of the hoity-toity tabletop houses, don't miss Bernardaud, which means Limoges china. Especially impressive are the newer contemporary designs with Art Deco roots. If you don't have to ship, you can save over New York prices. The tea shop is farther back in the *passage.*

CRISTAL LALIQUE
11 rue Royale, 8e (Métro: Concorde).

One glance at Lalique's crystal door and there's no doubt that you've entered one of the wonders of the world. Get a look at the Lalique-designed Olympic medals created for the 1992 Winter Games. The headquarters is sort of like a museum: People come to stare more than they shop. The prices are the same as at factory sources on the rue de Paradis, by the way, so don't think you may beat the tags here. Besides, you get to apply for détaxe, everyone is friendly and speaks English, and they ship to the U.S. This is an excellent case of a brand name that has expanded like mad—there's everything from jewelry to handbags to belts to perfumes.

DAUM
4 rue de la Paix, 2e (Métro: Opéra).

There's a lot more to Daum than large lead-crystal cars, and this two-level shop is a great place to discover how much more. The extra room allows the display of inventive glass art and colored-glass pieces that will surely become collector's items one day.

ROBERT HAVILAND ET C. PARLON CRISTALLERIES ROYALES DE CHAMPAGNE
Village Royal, 25 rue Royale, 8e (Métro: Madeleine).

This shop is a little bit hidden and very, very fancy. It's best not to bring the kids. Check out the way in which the printed patterns are mixed and matched—it's the essence of French chic.

PARADISE & MORE

The street for wholesale crystal, china, and tabletop accessories is the rue de Paradis, where many big names have their headquarters. There are just a few catches: This is a low-rent district, but prices are no different than in the high-rent districts. It's a bit of a walk from the nearest Métro stop in a not-so-interesting area (but not dangerous), or an $8 (7.35€) taxi ride from the 1er arrondissement. It's fun, true, but you might prefer a quick visit to Cristal Vendôme instead.

If you decide to head for rue de Paradis, be sure to take in the **Baccarat Museum.** Then just browse from one shop to the next. The factories generally fix prices; there is little negotiation. After a few shops, they'll all look alike to you. Many of the stores carry other European brands; all have bridal registries.

CRISTAL VENDÔME
1 rue de Castiglione, 1er (Métro: Concorde).

Right underneath the Hôtel Inter-Continental is a factory-direct store that will ship to the U.S. (You can phone in an order once you have bought in person, a service the factory will not offer.) It sells various lines (Baccarat, Lalique, Daum, and more), which makes shopping easy. The store offers tax-free prices, the same as at the airport. I priced a Lalique necklace and found it to be almost half the U.S. price.

EDITIONS PARADIS
29 rue de Paradis, 10e (Métro: Château d'Eau).

This is an enormous source with so much stuff that you'll be nervous if you are carrying a big, floppy handbag. It's fancy, with table settings on display to give you ideas. And, of course, it carries small Limoges boxes—the perfect collectible.

LA TISANIÈRE PARADIS
21 rue de Paradis, 10e (Métro: Château d'Eau).

A country-style resource on a street filled with more traditional showrooms, this porcelain shop offers stacks of kitchenware and tabletop items at fair prices. Some promotional items are downright cheap. Much fun.

ORIENTAL INSPIRATIONS

Paris went Zen in its craze for Japanese-inspired tabletop items and dishes about 3 years ago. Giorgio Armani's new home-style shop, **Armani Casa** (p. 222), has reinforced that look. If you don't want to pay $50 (46€) for a salad plate, try the resources below.

COMPAGNIE FRANÇAISE DE L'ORIENT DE LA CHINE
167 bd. St-Germain-des-Prés, 6e (Métro: Rue du Bac); 260 bd. St-Germain-des-Prés, 7e (Métro: Rue du Bac); 170 bd. Haussmann, 8e (Métro: Ternes).

This store has a few locations in Paris and some in other cities (such as Brussels); it sells clothes and tabletop accessories, sometimes in the same store, sometimes in separate stores. On the Left Bank, the stores are separate. The goods are mostly Chinese, as the name suggests, but are very chic.

MUJI
99 rue de Rivoli, 1er (Métro: Louvre).

This Japanese firm hit it big in London before coming to Paris, where its many shops sell a department store's worth of merchandise. They carry clothes, storage units, paper goods, gifts, and tabletop items. There are Muji stores in every major shopping district in Paris; some are better than others.

PROVENÇAL FABRICS

If you aren't headed for Provence, Paris has a selection of traditional country French prints. Most street markets sell less expensive wares.

BLANC D'IVOIRE
50 rue du Bac, 7e (Métro: Rue du Bac).

As the name might suggest, pale is the rule in this shop of reproduction French *boutis* (quilts) and classic antique linens from Provence. There are a few bright pieces, but no hot primary colors. This line is also sold in department stores. The machine-washable quilts cost a few hundred dollars and have a wonderful old-fashioned feel.

LES OLIVADES
95 rue de Seine, 6e (Métro: St-Sulpice or Odéon);
21 av. Niel, 17e (Métro: Péreire).

I have been told that Les Olivades was started in the mid-1970s when someone in the Souleiado hierarchy departed and started a new firm. Indeed, Les Olivades reminds me of the Pierre Deux–Souleiado look, although the colors (pastels and the like) are more muted. Les Olivades sells much the same merchandise—fabric by the yard, place mats, tablecloths, napkins, umbrellas, travel bags, and so forth.

While the goods are not cheap, they are about 30% less expensive than at Souleiado in France.

SOULEIADO
78 rue de Seine, 6e (Métro: Mabillon); Forum des Halles,
1er (Métro: Châtelet); 85 av. Paul-Doumer, 16e (Métro:
La Muette).

You have to be a real Pierre Deux freak to know that Pierre Deux is the name of the American franchise for these prints, but is not the name of the company in Europe. So remember the name Souleiado, which will get you happily through France.

The flagship rue de Seine shop is everything it should be. You will be in country French heaven. Be sure to see all parts of the shop (there are two rooms); the main shop winds around another showroom in the far back, where more fabrics are sold by the meter. There is a showroom for the trade next door. The Passy shop on avenue Paul-Doumer is almost as good but not quite as quaint. Nonetheless, it is chockablock with the look we love—plenty of fabrics plus clothing and all the tabletop accessories in the world.

TABLE LINENS

LE JACQUARD FRANCAIS
12 rue Richepanse, 1er (Métro: Madeleine).

Be still, my heart; this is flutter time if you love table style and fabrics and color as much as I do. The brand is well known (it's available at department stores, where you can use your tourist discount card), but this is the first freestanding store. It carries the entire line. There are hanging samples to touch and three video screens to watch. The patterns are all made with a jacquard loom (as you can guess from the name); they are incredibly sophisticated, very French, and fabulous for gifts. Large tablecloths cost 85€ to 155€ ($91.80–$167.40), but look like a million. The napkins cost about 10€ ($10.80) each.

BED LINENS

Continental bed sizes are metric, but why should that stop you? Just bring your tape measure. Or, if price is truly no object, have Porthault custom-make your sheets.

BLANCORAMA
12 rue St-Placide, 6e (Métro: Sèvres-Babylone).

This tiny shop is a regular haunt of mine because I always like to see what's in store at the discount shops that line the street. While there is bed linen in the shop, I buy bath mats here— very traditional French rugs for 8€ ($8.65) each.

DESCAMPS
44 rue du Passy, 16e (Métro: La Muette).

Descamps no longer has stores in the U.S., but higher-end American department stores sell its products. You may not find prices much better in Paris. Still, every time I visit Paris, I buy a few items (such as oblong terry-cloth bath mittens) that aren't available in the U.S. I also buy Primrose Bordier (that's the designer's name) home scent here. There's one in every trading area in Paris. The outlet shops are named Texaffaires; there's one on rue du Temple across the street from BHV (Métro: Hôtel de Ville).

D. PORTHAULT

18 av. Montaigne, 8e (Métro: Alma Marceau); 370 rue du Faubourg St-Honoré, 8e (Métro: Concorde); 163 bd. St-Germain-des-Prés (Métro: Rue du Bac).

Porthault was making fancy bed linens with pretty colored flowers on them long before the real world was ready for patterned sheets—or the notion that a person could spend $1,000 (920€) on bedclothes and still be able to sleep at night.

Porthault sells two lines in America: One is identical to what you can buy in France (it just costs more in the U.S.); the other is contracted by the Porthault family and is available only in the U.S. The French laminated products are not sold in the U.S.; the American wallpaper is not sold in France. One Porthault saleswoman swore that our pattern was not "theirs" because she was unfamiliar with the American wallpapers. The Montaigne shop has a whopper of a sale in January, when it unloads everything at half the retail price, or less! You cannot phone in orders from the U.S.

You may think that Porthault is totally beyond you and hurry by to avoid temptation; I beg you to reconsider. There are many affordable little accessories and gift items that are fun and speak volumes when presented. I always travel with my Porthault shower cap because it makes me smile and beats the plastic jobs. I gave my niece a traditional Porthault bib when she was born: $25 (23€). You have to know the Porthault name to appreciate items like these, but for those in the know, this could be your gift headquarters. They wrap.

I guess the shop on the rue du Faubourg St-Honoré is there to be more convenient to madame on her next spree, but it's tiny and doesn't have the selection or the feel of the mother store or the factory shop. It has a twin on the Left Bank. The flagship is far better.

If you are headed for Lille, note that discontinued prints cost a fraction of their regular price at the factory outside Lille. If you are a fan, this is a trip you will never forget. I am still drooling; thankfully I bought a lot of bibs.

FRETTE HOME COUTURE
49 rue du Faubourg St-Honoré, 8e (Métro: Concorde).

Very fancy new showroom for the Frette linens and home line. It also stocks pajamas, robes, and all your nesting needs.

OLIVIER DESFORGES
26 bd. Raspail, 7e (Métro: Sèvres-Babylone).

This is Descamps's main competitor, with fewer stores in France and none (to my knowledge) in the U.S. Sometimes the line has a country look to it. There are other locations in Paris; this one is a can't-miss.

YVES DELORME
Le Louvre des Antiquaires, 2 place du Palais-Royal, 1er (Métro: Palais-Royal).

Yves Delorme makes linen sold under the Palais-Royal label in the U.S.; he has a boutique on the street level of the Louvre des Antiquaires, and in Monaco and Lyons. This is luxury linen that isn't as wildly priced as other premium French luxury lines (such as Porthault and Descamps) but is still chic. Bed-linen freaks won't care about the prices; the total look has a certain French charm that makes it a must-have.

DEPARTMENT OF HOME STYLE

Naturally, the Parisian department stores carry many of the brands listed in this chapter. Furthermore, Au Printemps has a store, **Printemps Maison,** with many floors devoted to home wares. **Galeries Lafayette** sells linens on one floor and table-top items on another, and is said to be launching a home style store.

BHV has the largest selection of items for home decorating, from the basement (SS) hardware level to many floors of home and decor goods. It also has departments for storage style, furniture refinishing, and more.

Bon Marché is the most chic of the department stores and has many lines the others do not carry, including the Alain Ducasse kitchenware line. It even carries different patterns of mass-market merchandise—there's a Geneviève Lethu pattern that only this store keeps in stock.

La Samaritaine is in the middle of a makeover, so who knows what the future will bring; but the store currently has the best selection of bed linens of all the Parisian department stores.

For more information on the department stores, see p. 130–136.

Chapter Ten

·····················

PARIS BARGAINS

BARGAIN SMARTS

···

Prices in Paris are not low (especially now), so to sniff out the
bargains, you're going to need some background information:

- If you have favorite designers or acquisition targets, shop
  the major department stores and U.S.-based boutiques for
  comparison prices. Don't assume you will get a bargain on
  a Parisian-made purchase. Many international designers
  and retailers set prices that are virtually the same around
  the world.
- If you do not live in a city that has a lot of European merchandise, do some shopping through *Vogue* and *Harper's
  Bazaar*. In the ads for the designer boutiques, you'll find
  phone numbers and Internet addresses.
- Read French magazines to get familiar with the French
  look and the hottest shops. They can cost a fortune (sometimes $14 in the United States), but many libraries and
  French hairdressers have them. Most good newsstands sell
  them; I buy mine at Blockbuster.
- Understand the licensing process. Designers sell the rights
  to their names, and often their designs, to various makers
  around the world. Two men's suits may bear a well-known
  French designer's label but fit differently because they are
  manufactured differently.

- Don't assume a perfume bargain. Know prices before you leave home.
- Don't be fooled into thinking that merchandise with foreign-sounding names is made in Europe, or is French, or offers a bargain. Because Americans are so taken with European names, many American-made products have foreign—especially French—names.
- Conversely, don't be lured into buying an American brand in France that could be bought at home for less.
- French merchandise that might not sell well in the U.S. could be discounted in your hometown. I was just in Marshall's in L.A. and saw scads of French brands at way-low prices.

BEST BUYS IN PARIS

- **Perfumes, Cosmetics & Hair Care**   Perfume savings get to the heart-stopping level once you make the commitment to spend enough to qualify for the détaxe refund (183€/ $197.65). Beyond that, actual savings on discounted perfumes are getting hard to find because of changing business practices in France and a united crackdown on non-détaxe-related discounting by the big-name fragrance and makeup makers. This is aimed mostly at French locals, but may also affect you. Know your U.S. prices, and understand that new laws have been passed within the past year, so what you paid or how discounts were handled during your last trip could be very different now.

  But wait, let's talk about my wrinkles. I swear by Sisleya, which costs $300 a pot in the U.S. and can be yours for a mere (!) $110 (101.20€) in Paris if you take advantage of all the discounts. See, what you save with four jars pays for the airfare.

  If you are even more flexible on brand-name beauty creams, it may be time to visit a *parapharmacie*. These stores carry drugstore brands—no Chanel or Yves Saint Laurent—at a 20% discount. This is the place to load up on fancy hair-care products, skin creams, bath products, and possibly even face powder. Barneys New York has made T. Leclerc all the rage; now it's everywhere in Paris. (Note that Leclerc's new range of skin-care products is not yet available in the U.S.)

- **Limoges Boxes**   Buy Limoges boxes in pretty shapes—fruits, vegetables, animals, and so on. Each box costs $75 to $100 (69€–92€) in Paris, but twice as much in the U.S. (although I have seen them at Costco).

- **Hermès** · Prices in Paris (with a détaxe refund) are definitely lower than in the U.S. In addition, you can frequently find Hermès bargains at airport duty-free shops and in airline duty-free catalogs that are even better than Paris retail prices.

- **Baccarat**   All French glassware can be dramatically less expensive in France, but the cost of shipping it abroad voids the savings. However, have you seen the Baccarat crystal medallions and butterflies that hang from a silk cord? They are drop-dead chic and cost approximately $135 in the U.S. Get onto an airplane that has Baccarat in its duty-free catalog, and lo and behold, the same trinket sells for about $60. Or buy at regular French retail for about $70 (64.40€). This is a serious bargain.

- **Candies, Foodstuffs & Chocolates**   These make great gifts, especially when wrapped in the distinctive packaging of one of Paris's premier food palaces. I buy Maille's tomato soup–colored "Provençale" mustard in grocery stores (no fancy wrap for me, thanks) and give it to foodies around the world—it's unique and special. I haven't found it in any U.S. specialty stores yet. Some Maille flavors are available in the U.S. (and the U.K.), but not this one. Maille has a shop at place de la Madeleine (Métro: Madeleine).

- **Antique Junk**   It's pretty hard to give advice about the ever-changing collectibles market, but the things that caught my eye have all turned out to be bargains when I compared prices at American flea markets (why didn't I buy more?).

LESS-THAN-STELLAR BUYS

Some things are simply not a bargain in any sense:

- **Non–French-Made Goods:** Unless you are desperate, avoid buying American-made goods, whether they be designer items (such as a Ralph Lauren jacket) or mass-market items (like a Gap T-shirt or a pair of Levi's). Ditto for British goods (Aquascutum, Hilditch & Key, and so on), men's business attire, electrical goods (wrong voltage), and Coca-Cola at bars, cafes, or hotels.
- **Souvenirs:** Postcards priced at $1 (.90€) or more are no bargain (see p. 28 for how you can do better), and neither are massive amounts of Disneyland Paris souvenirs. Kitschy souvenirs vary in price—I have seen the same Eiffel Tower fake Limoges box for 4€ to 10€ ($4.30–$9.20).
- **Cheapie Fashion:** The French simply don't do this very well. That's why H&M, the Swedish firm, is so popular.

I bought an empty postcard album—probably from the turn of the century—at the flea market in Vanves, in perfect condition, for $10 (9.20€). I saw a similar one at a dealers' show in Greenwich, Connecticut, for $150. I bought a funky straw hat from the 1950s for $40 (36.80€) and a country-style tablecloth for $5 (4.60€). Museum-quality antiques offer few bargains.

SAVING GRACE

There are tricks that give you more bang for your euro. You can save on transportation, meals, and more. Combine your luxury hotel room with some down-and-dirty consumer facts, and enjoy the best of both worlds:

- Buy Cokes and mineral water at the grocery store and keep them in your minibar. Every chic Frenchwoman carries a large tote bag with a plastic bottle of mineral water. If you really want to save money, avoid drinking Coke completely—it's expensive everywhere in Europe. A whole six-pack costs almost as much as one minibar Coke!
- Buy food from fresh markets (one of Paris's most beautiful natural resources), supermarkets, and *traiteurs* (stores that sell prepared gourmet meals, hot or cold). You can eat a fabulous French meal for $5 to $10 (4.60€–9.20€) per person this way. An entire rotisserie chicken, which feeds four, costs no more than $10 (9.20€), depending on the size of the chicken. Pizza is another good buy.
- Eat your fancy meals at starred Michelin restaurants that offer fixed-price meals, usually at lunch.
- Get into the hotel dining-room game. Lately, it's become trendy for hotels to bring in a one-star (or more) Michelin chef to attract guests and locals. Some one-star chefs have even earned two stars! These hotel restaurants compete so fiercely with each other that they watch their prices carefully.
- Do your gift shopping in duty-free stores (not at the airport), *parapharmacies,* flea markets, or *hypermarchés;* don't scorn those tacky tourist traps for great $3 to $5 (2.75€–4.60€) gift items. You can also find small gifts at **Monoprix**—even at Métro stops. Actually, I buy a large percentage of my clothes and undergarments at Monoprix and have always bought baby clothes and kids' clothes here.

DEPARTMENT STORE DISCOUNTS & DEALS

The two major department stores in Paris, **Galeries Lafayette and Au Printemps,** offer a flat 10% discount to tourists on all nonfood items that are not marked with a red dot. You gain the discount by flashing your special tourist card at the cash register, before you pay.

This discount card has nothing to do with détaxe.

In order to get this discount, you need a card or a coupon for the card. These coupons are given away in most hotels and even through U.S. travel agents; they are also at the Paris Tourist Office on the Champs-Elysées. Or go to the welcome desk of either store and simply ask for the coupon or discount card.

Do not be surprised if you are asked to pay for each purchase at a central cashier rather than the nearest cashier; this has to do with the discount card and the store's accounting process. It's a pain, but nothing in life is free.

FIDELITY CARDS

Fidelity cards are used all over the world but seem to be particularly popular in France, especially in midrange designer shops, *parapharmacies,* and even some restaurants. The fidelity card is a small card, like a credit card, that is stamped or punched every time you make a purchase. Make a certain number of purchases or reach a total euro value and receive a discount or a gift. You get the card simply by asking for *une carte fidelitée.* No, department stores do not have them.

GETTING TO KNOW YOU

Personal relationships are very important in France. People continue to do business with the same people—indeed, the same salesperson—in the same stores and markets for years, even generations. This is cultural, but it also helps the customer make sure he or she is not cheated.

When you find stores you like, spend the time to develop a personal relationship. Reinforce the connection with faxes or little notes during the year, announcing when you will return to Paris. Go so far as to make an appointment, if you feel this is warranted. The more you are known—and this truly takes years of repeat business—the more chance you'll have of getting a discount or a family price and extra perks.

RENT A ROBE

In Paris for a special occasion, such as New Year's Eve, a big birthday, or your 25th wedding anniversary? Why not rent a couture gown for that big night out? The French do. Since French-women want only the finest quality but are too practical to buy a couture gown for a once-in-a-lifetime formal event, they rent. If it's been your dream to wear a couture gown, you can have a very good choice for about $100 to $150 (92€–138€). The place to rent is **Sommier,** 3 passage Brady, 10e.

DUTY-FREE SHOPPING STRATEGIES

Few shops use the word *discount*. The proper name to hide behind is "duty-free." Paris is famous for its duty-free shops. It is one of the few cities in the world where there is a lot of duty-free–style shopping, not just at the airport but on city streets. These shops take on a whole new importance now that duty-free between EU destinations has been outlawed and airport shopping has begun to change focus.

Most non-airport duty-free shops sell makeup, fragrances, and deluxe gift items—designer earrings, scarves, ties, and even pens. Some of the accessories have been created specifically for the enormous duty-free business and are not sold through the designer boutiques. Duty-free stores like to tell you that they give a 40% discount. In reality, expect to get a 20% discount without too much trouble, a 25% discount if you are lucky, and no further discount unless you qualify for a détaxe refund. If you do get a 25% discount and also qualify for a détaxe refund, your total savings will be 45%!

SPECIAL-EVENT RETAILING

Paris abounds with special shopping events. Ask your concierge for details and the exact dates, although events are advertised in magazines and papers. (I know you read *Madame Figaro* when you are in town, so you probably know it all anyway.)

Hermès has twice-yearly sales that can be described only as world-class sporting events. They take place in March and October (the exact dates are revealed only moments before, in newspaper ads). The sales have become such events that they are no longer held at the store. The average wait in line is 4 hours before admission; items are marked down to just about half price. Unfortunately, a code is worked into your purchase that tells the world your item was bought on sale. It is not obvious, but look for a teeny-tiny S in a scarf.

The latest trend comes from the New York sample sales. Catherine Max offers her **Espace Catherine Max,** 17 rue Raymond Poincare, 16e (Métro: Trocadéro), where she unloads designer this and that at unbelievably low prices. The catch is that in order to know the sale dates, you have to have a membership ($15/13.80€ per year) and then you get a postcard in the mail.

For antiques lovers, the event you really want to catch is the **Biennale Internationale des Antiquaires,** the single biggest, most important antiques event in the world. It's held only in even-numbered years, usually in September, at the Grand Palais, roughly halfway between the place de la Concorde and the Rond Point. Check the design trades for the actual dates or ask your concierge. You need not be a designer to attend; it's open to the public.

A number of antiques shows take place at the same time every year and become special events to plan trips around. April or May in Paris means only one thing: time for the **Brocante de Bastille.** Celebrated outside, in stalls planted around the canal at Bastille, it is truly magical. For more information, see "*Brocante* Shows," p. 121.

For information about big shopping events, look in *Allo Paris, Figaroscope, Zurban,* or antiques journals such as *Antiques, Alladin, or Chiner.* **The French Government Tourist Office** in New York (☎ **212/315-0888**) can supply the dates of special events, or you can do some online research at www. bonjourparis.com.

PRE-SALE SALES

As discussed, sale dates (Jan and June–July) are set by the government and announced in the papers a few weeks beforehand. What is not announced, or even discussed, is that regular customers can get the sale price a few days before the sale starts or can set aside merchandise to be held for the markdown.

PROMOTIONAL SALES

If there are only two sale periods during the year, how do you get a break? Well, you wait for the big promotional events. The department stores run them at least twice a year and give them very silly names such as "The Three Days" (which lasts 10 days), "The Days of Gold," or whatever. Note that like all promotional and produced sales, much of the merchandise is brought in to be sold at the sale price.

STOCK SHOPS

GR STOCK/GEORGES RECH
100 rue d'Alésia, 14e (Métro: Alésia).

REGINA RUBENS
88 rue d'Alésia, 14e (Métro: Alésia).

SR/SONIA RYKIEL STOCK
64 rue d'Alésia, 14e (Métro: Alésia).

These are the three best stock stores on a 2-block stretch on the rue d'Alésia. Also on this block are a Monoprix and several normal stores that seem to be discount stores, so it's confusing. The best approach is to just go, wander, and touch everything. Merchandise is usually from past seasons, but it does go on sale during the official sale periods.

VIDNA
9 rue St-Placide, 6e (Métro: Sèvres-Babylone).

This is one of the many discount and stock shops on the rue St-Placide (see "Discount Neighborhoods," p. 111). I point this one out specifically so you don't just walk by it. This is the stock shop for the brand Nitya, a chic line with stores all over France, including 327 rue St-Honoré, 8e. The look is slightly ethnic but monochromatic and easy for all figures to wear. Don't go by the sizes; try everything on. I'm a 42 here (sometimes) and a 46 in real life. You just never know.

STOCK GRIFFES
17 rue Vielle-du-Temple, 4e (Métro: Hôtel de Ville or St-Paul).

This is my new favorite stock shop in Paris; it has branch stores around town. I like this one because you don't have to go out of your way to find it—it's in the Marais near the Picasso Museum. Other stock shops are just a sneeze away, so if you strike out here, there's hope for you and your wallet.

Although this is a stock shop and is supposed to offer bargains, I am a spoiled American shopper, and I don't think that $150 (138€) for a dress is a bargain. But I happily paid that for an Irena Gregori dress, partly because I adore her stuff, partly because the dress was gorgeous—and mostly because the dress was machine washable. About half the stock is from a brand called Lillith, sold in a Left Bank shop and Au Printemps, which personifies droopy chic. I am mad for it.

You may not recognize the names on the labels here, and sometimes the labels are cut out; but the merchandise is often fashion forward and less expensive than in regular retail sources.

FACTORY OUTLET MALLS

By definition, factory outlets lie outside of major metropolitan areas. As the outlet mall craze grows in Europe, more and more are opening closer to Paris. A few are within an hour of the city, although only the one at La Valee was created with public transportation in mind; it uses the same RER line that serves Disneyland Paris.

LA VALEE

This is the newest outlet mall, 5 minutes from Disneyland Paris and 45 minutes from the city. Among the brands with outlet shops here are Anne Fontaine, Muriella Burani, Charles Jourdan, Max Mara, Camper, Lamarthe, Robert Clergerie, and Ventilo.

The mall is open Monday through Saturday 10am to 8pm, Sunday 11am to 7pm. For information, call ☎ 01/60-42-35-00 or e-mail marketing@valueretail.fr.

By car, take the Autoroute A4 east in the direction of Nancy; take Exit 14, "Disneyland."

Or take RER line A4 direct to Val d'Europe in the Disneyland direction. Go out through the mall (Commercial Centre Val d'Europe) to the outlet center on the far side. It is a hike.

PARIS NORD2/USINES CENTER X

You will pass this center (☎ 01/48-63-20-72) as you drive between Paris and CDG Airport in Roissy. It's about 40 minutes from Paris. Open weekdays 11am to 7pm, weekends 10am to 8pm. There are 120 boutiques here.

Directions: A1 Autoroute in the direction of Roissy, Exit ZI (Zone Industriel) Paris Nord 2.

Troyes

Troyes is a city, not an outlet center, and is home to two large outlet malls. The one owned by McArthur Glen offers a bus (☎ 0800/80-92-43; www.eva-voyages.com) each Saturday. The round-trip fare for the 90-minute trip is 14€ ($15.12) per person. It departs from the place de la Bastille in front of the Opéra (Métro: Bastille) at 9:30am and returns to Paris at 7pm.

BARGAIN BASEMENTS

I am calling stores that sell many brands at lower-than-average prices "bargain basements" and listing the best ones here. Stores that concentrate on one brand are known in France as "stock shops"; see p. 250. See "Resale & Vintage," below, for information on resale shops, which can offer bargains on preowned designer clothing, and the "Discount Neighborhoods" section of chapter 6, "Left Bank Shopping Neighborhoods."

Paris has seen a lot of stock and so-called discount stores open in the past few years. Some even call themselves outlet stores. Often they are regular mom-and-pop stores that carry name brands but cut their profit to appeal to shoppers who are disgusted by the high regular retail prices in France.

I don't need to give you the lecture about the nature of bargain shops, but I will say that on my last research trip I noticed two new addresses in popular tourist magazines (no names, please). I eagerly went off to these sources—each in the heart of Paris's best shopping district and convenient for any visitor. Maybe I hit a bad day; maybe I am too big a snob. I hated both of them so much that I refuse to list them in this book. On the other hand, that doesn't mean that the sources I have listed are going to be super on the day you visit. Bargain hunting in Paris is even harder than in America, so think about how much time you want to invest in this pursuit. Good luck.

Finally, a word about sizes—if you are larger than a size 12 (U.S.), you may not find a fit.

ANNA LOWE
104 rue du Faubourg St-Honoré, 8e (Métro: Miromesnil).

For more than a decade this has been a terrific store; now people visit for clothes and pashmina. Aside from a few Chanel accessories, there were no name clothes, but I still spent $500 (460€) on a suit without a label—which turned out to be a $1,200 (1,104€) designer suit I saw at full price in another store. Open Monday through Friday 10:30am to 6pm.

ANNEXE DES CRÉATEURS
19 rue Godot-de-Mauroy, 9e (Métro: Madeleine).

This crowded shop lacks charm, but it is crammed with clothes and bolts of fabric. It carries sizes up to 44 (12 U.S.). You won't have to make a special trip; it's close to many places in every woman's journey through Paris—halfway between boulevard Madeleine and the big department stores on boulevard Haussmann.

It tries to specialize in younger and kickier designers, such as Moschino and Mugler; pieces are a season old and priced at 30% to 40% off regular French retail. Stop in to check out hats and accessories as well—the good stuff begins at $100 (92€).

LA BRADERIE
38 rue de Rivoli (at rue Vielle-du-Temple), 4e (Métro: Hôtel de Ville or St-Paul).

Although this small chain has almost a dozen discount shops in Paris and has separate shops for men and women, I have listed this one because it is half a block from a great stock shop, Stock Griffes. While I personally struck out when I last visited, it carries some French brand names and has plenty of choices at realistic prices. There's a men's shop a few stores away at 11 rue Vielle-du-Temple.

MODA
79 rue de la Victoire, 9e (Métro: Chaussée d'Antin)

Before you don't recognize the address and ignore this listing, let me confess that this is one of my best sources in Paris. You'd be foolish to miss it. The store is also right behind Galeries Lafayette, so it's not hard to find.

Moda sells brand-name shoes for men, women, and children, and some handbags. By brand name I mean basics like Prada, Chanel, YSL, Tod's, and Hogans. Prices are about half the regular European price. The shop takes credit cards but does not give détaxe refunds.

Mouton à Cinq Pattes

15 rue Vielle-du-Temple, 4e (Métro: Hôtel de Ville or St-Paul); 18 rue St-Placide, 7e (Métro: Sèvres-Babylone); 138 bd. St-Germain (Métro: Odéon).

This is a small chain of stock shops; I have always called it "The Lamb Chop Store." Actually the name means "a lamb with five paws." I guess that's the kind of misfits it sells or considers itself to be, because of the unusual savings. You will find big names.

I have been shopping at the St-Placide store for about 20 years and had never been very impressed, then suddenly I hit pay dirt. So you just never know. The St-Placide store is handy to Bon Marché department store and is on a street with other bargain stores. My friend Bob, who lives on the Left Bank, likes the St-Germain store, which is famous for its menswear.

Mi-Prix

27 bd. Victor, 15e (Métro: Porte de Versailles).

This store is far from fancy. It's also far from central Paris. You may make a long trip for nothing, but that's life in the bargain fast lane. But the bargains? Mi-Prix carries a weird combination of items—the junkiest of no-name merchandise, some very nice skiwear, a fabulous collection of Maud Frizon and Walter Steiger shoes and boots, Bottega Veneta closeouts, and Philippe Model hats—at almost giveaway prices. The store is packed with merchandise, much of it current. The shoes are a different story. Some could be as current as last season, others as old as your grandmother.

If you are attending a trade show at the Porte de Versailles, this is a must. Also check the newspapers for *brocante* and antiques shows that may be held in this area, so you can combine agendas. It's hard to convince yourself to come all the way out here for one store, but I've never been sorry I did. Walk from the convention center along boulevard Victor about 2 blocks; you may also want to check out some other shops and discounters along here. You can also take the PC1 bus to the door.

RIVOLI 44
44 rue de Rivoli, 4e (Métro: Hôtel de Ville).

This is a little shop that doesn't look like much. The owner doesn't speak much English, but she's very sweet and will explain everything to you. The store carries only the Arche brand of shoes. I wear this line, but I never pay $265 per pair at Nordstrom. The prices here vary with the style, but they are current season and cost about 10€ ($10.80) less than in department stores.

GARMENT CENTER

I gave up trying to find a bargain in Paris's garment district (the Sentier; p. 92) years ago, but every now and then I poke into some of the jobbers and cut-rate dealers who say they sell wholesale. My friend Abby took me to a good find for low-cost handbags, below. Forget Hermès, Princess Grace.

CELYSA FRANCE
28 rue du Temple, 4e (Métro: Rambuteau).

This entire street is 2 blocks of handbag jobbers; you can buy individual pieces or go mad. I got a great-looking fake croc bag in lavender plastic for about $15 (13.80€).

RESALE & VINTAGE

....

The French pride themselves on being a practical people. They rarely throw anything away; they buy only the best quality and use it forever; they hate waste of any sort. But if someone in the family dies or if someone falls on hard times, he can sell his fine possessions at a *dépôts-vent*. Or, knowing that good merchandise is being sold, he will frequent a *dépôts-vent*. No one in Paris is ever ashamed to be seen buying used items. They think it's smart. I do, too.

Do note that designer clothing that you may not consider purchasing at regular retail can be sale priced at the end of a season at virtually the same price you might pay at a *dépôts-vent*. *Dépôts-ventes* traditionally sell used clothing of current styles, while vintage shops sell older clothing. These days, with so many retro looks in vogue, it's hard to tell one from the other. The two big flea markets, St-Ouen and Vanves, each have dealers who sell vintage clothing. The term *fripes* generally refers to nondesigner used clothing from the 1970s—not vintage Chanel or Balenciaga.

RÉCIPROQUE
89, 92, 95, 97, 101, and 123 rue de la Pompe, 16e (Métro: Pompe).

Réciproque has grown at an alarming rate—there are now more storefronts bearing this store's name along rue de la Pompe than ever before. The main shop, at no. 89, has two floors; don't forget to go downstairs.

There are racks and racks of clothes, all of which are clean. You'll find separates, shoes, evening clothes, and complete ensembles. You must look through the racks carefully and know your merchandise, although the labels are always in the clothes. Not everything is used or seriously used—many designers sell samples here. Every big name is represented; this is the best single resource for used couture clothing. Prices are not dirt cheap—a Chanel suit will cost over $2,500 (2,300€).

There's a shop for men's clothing; there are accessories, furs, and things for the home. There are sales too. It can be overwhelming; you need patience as well as a good eye.

Dépôts-vent Dix-Septieme
109 rue Courcelles, 17e (Métro: Courcelles).

This is the best resale shop in Paris, and the only chic one. It carries men's and women's clothing and a few home items all in one shop. The prices are sometimes a tad high—I paid about $400 (368€) for a used Chanel handbag (compared to $500/460€ for a brand-new Chanel handbag the same size at the July half-price sale). Some Chanel bags are $600 to $700 (552€–644€). You'll see designer costume jewelry, a large selection of Chanel suits, and a little bit of everything else. Sales take place during the regular sale periods. No détaxe. Open Monday at 2pm; otherwise, 10:30am to 7pm.

Dépôts-vent Passy
14 and 25 rue de la Tour, 16e (Métro: Passy).

Another contender in the used-designer-clothing wars. Catherine Baril has two shops with top-drawer stuff—YSL, Chanel, the works. One shop is for women, the other for men. They are a few yards from each other. They carry a fair number of samples. On my last visit, I found tons of Chanel straight from the runway. The prices were generally high, but I found a few bargains. A Chanel suit (summer weight) for $1,500 (930€) seemed like a good buy, whereas a Chanel camisole for $200 (184€) was overpriced, at least to me.

The best part about this shop is its location. You can easily combine a stroll along the rue de Passy with a shopping spree here and have a fabulous time. Open Monday 2 to 7pm, Tuesday to Saturday 10am to 7pm. In July, Monday to Saturday 2 to 7pm.

DIDIER LUDOT
24 passage de la Galerie Montpensier, Palais-Royal, 1er (Métro: Palais-Royal).

This shop is not easy to find, so have patience and remember that it is on the gallery side of the building, not the street side. Ludot tries to sell only top-of-the-line used designer goods, and specializes in Hermès, Céline, and Chanel. You may find Hermès bags from the 1930s, as well as vintage Vuitton luggage. This store is a standout for old-clothes junkies. Prices are high for quality items, but not unfair: a Pucci in perfect condition, just over $1,000 (920€); a wool Chanel suit (no blouse), $2,000 (1,840€).

Leaving the Métro, zig to the right into the open arcade, then hug the left-hand side of the arcade (where it is covered). Shops line the walkway. Ludot is among them. Do not confuse the vintage clothing with his new Little Black Dress line.

SCARLETT
10 rue Clement-Marot, 8e (Métro: Alma Marceau).

If you are a regular at the flea market at Vanves, you already know Scarlett; she's the one with the little tent and the big-name designers. Her shop carries gently worn clothing and accessories, mostly from Hermes, Chanel, and Vuitton. She still has the tent at Vanves.

Chapter Eleven

························

PARIS SHOPPING TOURS

TOUR 1: THE DO-IT-ALL-IN-A-DAY TOUR

This tour takes you by most of the best shopping in Paris and gives you a good workout as well. Since some of these stores are quite expensive, you may find yourself mostly window-shopping. If that's the case, you can complete the tour in half a day.

Begin at **Printemps Maison** on boulevard Haussmann. It opens at 9:35am. Don't mind the perfume and makeup on the street level; just get a free spritz and take the escalator up. Shop the three floors of housewares, being careful to ignore the non-French merchandise, of which there can be a lot.

Now head over to **Galeries Lafayette.** Pick up a free guide to the store at the Welcome Desk. Check out the stained-glass ceiling, the tabletop and housewares area, and the designer floors. You might want to take notes on new styles and trends. Although you can spend a week at Galeries Lafayette, when you're ready to move on, head for **Lafayette Gourmet,** which is upstairs in the Men's Store.

Exit Lafayette Gourmet through the back door onto the rue Provence. Head west, back toward Printemps. At the corner stop to stare, and maybe shop, at **Citadium,** a sports-shoe complex.

The tiny pedestrian street Havre-Caumartin is very junky looking, but who cares, right? This is a super little alley, especially if you like low-end junk. If you are the Chanel/Armani type, you may not be nearly as enthusiastic as I am. **Monoprix** is here, underneath Citadium. The mall Passage du Havre contains several branches of French multiples (chain stores) and a big FNAC. In short, everything you need in life is in this little area.

I can spend the better part of a day in these places alone, but I can also trim down to a few quick hours and be out by lunchtime. It's your call.

If you want to do this slowly and carefully, then you will make a day of it—eating in any of the many restaurants in the department stores or at **Toastissimo** in the basement of the Passage du Havre mall. If you zip through all of this by lunch, continue.

Follow rue Tronchet toward the Seine; you are headed to place de la Madeleine, which you will reach in a block. There are a number of fancy food shops around here; surely you have time to press your nose to the glass at **Fauchon,** 26 place de la Madeleine, and **Hédiard** (no. 21).

If it's lunchtime or even a little before (beat the crowds), try the famous tearoom **Ladurée** on the rue Royale. After you pass the place de la Madeleine, rue Tronchet becomes rue Royale. Ladurée looks like the kind of tearoom your grandmother would take you to; it has desserts galore, but also salads and omelets at moderate prices—plus a great-looking clientele.

Walk or cross over to the far side of the place de la Madeleine, where you'll see the famed **Lucas-Carton** restaurant. Swing around onto the boulevard Malesherbes so that you are across the street from Burberrys. This is Paris's newest block of retail shops, which holds **Sai, Resonances,** and **Shiseido,** 3–5 bd. Malesherbes.

On the rue Boissy d'Anglas, another tiny street known only to locals, are several great stores, among them **Territoire** (no. 30).

Shop your way to the rue du Faubourg St-Honoré, and *voilà,* you are at the door of **Hermès!** This is one of the swankiest streets in Paris; you will want to window-shop, if nothing else.

Keep walking east until the Faubourg becomes the rue St-Honoré. Continue walking—or dragging your feet. At the rue Castiglione, turn right and plop down at **Catherine,** the discount perfume shop that also sells great handbags for not much money.

Celebrate your strength, your purchases, and Paris by having a drink around the corner in the new bar at the **Hotel Meurice,** 228 rue de Rivoli.

TOUR 2: SHOPPING CHAMPS TOUR

Begin this tour by emerging from the F-D-Roosevelt Métro and promenading on the Champs-Elysées, stopping at whatever stores interest you. Be sure to hit **Monoprix** and the flagship **Sephora.**

Work your way toward Etoile, being sure to get to the new **Petit Bateau** shop (no. 116).

Head back down toward Rond Pont on the other side of the street.

Turn right onto the avenue Montaigne and stroll the entire length of the avenue (only 2 or 3 blocks). Don't miss **Joseph, Christian Lacroix,** and **Porthault.**

When you get to the end of avenue Montaigne, you have choices: You can either double back and hit the other side of the street, ending up at Rond Point, or follow the signs to the *bateau mouche* and collapse on a boat tour of Paris while you wave to the Princess Diana memorial.

Or hop on the Métro at Alma Marceau, at the end of avenue Montaigne. There's a cafe inside the **Joseph Store** (no. 14).

Or take a peaceful walk through the green paths that lead toward the American Embassy and the place de la Concorde.

Now it's time for your reward for not buying too much: Hit the gift shop at the **Hôtel de Crillon.** If you're really exhausted, maybe you need a refreshing wrap and treatment at the hotel's Guerlain spa.

If you're not staying at the Crillon (well, maybe next trip), you'll note that a few meters beyond the hotel's entrance is the Concorde Métro stop. *Voilà!*

TOUR 3: MAKE MINE A DISCOUNT TOUR

This tour uses a lot of taxis, which may seem antithetical to bargain shopping. But when you see how much time they save and the kind of bargains you can get on designer and big-name merchandise, cab fare may strike you as positively thrifty by the time you're finished.

Begin your day with a croissant or two loaded with jam (you'll need the sugar) and a strong cafe au lait. Wear your most comfortable shoes and take a taxi to **Réciproque,** the grandmother of Paris resale shops. Now you are French. Réciproque begins at 95 rue de la Pompe; don't miss its other shops up the street or the fact that there are clothes upstairs and downstairs in this temple to designer resale. Prices are average to high, depending on the age and condition of the garment and the designer. One rack holds a virtual library of Sonia Rykiel.

If you can manage all of your packages, hail a taxi now. If not, head back to your hotel, unload, and grab a bite to eat.

From the 16e, move over to the 17e and the Dépôts-Vente Dix-Septieme, 114 rue de Courcelles.

If you can still manage, have a taxi take you to the rue d'Alésia, where you will find the **Sonia Rykiel** outlet store (no. 64). Check out the whole 2 blocks of stock shops.

After all those bargains, you may need a pit stop or a trip back to your hotel to unload your packages.

For your discount afternoon, you can either do some more Left Bank shopping or ride the Métro to Sèvres-Babylone. Dash into the indoor flea market at **Le Bon Marché,** the department store, to round out your bargain hunting by negotiating with a few of the 35 antiques dealers here.

Then walk along the rue St-Placide, where you'll find even more stock shops. Be sure to check out **Mouton à Cinq Pattes** (nos. 8, 14, and 18), with three shops selling kids', men's, and women's designer clothes at discount. The merchandise is in bins or crammed onto racks, but there are big names and big savings to be had.

Finally, walk on the rue de Rennes toward the Commercial Centre Montparnasse, which you will pass as you head into **Inno**. This dime store, with a grocery in the basement, has afforded me some of my best bargains in Paris. The rue de Rennes becomes the rue Depart after you cross the boulevard Montparnasse at the base of the Commercial Centre.

TOUR 4: LEFT BANK IN A DAY TOUR

The best way to see the Left Bank is to live there. Failing that, try to spend the best part of a day there. Get an early start, because after noon, the Left Bank's neighborhoods take on the hustle and bustle of any busy part of town. Early morning has a slowness that allows you to absorb the vibes.

Here's an optional preliminary for early birds: Any early morning but Monday, start at the street market in the rue de Buci, behind the church St-Germain-des-Prés. Get out of the Métro at St-Germain-des-Prés and hang a left on the rue de Seine. This will take you right into the thick of the street market. After you've checked out all of the wonderful fruits, vegetables, and fresh flowers, grab a table at **Café de Flore.** The name is on the awnings; you can't miss it. There's a kiosk just past it if you need a morning newspaper. There isn't much of a crowd for breakfast—all the better for you, my dear. You may eat outside, even if you don't see other people outside. If you are indoors, certainly sit near the glass walls—you come here to watch the parade. Since most stores don't open until 10am, and some don't open until 11, you can sit and sip, write postcards, read the news, and watch the world go by. This is what you came to Paris to do; take your time and enjoy.

When you're finished, head back toward the rue de Seine and catch the street market at the rue de Buci, if you didn't see it before. If you've already seen it, cut onto the rue Jacob, making sure not to miss the tiny place de Furstemberg. Walk the narrow streets, full of antiques shops, behind the church. Take the rue Jacob to the rue Bonaparte, and turn right. Shop, shop, shop.

Now, take the rue Bonaparte all the way back toward the church (all of 2 short blocks). Before you get to Deux Magots, hang a quick right onto a street that's only half a block long. Get a good hard look at the Art Nouveau tile-front cafe on the corner to your right, then turn left so you can shop at the retail store alongside the **Café de Flore.**

You have now come full circle and are on the boulevard St-Germain. Cross the street and head downtown toward the Musée d'Orsay. But don't go that far; you're stopping at **Sonia Rykiel** (no. 175). Just beyond here, turn left onto rue des Sts-Pères and work the shoe stores. Segue from rue des Sts-Pères onto the rue Dragon, which hits it at an angle, and work your way through more boutiques. Take the rue Grenelle (more Sonia) when you reach it, and you'll eventually end up on the rue de Rennes.

Walk up one side of the rue de Rennes (toward the black office building you see in the background) and down the other side. Be sure to get as far as **Geneviève Lethu** (no. 95), then head back toward St-Germain-des-Prés.

Back on the rue des Rennes, look for the left-hand fork once you reach rue du Four; you'll see **La Bagagerie,** 41 rue du Four, as you turn. Explore all the trendiness you can stand. Then turn right onto rue Bonaparte, a street filled with the sights you came to Paris to enjoy. At the corner of rue du Vieux Colombier, you'll see the church of St-Sulpice. Before you go there, shop the stores on Vieux Colombier, including Hervé Chapelier.

At the corner of the Jardin de Luxembourg and rue Bonaparte, make a quick left, go two or three storefronts, and stop by **Pierre Herme's** pastry shop to drool, buy a snack, or just worship the rose-flavored *macarons*. Then hit place St-Sulpice and all the good stores there.

Leave place St-Sulpice on the rue St-Sulpice. You'll pass a few wonderful shops and even the new branch of London's **Muji,** which sells minimalist chic.

Eventually, you'll come to the mall **Marché St-Germain** and rue de Tournon. There's a **Souleiado** shop here. Rue de Tournon becomes the rue de Seine on the other side of the street. Take the rue de Seine toward the Seine. It dead-ends at the quai Malaquais.

Hang a quick left for a block to reach the quai Voltaire and some fancy antiques shops. Follow the quai uptown, toward the Cathédrale de Notre-Dame. The antiques stores will peter out, but the stalls along the riverfront sell wonderful, touristy jumble—postcards (old and new), books, prints, and old magazines. Stop at a few, and don't forget to make a wish as you stare into the Seine.

TOUR 5: THESE FEET WERE MEANT FOR WALKING TOUR

This tour resembles the tours above, so it's best to read the others first. The advantage of this one is that it walks you across Paris quickly, covering only the best and the brightest shops. It's a very tony tour.

Begin at the duty-free shop **Catherine,** 7 rue Castiglione, 1er. This tiny shop gets crowded during the day, so arrive first thing in the morning. Ask the staff to hold your purchases for you—you have a big day ahead and don't want to schlep too many heavy bottles. If you've bought only a few small items, consider having them mailed to you in the United States—you'll get a bigger duty-free discount, and the postage may not be as expensive as you think.

From the rue Castiglione, walk toward the Tuileries (half a block) and hang a left to walk along the rue de Rivoli. This gives you ample opportunity to shop at every tourist trap in Paris. When you see the gold statue of Joan of Arc in the middle of the road, right before the Hôtel Regina, turn right and walk alongside the Musée du Louvre. Take the bridge across the river and turn right onto rue du Bac. Welcome to a very fancy, private part of the Left Bank.

Prowl every inch of the rue du Bac, which twists and turns a little. You will pass the Hôtel Port-Royal, where the road curves, but don't let that throw you. The first blocks of rue du Bac are a tad slow, with just a few antiques shops and real-people places. By the time you hit the Port-Royal, things are sizzling. But before the sizzle, there are some quiet statements of style you shouldn't overlook. They include **Beauvais** (no. 14), one of the oldest engraving and print shops in Paris, and **Laure Japy** (no. 34), for stylish tabletop designs. Japy doesn't open until 10:30am, so take your time and don't rush to get here. At no. 38, you'll find **Myrène de Trémonville**, a designer who sells hipper-than-thou clothing to Henri Bendel and Barneys in the U.S.

At no. 43, I have a specialized find that may not be for everyone. **Deyrolle** (upstairs) is where you go to buy dead stuffed chickens. Don't snicker. They happen to be gorgeous, fabulous, expensive, and very country French. And, no, I have no idea how to get yours home with you. At least you won't ruffle any feathers at U.S. Customs, since the animals are quite dead. Deyrolle closes for lunch, so don't spend too much time in the previous stores if you plan to stop here.

Very shortly, you will be at the crossroads of boulevard St-Germain. To your right, on the corner, is a leather shop that opened in 1815. **Atelier Schilz** is like Hermès without the hype. They sell a gorgeous handbag for 600€ ($648), which isn't cheap, but does enable you to get a détaxe refund and is less than Hermès.

Cross St-Germain and continue along the rue du Bac. At this junction, the street gets even better, so if you must modify this tour, you can start here (Métro: Rue du Bac).

Walk along rue du Bac, enjoying every minute of it. If you need a spiritual moment, tuck into Chapelle Nôtre-Dame de la Medaille Miraculeuse, where you can buy medallions at the gift shop and say a prayer in the chapel. This is as magical as it sounds.

Once back on the street, you are half a block from the big department store **Le Bon Marché.** You can spend the rest of the day at Bon Marché, shopping its boutiques, eating lunch at **La Grande Epicerie,** and checking out the antiques market upstairs. Just be sure to keep up your strength, because you must—*must*—make time afterward to hit the rue St-Placide. It's across the street from Bon Marché and to your left 1 block.

The most interesting segment of St-Placide is only a block long, but it houses several discount shops where you may snap up a big-name designer garment. Because the rue St-Placide is dumpy and can be depressing, you'll need a pick-me-up once you're finished. Walk 1 block along the rue de Sèvres right into the **Hôtel Lutétia** and plop yourself down in the Art Deco lobby for a glass of champagne. Then you can face the Métro ride back to your hotel. You're staying at the Lutétia? Clever you.

Size Conversion Chart

Women's Clothing

American	8	10	12	14	16	18
Continental	38	40	42	44	46	48
British	10	12	14	16	18	20

Women's Shoes

American	5	6	7	8	9	10
Continental	36	37	38	39	40	41
British	4	5	6	7	8	9

Children's Clothing

American	3	4	5	6	6X
Continental	98	104	110	116	122
British	18	20	22	24	26

Children's Shoes

American	8	9	10	11	12	13	1	2	3
Continental	24	25	27	28	29	30	32	33	34
British	7	8	9	10	11	12	13	1	2

Men's Suits

American	34	36	38	40	42	44	46	48
Continental	44	46	48	50	52	54	56	58
British	34	36	38	40	42	44	46	48

Men's Shirts

American	$14^1/_2$	15	$15^1/_2$	16	$16^1/_2$	17	$17^1/_2$	18
Continental	37	38	39	41	42	43	44	45
British	$14^1/_2$	15	$15^1/_2$	16	$16^1/_2$	17	$17^1/_2$	18

Men's Shoes

American	7	8	9	10	11	12	13
Continental	$39^1/_2$	41	42	43	$44^1/_2$	46	47
British	6	7	8	9	10	11	12

INDEX

FROMMER'S® COMPLETE TRAVEL GUIDES

Alaska
Alaska Cruises & Ports of Call
Amsterdam
Argentina & Chile
Arizona
Atlanta
Australia
Austria
Bahamas
Barcelona, Madrid & Seville
Beijing
Belgium, Holland & Luxembourg
Bermuda
Boston
Brazil
British Columbia & the Canadian
  Rockies
Budapest & the Best of Hungary
California
Canada
Cancún, Cozumel & the Yucatán
Cape Cod, Nantucket & Martha's
  Vineyard
Caribbean
Caribbean Cruises & Ports of Call
Caribbean Ports of Call
Carolinas & Georgia
Chicago
China
Colorado
Costa Rica
Denmark
Denver, Boulder & Colorado
  Springs
England
Europe
European Cruises & Ports of Call
Florida

France
Germany
Great Britain
Greece
Greek Islands
Hawaii
Hong Kong
Honolulu, Waikiki & Oahu
Ireland
Israel
Italy
Jamaica
Japan
Las Vegas
London
Los Angeles
Maryland & Delaware
Maui
Mexico
Montana & Wyoming
Montréal & Québec City
Munich & the Bavarian Alps
Nashville & Memphis
Nepal
New England
New Mexico
New Orleans
New York City
New Zealand
Northern Italy
Nova Scotia, New Brunswick &
  Prince Edward Island
Oregon
Paris
Philadelphia & the Amish Country
Portugal
Prague & the Best of the Czech
  Republic

Provence & the Riviera
Puerto Rico
Rome
San Antonio & Austin
San Diego
San Francisco
Santa Fe, Taos & Albuquerque
Scandinavia
Scotland
Seattle & Portland
Shanghai
Singapore & Malaysia
South Africa
South America
South Florida
South Pacific
Southeast Asia
Spain
Sweden
Switzerland
Texas
Thailand
Tokyo
Toronto
Tuscany & Umbria
USA
Utah
Vancouver & Victoria
Vermont, New Hampshire &
  Maine
Vienna & the Danube Valley
Virgin Islands
Virginia
Walt Disney World® & Orlando
Washington, D.C.
Washington State

FROMMER'S® DOLLAR-A-DAY GUIDES

Australia from $50 a Day
California from $70 a Day
Caribbean from $70 a Day
England from $75 a Day
Europe from $70 a Day

Florida from $70 a Day
Hawaii from $80 a Day
Ireland from $60 a Day
Italy from $70 a Day
London from $85 a Day

New York from $90 a Day
Paris from $80 a Day
San Francisco from $70 a Day
Washington, D.C. from $80 a Day

FROMMER'S® PORTABLE GUIDES

Acapulco, Ixtapa & Zihuatanejo
Amsterdam
Aruba
Australia's Great Barrier Reef
Bahamas
Berlin
Big Island of Hawaii
Boston
California Wine Country
Cancún
Charleston & Savannah
Chicago
Disneyland®
Dublin
Florence

Frankfurt
Hong Kong
Houston
Las Vegas
London
Los Angeles
Los Cabos & Baja
Maine Coast
Maui
Miami
New Orleans
New York City
Paris
Phoenix & Scottsdale

Portland
Puerto Rico
Puerto Vallarta, Manzanillo &
  Guadalajara
Rio de Janeiro
San Diego
San Francisco
Seattle
Sydney
Tampa & St. Petersburg
Vancouver
Venice
Virgin Islands
Washington, D.C.

FROMMER'S® NATIONAL PARK GUIDES

Banff & Jasper
Family Vacations in the National
  Parks
Grand Canyon

National Parks of the American
  West
Rocky Mountain

Yellowstone & Grand Teton
Yosemite & Sequoia/ Kings Canyon
Zion & Bryce Canyon

FROMMER'S® MEMORABLE WALKS

Chicago	New York	San Francisco
London	Paris	Washington, D.C.

FROMMER'S® GREAT OUTDOOR GUIDES

Arizona & New Mexico	Northern California	Vermont & New Hampshire
New England	Southern New England	

SUZY GERSHMAN'S BORN TO SHOP GUIDES

Born to Shop: France	Born to Shop: Italy	Born to Shop: New York
Born to Shop: Hong Kong, Shanghai & Beijing	Born to Shop: London	Born to Shop: Paris

FROMMER'S® IRREVERENT GUIDES

Amsterdam	Los Angeles	San Francisco
Boston	Manhattan	Seattle & Portland
Chicago	New Orleans	Vancouver
Las Vegas	Paris	Walt Disney World®
London	Rome	Washington, D.C.

FROMMER'S® BEST-LOVED DRIVING TOURS

Britain	Germany	Northern Italy
California	Ireland	Scotland
Florida	Italy	Spain
France	New England	Tuscany & Umbria

HANGING OUT™ GUIDES

Hanging Out in England	Hanging Out in France	Hanging Out in Italy
Hanging Out in Europe	Hanging Out in Ireland	Hanging Out in Spain

THE UNOFFICIAL GUIDES®

Bed & Breakfasts and Country Inns in:	Southwest & South Central Plains	Mid-Atlantic with Kids
California	U.S.A.	Mini Las Vegas
Great Lakes States	Beyond Disney	Mini-Mickey
Mid-Atlantic	Branson, Missouri	New England and New York with Kids
New England	California with Kids	
Northwest	Chicago	New Orleans
Rockies	Cruises	New York City
Southeast	Disneyland®	Paris
Southwest	Florida with Kids	San Francisco
Best RV & Tent Campgrounds in:	Golf Vacations in the Eastern U.S.	Skiing in the West
California & the West	Great Smoky & Blue Ridge Region	Southeast with Kids
Florida & the Southeast	Inside Disney	Walt Disney World®
Great Lakes States	Hawaii	Walt Disney World® for Grown-ups
Mid-Atlantic	Las Vegas	Walt Disney World® with Kids
Northeast	London	Washington, D.C.
Northwest & Central Plains		World's Best Diving Vacations

SPECIAL-INTEREST TITLES

Frommer's Adventure Guide to Australia & New Zealand
Frommer's Adventure Guide to Central America
Frommer's Adventure Guide to India & Pakistan
Frommer's Adventure Guide to South America
Frommer's Adventure Guide to Southeast Asia
Frommer's Adventure Guide to Southern Africa
Frommer's Britain's Best Bed & Breakfasts and Country Inns
Frommer's Caribbean Hideaways
Frommer's Exploring America by RV
Frommer's Fly Safe, Fly Smart
Frommer's France's Best Bed & Breakfasts and Country Inns
Frommer's Gay & Lesbian Europe

Frommer's Italy's Best Bed & Breakfasts and Country Inns
Frommer's New York City with Kids
Frommer's Ottawa with Kids
Frommer's Road Atlas Britain
Frommer's Road Atlas Europe
Frommer's Road Atlas France
Frommer's Toronto with Kids
Frommer's Vancouver with Kids
Frommer's Washington, D.C., with Kids
Israel Past & Present
The New York Times' Guide to Unforgettable Weekends
Places Rated Almanac
Retirement Places Rated